Horace Williams

GADFLY OF CHAPEL HILL

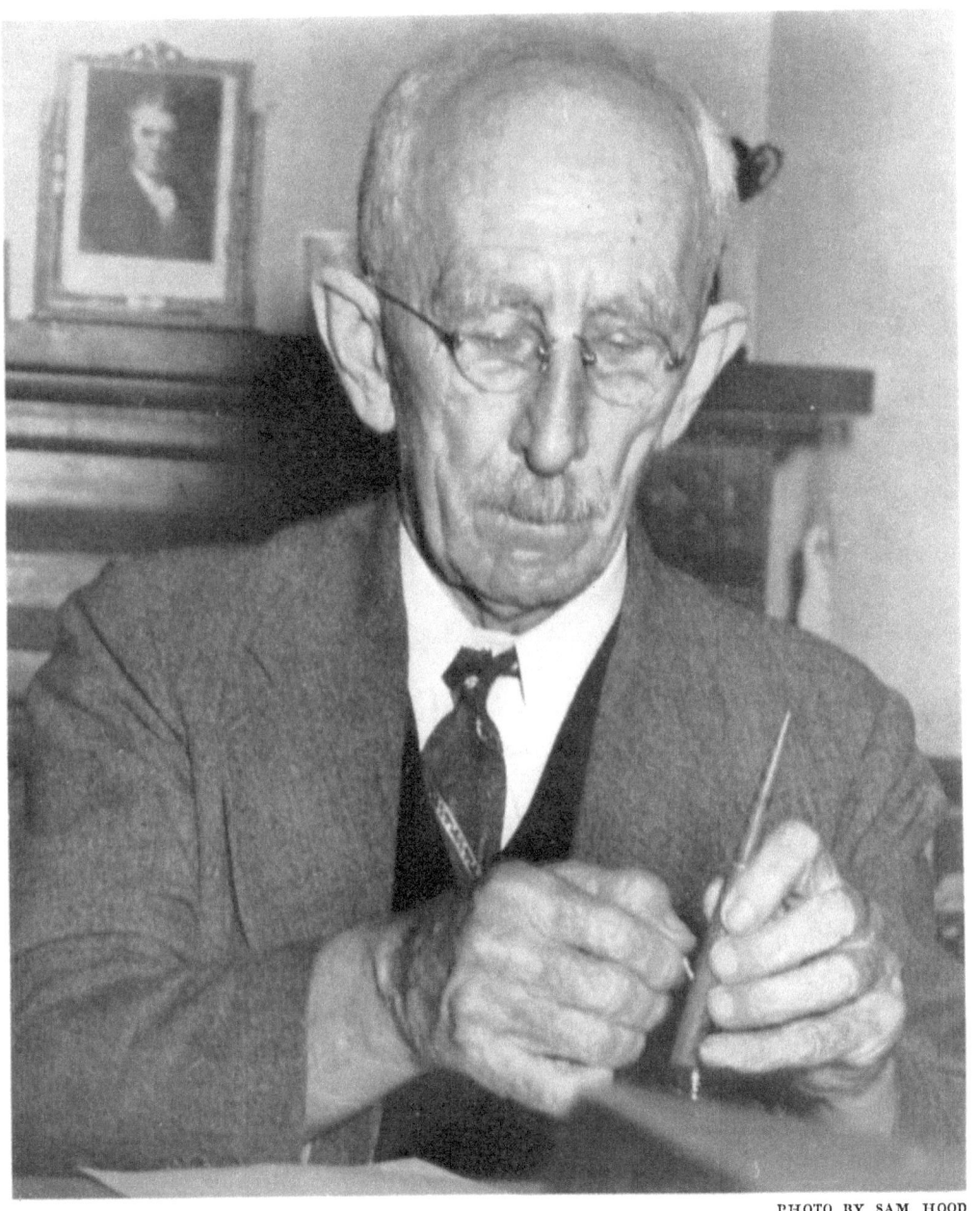

PHOTO BY SAM HOOD

PHOTO BY SAM HOO

PHOTO BY SAM HOOD

PHOTO BY SAM HOOD

Horace Williams

GADFLY OF CHAPEL HILL

———•◆•———

By

Robert Watson Winston

> O men of Athens: I am a sort of gadfly, if I may use such a ludicrous figure of speech, attached to the state and always fastening upon you, arousing and persuading and reproaching you.
> —Socrates, *Apology*

Chapel Hill

THE UNIVERSITY OF NORTH CAROLINA PRESS

1942

Copyright, 1942, by
THE UNIVERSITY OF NORTH CAROLINA PRESS

PREFACE

SOME TWENTY YEARS AGO, when I had attained the ripe old age of sixty, I accomplished an unusal feat. I closed my law office and reëntered college.

Now one evening, shortly after this daring plunge, a rather amusing episode occurred. The Phi Society was holding its annual celebration to induct new members, an occasion of much interest, and Professor Horace Williams and I had been asked to do the talking. My turn came first and I rose and faced five hundred youngsters with the confidence of mature experience. After I had cracked a few jokes, of the vintage of the seventies, I got down to business and roundly attacked the new order of things in my old college—the careless and indifferent manner in which the students were going about their work and the general lack of interest in life and its responsibilities.

"Why, boys," said I, "you seem slack-twisted, lackadaisical. You don't buck the line as we did in my day. The motto of my oratory medal, won at graduation, tells the whole story: *Non Palma sine Pulvere*, 'No reward without getting down into the dust for it.' To change the figure, young men, I quote another maxim: 'The cat loves fishes but does not love to get its feet wet.'

"Hear me, young gentlemen! Hit the line and hit it hard! Bowl your opponent over. Beware of entrance into a quarrel, but being in, bear it that the opposed may beware of thee. The little success which I have won, how did I do it? Why, I stood up like a man. I gave blow for blow. Yes, I took it on the chin, and if you would win, you, too, must give punch for punch, till your adversary is knocked into the ropes." Evidently I had made a hit, for the applause was loud and long.

In a few minutes the presiding officer rapped for order. "The Chair recognizes Professor Horace Williams, head of our School of Philosophy," he said. Slowly the caustic Philosopher rose to his feet, indignant, his feelings wounded, a fire burning in his deep-set eyes. He was provoked. I had preached heresy. I had given bad advice. I had glorified the material and trampled on the spiritual. Such conduct he would not stand for. In a smooth, soft-speaking voice he began.

"Young men," he said, and an em quad might have been placed between the words, "you have just listened to an exaltation of the material, a worship of force. On that level a dog is your superior; he has a keener scent than yours. A bull is your master; he is stronger than you are. The horse is your better; he can run faster than you can." Here the speaker paused and gazed sadly about him, as the boys chuckled and nudged each other. As for myself, I wilted away and prayed that the floor would open up and swallow me. The Professor continued. "Our learned brother," he said, "has missed the mark. His concept of life is not founded in wisdom; it is hasty, and he will so conclude, I am sure, upon further reflection. The material is the shadow of things, the spiritual alone abides."

Thus on and on the speaker went, to my utter confusion. Discarding his gadfly attack he insisted that not the material but the spiritual should be the goal. He asked what had become of those ancient nations which glorified the material and extolled force. The vast empire of Xerxes, of Alexander, of Caesar, have they not crumbled in the dust? On the contrary, the spiritual nations still abide: the gentle Hindu, the loyal Chinese, the law-abiding Hebrew. Not the material but the spiritual counts. Truth should be the aim of the individual, Truth, whose pathway is the thinking process. Physical existence cannot attain the truth. Religion finds itself as Christianity, which is the process of civilization and is grounded in the perfect individual.

Life is a vital process in which the individual lives and moves. As the insect exhibits life in terms of the insect type, so the thinker exhibits life in terms of truth. A mosquito is always true to type; the horse is always a horse; water, always H_2O. Must man alone of all creatures wobble along the best way he can? Shall it be said that the material world is orderly and loyal to itself, but the spiritual is chaotic, haphazard, and dependent on violence? If it is possible to build a good boat or to organize and administer a business, shall it be admitted that the beautiful life is beyond us?

"No, young men," the Philosopher concluded, as the students' eyes were fixed on his glowing, enraptured face, "force is not the key to success. The spiritual has not gone into bankruptcy. It is possible to live reasonably and beautifully. I invite you to ascend the heights. I ask you not to dwell in the valley."

The speaker finished and there was not a ripple of applause. Feeling ran too deep for conventionalities. Stillness as of the grave ensued. My own resentment had faded away. I was swallowed up in the deep emotions of the occasion. Slowly and sadly the wise, prickly-tongued Philosopher wandered from the speaker's desk and came and took a seat by my side. I rose and shook his hand. I did more. I thanked him. Indeed, I candidly admit that he had opened my eyes and my heart. So greatly had he impressed me that I immediately enrolled as a student in his classes and sat under him for two full years. I likewise admit that the drubbing which the Socratic Gadfly gave me that October night is the source and inspiration of this book.

Another confession I must make. Much of the book is without quotation marks though quoted from Horace's teachings in which it must be said he has had few equals. The art of writing he did not possess.

When Sydney Smith, the wittiest man of his time, reviewed Jeremy Bentham's abstruse work, *Fallacies of Reformers*, he remarked that by selecting and omitting, an admirable style may be formed from the text. Using this liberty, I have endeavored to give an account of Horace Williams' teaching, for the most part in his own words. Wherever an expression is particularly happy, let it be considered Horace's—the dullness I take to myself.

ROBERT WATSON WINSTON

University of North Carolina
Chapel Hill, N. C.

CONTENTS

	Preface	vii
1	Preview	3
2	Plowboy of the Dismal	8
3	As the Twig Is Bent	13
4	At Chapel Hill	17
5	Expanding Horizons	23
6	Yale, Harvard, and Germany	28
7	Return of the Native	40
8	A Gift of the Gods	46
9	Mental Midwife	55
10	The Reach and the Grasp	63
11	Begriff in Action	70
12	Struggle and Conflict	80
13	The Good Teacher	90
14	My Boys	103
15	Horace on the Bible	114
16	And So It Goes	125
17	Deep Calling unto Deep	140
18	Confounding His Adversaries	150
19	Imp of the Perverse	161
20	Horace's Philosophy Examined and Simplified	171
21	Solipsist	185

	CONTENTS	
22	Humiliation and Triumph	195
23	By Their Fruits	205
24	The Passing Years	216
25	The Human Touch	230
26	What the Good Teacher Taught Me	245
27	A Love Letter	254
28	The University under Three Presidents	268
29	Conclusion of the Whole Matter	287
30	Hail and Farewell	301

To the student of Horace Williams who employed his Good Teacher's dialectic method to vitalize democracy and make America safe for differences,

FRANK PORTER GRAHAM

CAVEAT LECTOR

Throughout the book it will be observed that the class discussions in which Horace Williams and successive generations of students participated are composite pictures put together with no attempt at a strict chronology or the separation of one class from another.

1

PREVIEW

THE TASK I am undertaking is necessary and difficult. Necessary, in that it goes to the root of the intellectual revival in North Carolina and the South. Difficult, because of its complexity. For fifty years Horace Williams was the head of the department of philosophy at the University of North Carolina and, during that long period, was a veritable gadfly, waging a never-ending warfare against ignorance, superstition, intolerance, and orthodoxy.

"He's a slick brother and will bear watching," said the preacher. "He's the most interesting, thought-provoking and useful teacher in America," retorted his boys.

How is it possible to make heads or tails of a man who bore no label, had no religious or political bias, was equally Vedantist, Egyptian, Jew, Hegelian, and Christian, and whom some associates considered a rank fraud and others a profound thinker?

Though an innovator and a thorough-going idealist he was so old-fashioned in his ways and so unconventional that, after the simple manner of his Yogi friends, he lived in an old, unsightly, rambling, uncomfortable dwelling, off in a grove by itself, without screens, telephones, bath-tubs, steam heat, or toilets—a situation he stoutly justified in the name of his inalienable rights, as a free-born man, to be individualistic and live his life in his own way.

Perhaps there were two Horace Williamses, as Emerson said of Bronson Alcott, and no one could ever make the least guess as to which one of the two would turn up on a given occasion. "Very tedious and prosing and egotistical and narrow, I do not want any more such persons to exist," said Emerson of Alcott. Yet, as Emerson concluded, "the highest genius of the time."

Are these words concerning Louisa May Alcott's father a true picture of Horace Williams, beyond all doubt one of the most stimulating, widely beloved and hated characters who ever puzzled a philosophy class, day in and day out, year in and year out, standing them on their heads, shocking or delighting them, prodding them out of mental lethargy, often expounding theories which they knew were fallacious, but could not refute; always insisting that the students take nothing for granted, accept nothing as true simply because it was stated, urging them to rise superior to the group-mind and, with Hegel and the masters, adopt the dialectic method and learn the value of forming concepts, the only gateway to the infinite and the absolute?

While it must be frankly admitted that such teachings were neither new nor revolutionary in Europe or in New England, they were anathema in the unchanging South of fifty years ago. Indeed they were dynamic and diabolic.

Now, in the clash of opinions respecting the professor's real worth and his call on fame there was a clear-cut cleavage. The students and trustees, as a whole, were Horatians, devoted to Horace, to his biting tongue and stimulating thoughts. On the other hand, some members of the faculty and their wives were skeptical or hostile. Mothers, in particular, were up in arms against what they had heard was the faith-shattering, youth-corrupting, unorthodox professor.

"Why, I would much rather haul my son's dead body off to its grave than let him go to Chapel Hill and study under that atheist, Horace Williams!" Thus protested one of dozens of mothers who knew the professor by hearsay only. A pupil of his, however, declared that he had given her a new vision of life; he had made religion vital. "In truth, when Mr. Williams taught me that God was not distant, not millions of miles away, in the far-off, but in my own heart, a part of me, bone of my bone, flesh of my flesh, spirit of my spirit, I shouted for joy and almost jumped out of my skin."

In 1891 when Horace Williams, having graduated with honor at the University of North Carolina and at the Yale and Harvard divinity schools, came back to his old college to teach philosophy he had a definite, a fixed purpose. Let me set down some of the reasons which influenced him to give up a promising career elsewhere and come into the Bible Belt of the static South.

To begin with, as the youthful innovator insisted, the South had not had an intellectual upheaval and he proposed to inaugurate such a movement. Besides, the South boasted of its orthodoxy, and to him orthodoxy was dead formalism. Or, as the merciless critic charged, orthodoxy has a keen sense and a deadly anger. Orthodoxy cracks down. Orthodoxy was the source of the death of Jesus. "I knew that the grip of orthodoxy in the South must be broken," he declared.

The University of North Carolina could not do its work, he maintained, until liberalized. But such a movement generally meant bitterness and violence. He was confident he could work this great liberalizing movement without violence. At all events to help in this process was an opportunity and a test.

"The South is a goodly land, though dogmatic and poorly led," he declared. "Its people are my people, and my mother, noble and godly, rests in its bosom." The decision was therefore made. In response to letters from Winston, his old Latin teacher in the University of North Carolina, and from Colonel Steele, president of the board of trustees, and Battle, president of the University, the young innovator abandoned his dream of growing up with the expanding Pacific coast and came down to the little village of Chapel Hill, where he lived and taught and wrought for half a century, isolated and lonesome, a puzzle and an enigma and oftentimes a terror.

Always and everywhere, he spread the gospel of unorthodoxy, lambasted worn-out traditions, acclaimed the dignity of the individual, the persistence of the One among the many, the exaltation of quality above quantity and, beyond all other considerations, the passion for truth. Indeed, to Horace Williams truth was God. And there must be a ceaseless effort to reach the truth and full confidence that it could be attained.

These principles Horace Williams not only expounded, but lived and put into practice. In a community which was thoroughly solid and unbroken, and where to be a Republican was a sin unpardonable, he cast his ballot for William McKinley and against William J. Bryan. In a section of the nation which considered the Bible the literal Word of God he rejected physical miracles, taught that Jesus was the most perfect individual who ever lived, but not God, insisted that life is evolution, and civilization is the process of life.

"God is more than a business man," he proclaimed. "God has color, charm, imagination. God is the glory of variety. The skies, the sea, the mountain, the primrose, the poet, the terrible forms of power, the light and the darkness, the gentle breeze and the world currents are all His. The individual as an ultimate unit in the process of life must exhibit in himself the universal attitude of life."

A monotheist, opposed to dualism and glorying in the dialectic, he was an Hegelian and a Trinitarian. Since the Council of Nicea, as he affirmed, no universal truth had been promulgated. That council put the Holy Ghost into religion; it humanized religion, relating the Father to the Son. The structure of God is not a simple quantity, but a living synthesis, a Trinity. God in Man, Man in God.

"I do not know a greater saying," declared Horace Williams, "than that of Jesus, 'I am the Truth.'" Hence, as he went on to declare, his aim should be to exhibit truth. And by the word truth he implied unity in structure difference. "The day of the Priest and the Dogma is finished," he boldly proclaimed. "The day of the scholar begins." Of religion he asserted that there is no power in life to be compared with its fertilizing power. Religion is the source of all the master ideas. To limit it to the forms of life, to any form, is to limit the sun to a favorite flower. How a Christian can be orthodox is the hopeless problem in Logic. How an intelligence that has stood upon the Mountain, has seen the beautiful life, can limit itself to any form, Jewish, Greek, Roman, or Christian, is the problem. Yet the South has boasted of its orthodoxy, and has made no contribution. "Being orthodox is our most expensive luxury."

Thus did the brave, unorthodox young teacher go about his task, bearing aloft a banner inscribed with the words, Truth, Goodness, Beauty. This banner he never lowered. Regardless of friend or foe, of powers or principalities, he went his undaunted way. Was he destined at last, like Socrates, his beloved master, to drink the hemlock?

2

PLOWBOY OF THE DISMAL

ON THE sixteenth day of August, in the year of our Lord, one thousand eight hundred and fifty-eight, in a commodious, unpretentious dwelling a score of miles distant from the marts of trade, on the edge of a vast pocosin around which William Byrd of Westover once surveyed, calling it the Dismal, a child was born to Elisha Williams and Mary, his wife. It was their first-born, a raw-boned, deep-chested, virile youngster whom they named Henry Horace.

Nothing in the boy's ancestry presaged or even remotely suggested his future. His father was an ordinary country doctor, quite content with his lot, opposed to much booklearning, and, as the neighbors said, rather sot in his ways. Tradition does have it, however, that Dr. Williams was a kinsman of General Lee in the same line as Cousin Markie Williams, to whom the General frequently wrote interesting letters, since collected and published under the title of *Markie Letters*.

Horace Williams' mother was a Taylor, her husband's second wife, bearing him eight children, two girls and six boys, none of whom, except the eldest, attained any distinction. Mrs. Williams was a woman of deep sympathy, the exact opposite of her husband in her outlook on life, and she possessed those sterling qualities of motherhood which made her the idol of the family. It was to his mother, therefore, that young Horace turned for guidance, encouragement, and inspiration. His mother was likewise the sole cause of his obtaining an education.

From this description of Horace's parents it might be inferred that the doctor was the forthright, dogmatic Baptist and his wife the plastic Methodist. But the doctor was the Methodist and Mrs. Williams the Baptist.

If the ancestry of the lad failed to adumbrate his future, what shall be said of his environment? Gates County, North Carolina, the home of the Williamses, lies on the Virginia border and is somewhat below the average in fertility. The western portion, which is elevated and well drained, is the more desirable, but Dr. Williams' home was in the eastern section and in Holly Ridge Township, adjoining the Great Dismal Swamp. Writing of this eastern section, a recent historian records that swamps and pocosins predominate.

In Dr. Williams' day, a few hogs were raised, but they had to be penned to guard against the bears that roamed the Dismal. Between the swamps there were numerous sand-ridges rank with weeds for fattening cattle, but these lands were almost valueless, for in winter they were often flooded and in summer flies and mosquitoes stung the stock unmercifully. Cotton and peanuts were the money crops. The county was sparsely settled, and the population was divided about equally between whites and blacks. Before the deep wells were sunk and screens provided, the drinking water, taken from shallow wells, was sometimes filled with deadly germs. Mosquitoes, as is now known, caused the chills and fevers.

Despite these drawbacks and others, such as the pestilential miasma of the Dismal—a wilderness thirty miles long from north to south and varying in width, where, as William Byrd records, "no beast or bird approaches, nor so much as an insect or reptile. . . . Nor indeed do any birds fly over it . . . for fear of noisome exhalations"—despite these disadvantages, the home county of Horace Williams did possess certain attractions. Its western boundary is the majestic Chowan, a river deep, wide, and madeira-colored, which, at its mouth not far from the historic town of Edenton, is one of the most inspiring sheets of water known to the navigators of inland waters. On the eastern boundary of the county, and very near the Williams home, ran a post route, now an excellent highway, stretching from Suffolk, Virginia, to Edenton, North Carolina, and thence south to Wilmington. This road is nearly two hundred years old, the most ancient highway in the State.

Down this thoroughfare once traveled George Fox, and later John Woolman, Quakers and friends of peace, on their way to visit the Society of Friends in and about Durant's Neck in the adjoining county of Perquimans. George Washington, as a young surveyor, spent considerable time in and upon this highway while he was laying plans to establish the waterway later to become the Dismal Swamp Canal. A one-time resident of Gates County invented the Gatling gun, and a native son, a youth of twenty-odd, became the youngest brigadier in Lee's army.

Near the center of the Dismal there is a sheet of water known as Lake Drummond. To its shores came Tom Moore and spun a pathetic tale called "The Lake of the Dismal Swamp," which tells the story of a maiden who had wandered off into the Dismal and become lost. Her lover went to find her. Through tangled juniper and beds of reeds he wandered, through many a fen where the serpent feeds and man never trod before. Though the lovers were never found, they live on, . . .

> *And oft from the Indian hunter's camp*
> *This lover and maid so true*
> *Are seen at the hour of midnight damp*
> *To cross the Lake by a firefly lamp*
> *And paddle their white canoe.*

In Gates County, there were several Baptist and Methodist churches and one Christian church. The Methodist church at Sunbury (Philadelphia) was generally attended by Dr. Williams and his family. Here, in an earlier day, Francis Asbury, renowned missionary Bishop of the Methodist church, had preached. In his diary the good Bishop makes this record: "Alas for this place! Five souls of the Whites—some poor Africans, are seeking the Lord." Mrs. Williams' Baptist church likewise had its ups and downs. Young Horace could remember an occasion when a stove was put in one of these churches. "Another ungodly innovation!" protested the faithful; and indeed this innovation came near destroying the brotherly sentiment of the people and, but for wise leadership, would have done so.

Such were the advantages and disadvantages of the birthplace of young Horace, a community of easy-going folk, uncommercialized, never worried, whose motto was "Live and be happy," who read only such great books as *Pilgrim's Progress*, Baxter's *Saints' Rest*, Taylor's *Holy Living* and *Holy Dying*, and the Bible.

During the war years, the boy Horace suffered with others, often lacking the bare necessities of life. When his father's yard was filled with Union cavalry, soon after the war, not a pig, not a cow, not a grain of wheat or corn, as he afterwards declared, remained. During the next two years the Williams family, to quote Horace, "lived by the week": they did not know whether there would be anything to eat next week.

Until Horace was almost free, he was a plowboy on his father's farm, and a number-one hand he was. In the hot, exhausting work of pulling and saving fodder, he so far outdistanced the half-dozen Negroes that they were soon off in the bushes begging for rest. In the cotton patch he chopped more cotton than any Negro who came to the farm.

After these difficult years, the young man's capable mother and other relatives gathered together enough money, with a small sum he had laid by, to send him off to school. Before the war, Gates County had possessed good private schools and public schools which ran for seven months every year. But the war, as war always does, substituted bullets for books. Horace Williams was nineteen years of age, tough, ambitious, and original, when he quit the paternal roof, crossed the Chowan River into Hertford County, and entered the Boys' School in the beautiful town of Murfreesboro, North Carolina.

3

AS THE TWIG IS BENT

GENERALLY speaking, young people are slow in selecting their life work. Ask the average college boy of eighteen or twenty what he intends to be, and nine times out of ten he will answer, "Oh, I don't know. I'll settle that matter when I get to it." But not so with Horace Williams. Almost from childhood he had made up his mind: he was going to be a teacher, a decision more firmly fixed at the school he had now entered.

In the 1870's the Boys' School at Murfreesboro was administered by a Methodist preacher, but its teacher and inspiration was C. P. Conrad, a graduate of the University of Virginia, which at that early date was far-and-away ahead of any other southern college. At the University of Virginia Conrad had come under the influence of those master minds, Gildersleeve, Holmes, Mallet, Minor, and others. Now he was a teacher himself and a source of inspiration to his pupils. Naturally such a scholar and so callow a youth as Horace Williams were unable to agree. Conrad's intellectual process and Horace's farming process were soon at loggerheads. The practical Gates County farm boy could not understand the idealistic college-bred Virginian, nor could the student of Plato and Homer appreciate the plowboy of the Dismal.

Wider and deeper grew the break between teacher and pupil until they finally quarreled and parted company, the rebellious youngster taking his foot in his hand and setting out along the dusty highway for his far-away home beyond the unbridged Chowan. Fortunately the principal got wind of the affair and went in pursuit, finally overtaking the runaway. A pleasant interview followed. Horace agreed to return to the school and have a talk with Conrad, provided the principal would be present as a witness. The upshot of the episode was satisfactory. Conrad made his position clearer, explaining that the basis of civilization is intellectual and aesthetical and not materialistic. The material is but dust in the balance in comparison with the spiritual. This statement satisfied young Horace and he and his teacher soon became the best of friends. "Mr. Conrad showed me the intellectual process," he said, "and it became as real as the process of work."

Thus did a great thought take root in young Horace's mind and so germinated that in after years, like Pythagoras, he found sermons in arithmetic and truth in algebra.

Conrad was indeed more than a teacher to Horace; he was a stimulus and a counselor. He urged the brilliant young fellow not to return to the farm, where he would pick cotton or hoe corn for a few dollars a week, but to go off to college and educate himself for a larger life. This course, however, was beset with difficulties. The Williams family were very poor. Eight children had to be fed and clothed. The father, not being a college-bred man, was not keen on education and wished his son to work in the cotton patch and the cornfield, where things had been much better when Horace led the slothful hands.

In this situation Mrs. Williams came to the rescue. She insisted that her son be allowed to gratify his ambition to get a college education. But again the old difficulty arose: Where was the money to come from? At this low ebb in the fortunes of the young fellow a favorable break occurred. At Belvidere, a village not far away, Josiah Nicholson, a benevolent old Quaker, wanted a clerk for his store. Horace applied for the job and, when Mr. Nicholson insisted upon experience, proposed a thirty-day try-out without pay.

"If I cannot do the work, Mr. Nicholson," said the boy,

"I do not wish the position. And until the thirty days are out I ask nothing but a bed to sleep in and something to eat."

The canny old Quaker eyed the youth with satisfaction and then slowly replied, "Thee can try. When can thee come?"

"In the morning," answered Horace.

The bargain was struck, and so well was the work performed that the business greatly increased and sales multiplied. At the end of the year Horace's salary was raised to one hundred and seventy-five dollars.

At the end of the second year the young clerk had saved two hundred dollars, a sufficient sum to pay expenses for a full nine months' session at the University of his State. His eagerness to reach Chapel Hill is illustrated by the unearthly hour of his departure from home and the difficulties he surmounted.

On a December midnight he and his brother Herbert set out from Gates County to catch the morning train due at Suffolk, Virginia, at 9:30. The weather was cold, the roads muddy, the streams had overflowed their banks, and the distance was twenty long miles. Their vehicle was a two-wheeled cart without springs or top and hitched to a mule. They were seated on a rough plank stretched from one side of the cart to the other.

On the way they encountered a dangerous-looking stream, out of its banks, with its bridge washed away. The younger brother hesitated to make the plunge. "We must make it," said Horace. "The mule can swim." On and on they plugged, through mud and slush, into the darkness. At length they struck the outskirts of Suffolk and heard the whistle of the engine nearing the station.

Urging on the mule with whip and coaxing, they reached the depot, where the antiquated, wood-burning engine was puffing and wheezing, ready to move off. Horace rushed into the office and bought a ticket. Herbert got a check for the trunk. The brothers waved goodbye, the younger returning to his home, and Horace boarded the train with the aid of an interested passenger. After an all-day run to Raleigh, where he spent the night, and thence next morning by another train to Durham, and finally aboard a venerable, well-worn plush-upholstered hack operated by a jocular colored Jehu, the young searcher after knowledge reached Chapel Hill. Such were the means of travel in the good old days.

4

AT CHAPEL HILL

DURING the Christmas season of 1879 Horace Williams and I met for the first time. I was then a senior and he a freshman. Though he was more than two years my senior in point of age, I was four years further along in the college course. At this time we saw little of each other. During the session of 1880–81, when I was a law student and a tutor and he a rising junior, we became better acquainted. It must be said, however, that Williams had few acquaintances, fewer friends, and no intimates. But though his friends were few, his admirers were many, and he soon became an acknowledged leader in the intellectual life of the college.

No one, indeed, could forget the strange individualistic fellow: tall, spare, erect, with expansive chest and dome-like brow. Ears twice the ordinary size and bulging out as if to catch the news. A face lean, hungry, inscrutable, a veritable interrogation point. A cold, steel-gray eye, curious and searching. A voice soft, persuasive, restrained, and muffled, but of great carrying power. His intangible qualities were no less remarkable: a far-away, mystical manner, a personality intriguing, and a spirit undaunted.

His reputation had preceded him. It was understood that he had made good as farmer, merchant, and student under Conrad. Moreover he was older and more mature than any other member of his class. He was soon snugly incorporated into college life and chose the Arts course. In his freshman year he won the Greek medal and stood well in German. For the sciences and literature he had little relish.

Poetry was an unknown country to him. Though he afterward declared that entering the University was a birthday, as a matter of fact he found little that was satisfying. He was in search of general principles. He cared little for facts or details. He wished to cultivate his mind and not his memory.

He found no courses in logic or philosophy or comparative religions. Latin, Greek, and mathematics were about all the venerable, conservative, delightful University had to offer. He did, however, bring away something of value from mathematics. "My education began," he said, "in the mathematics class." How a radius, moving about a fixed point, achieves a perfect circle, puzzled him and put his mind to work. That one inanimate line crossing another inanimate line can create an angle was beyond his comprehension. The famous proposition that the square on the hypotenuse of a right-angled triangle is equal to the sum of the squares of the other two sides was illuminating. "I had my first view of knowledge." This, indeed, was the moment of transcendence. "Things, objects, the present were not important." He wished to go to the bottom of a subject. "Homer, Sophocles, Plato were the great ones."

If instruction at the University was not entirely satisfactory to the young man from Gates County, the literary societies were adequate. The Phi and Di (Philanthropic and Dialectic) were the center and heart of University life. They appointed the monitors, kept order, elected marshals, ball managers, debaters, essayists, and declaimers. They were the inspiration and the custodian of the honor system.

At the end of his freshman year Horace was elected college librarian, and simple quarters on the west end of the library building (now the Playmakers Theater) were cut off as a sleeping place for him. He ate about in the village, wherever food was the cheapest. He was frugal; he neither smoked, drank, nor danced. The students considered him close in money matters. Years of hard work were calculated to make the lad a bit careful.

During his first year he had lived in a rent-free cabin where he and his roommate, the pious, well-beloved "Bishop" Betts, did the household drudgery, cooking, kindling the fires, sweeping, dusting, and tidying up the shuck mattress.

Yet he dressed in good taste, almost in the garb of a staid Methodist preacher. On Sundays he wore a starched shirt, a stiff clerical collar, a white tie, and a sombre-colored suit. He was not certain whether he would add preaching to the job of teaching. He was a regular attendant at the Methodist church and Sunday school.

Young Williams was fond of the society of women and soon became engaged to one of the most eligible ladies of the village. When she broke off the affair and returned his ring, he was not in the least cast down. His heart had not been touched; he was an intellectual, not a lover. Not made to court an amorous looking glass. Nor could he

> ... *caper nimbly in a lady's chamber*
> *To the lascivious pleasing of a lute.*

The little village of Chapel Hill, where Williams now found himself, was in a class all its own. There was no place in the land quite its equal, abounding as it did in hospitality, graciousness, and freedom from caste, snobbery, or corroding wealth. The faculty were poor, students poorer, villagers poorest of all—conditions which made little difference however. Did not Chapel Hill possess traditions rich and sacred, and were not its natural advantages unmatched? A plateau, nearly five hundred feet above sea level, remote, far from the noise of town or city, drained in all directions and set in giant oaks and hickory and in lovely shrubs and plants and flowers.

And yet how scant and primitive was the equipment of the University. In the winter time, beautiful little Gerrard Hall, the college chapel, with compulsory prayers at seven o'clock every morning was without a spark of fire. During a portion of his college career, Horace waited on himself, slept all winter in a room with no heat, and bathed once a week in a tin tub filled with cold water drawn from the rock-ribbed college well. But the hardy youngsters of that day were not cast down. They realized that a devastating war had recently ended. The University was without endowment or one copper of aid from the State. The denominational colleges were jealous and hostile.

There were some bright spots in the cloudy sky. In the University a determined struggle was beginning, to overcome obstacles and to grow in usefulness. The alumni association was becoming active. Athletics were encouraged. A strong chemistry department, of which F. P. Venable was the head, had been organized. A law school presided over by John Manning, an impressive, beloved man, was beginning to function. A short railroad, leading from the village, by General Hoke's iron mine and out to the Southern Railroad at University Station had been put in operation.

The chief improvement of Horace Williams' day was an appropriation by the State of the sum of $5,000 for the support of the University. This act marked the beginning of a new era for higher education in North Carolina. A few years later the annual appropriation was increased to $15,000. But these measures had been adopted after a struggle of nearly a quarter-century.

I was fortunate in being present in the hall when Williams was admitted into the Phi Society, a ceremony which so impressed the young fellow that he rated it above joining the Methodist church. Aycock was president. "As that man" (and I quote Williams) "stood before us challenging us to achievement, . . . I was found in two new centers of being. The doors opened by that experience have not been closed. My life was enriched."

The chief attraction for Horace Williams in the Society was the honor system. There he discovered that "character is the integrity of the I, the genuineness of the One. Under any circumstances, in any jam, the individual will be himself." The influence of Aycock was "elemental"—when a group in the Society tempted him to lower the standard, "he left the president's chair, took the floor, and made the most stirring speech it has been my fortune to hear."

A few years after Aycock had left the University and Williams was president of the Society, a resolution was introduced to suspend the honor system. The best speaker in the hall advocated the resolution and it seemed an easy victory. Williams called the vice-president to the chair and took the floor in opposition. The honor system won out by a majority of thirteen votes.

In Horace's senior year an episode occurred which may illustrate his secretive tendencies and growing mysticism. He fell under the spell of a little girl, a child in pigtails, Mary Anderson, the favorite of the village, whose beautiful eyes, gracious manners, and vital personality made her irresistible. At this time Mary—Horace was calling her his Highland Mary—was a pupil of that famous southern beauty, Emma Graves, and was very busy with the three R's.*

After four and a half years of poring over books, composing essays, engaging in heated debates, conducting the college library, teaching Sunday school, and generally observing men and events, Horace Williams graduated, having garnered the highest honors of the institution. So efficient was he as a debater and a writer of essays that coveted medals in those departments were awarded him. When he reached the senior grade he was chosen by his mates as president of the class.†

---

* Mary Anderson is the great-niece of Major Robert Anderson of Fort Sumter fame.

† Perhaps not the least useful portion of his college course had been one not previously mentioned—the summer normal school of 1879, which had been established at the University two years earlier, the first university summer school in America. The instruction was neither thorough nor profound, but the atmosphere was uplifting. A wide-awake, enthusiastic, homogeneous group had come together for the purpose of magnifying the office of teacher, dignifying their profession, and popularizing education and selling it to the masses.

The commencement of 1883, when Williams graduated, was a memorable one. Country people filled the campus, arriving in covered wagons, in buggies, in carts, on horseback, and afoot—all eager to hear the music of a brass band. Interested spectators, coming all the way from Asheville to Wilmington, filled Gerrard Hall and jammed its galleries. The rostrum and the famous Bull Pen were occupied by visiting statesmen. The Chief Justice of Louisiana delivered the address. Seven graduates spoke. Horace's subject was "The English Middle Classes."

After the speaking, President Battle came forward, beaming with a sense of duty well done. "On this interesting occasion," he said, "for the first time in the history of this institution, there will be awarded, in course, both the degree of Bachelor of Arts and the degree of Master of Arts. Hitherto the Master's degree has been purely honorary. Hereafter it will stand on its merits. The recipient of these unusual honors is Henry Horace Williams."

The president of the University here passed out the two diplomas, and as the young student came forward to receive them, confident, resolute, unruffled, the audience took cognizance of a man. And well they might. The younger students had come to look upon him as a member of the faculty. His scholarship was such that his college mate, Joyner, afterwards president of the National Educational Association, invited him to become a partner in the La Grange Collegiate Institute, where he taught for two sessions. "During these months of intimate association, occupying the same room and the same bed with him," said Joyner, "we opened our hearts and minds to each other. I learned to love him as a golden-hearted man of noble impulses and lofty aims, and to admire him as a courageous seeker after truth: a clear, unfettered, liberal thinker and a remarkable and thought-provoking teacher."

5

EXPANDING HORIZONS

COMMENCEMENT over, and before taking up his work at La Grange, the young graduate went down to visit his father's home in Gates County and received a warm welcome, his mother and his little sister Lizzie especially giving him a greeting which he cherished to the end of his days. After breakfast, he knocked on his mother's door and presented her with the three medals he had won. Her heart was touched, and the following week when her son delivered a fine address at the local school commencement and was greeted with rounds of applause, her face shone. "Life has not brought me a richer moment," he said. "To make glad the heart of a great Mother is the highest joy."

Lizzie, not yet out of her teens, was captivated by her strange, learned brother. But down in that remote section the young man soon discovered that he did not have the importance which he had attained at the University. On the Sunday after his arrival, he and the family attended Philadelphia Church, where he expected something of an ovation. He was disappointed. Though he was greeted kindly, there was no enthusiasm. A neighbor would come by and shake hands and then stand quite silent—there was no point of contact with the new arrival. Gathered about in groups, the church members discussed the weather and hog cholera, sore-shin, and other interesting topics, totally unmindful of the presence of a distinguished Master of Arts. This treatment was an awakening experience and cut the young fellow's comb. He found himself a freshman again. He must begin life at the bottom.

Later, up at La Grange, from day to day in the schoolroom he learned more and more about teaching. He concluded that the work of a teacher is to teach, to impress his personality on the students, and to show in terms of knowledge the process being considered. "The thinking act is the highest reach of intelligence, but it is rarely exhibited." Such reflections as these caused him to reëxamine his own life and to ask himself if he were really educated or a mere smatterer. "The result of the University classroom was being challenged." Cramming the mind with isolated, disconnected facts was not education.

One day a bright young boy rose and asked why it was that minus three multiplied by minus three gave a plus nine. The teacher was stumped. But he must find that plus or resign. When school turned out for the day, the teacher fled to the forest. Would the tall pines aid him? On and on he strolled as the shadows lengthened. After a while night overtook him and in the solitude of the woods he located the plus. What is a minus sign anyway but a moment of negation? Let this moment clash with another moment of negation and the negative disappears and the plus emerges—an explanation as clear as mud, no doubt, to the inquiring schoolboy.

About this time another interesting experience came Horace's way. Hitherto going to church and Sunday school had been a mere matter of course, like breakfast and clothes. Religion was a sacred subject and must not be questioned or disputed. But now he was beginning to use his reasoning faculties and to delve into these deep mysteries. One Sunday after church he asked his aunt, whom he greatly cherished and who read her Bible with diligence and satisfaction, how the Bible came about, who wrote the Book, and by what authority? The good woman was shocked.

"Why, Horace!" she replied, as she sadly gazed at him over her silver-rimmed spectacles, fallen down to the tip of her nose. "Every word of the Bible is a message: It is a letter from God. There is no problem of understanding the Bible."

Now the teaching of Professor Conrad had made it impossible, as Horace afterwards asserted, for him to go with his aunt in this matter. He was unwilling to take for granted or to assume as true the very matter under discussion.

There were also other subjects which agitated young Williams' mind. At that time the intellectual world was in commotion and the foundations of belief were undergoing revision. The spirit of nationalism had swept over the civilized world. England was becoming a far-flung Empire. Germany and Italy were nationalized. The United States were no longer a confederation of states but a Nation, unified, concentrated; and the South was still conquered territory. State socialism was challenging the democratic dogma. Liberalism was gaining ground and the social conscience of mankind was quickening.

Great seats of learning were examining such startling innovations as Darwin's theory of evolution, investigating the mistaken treatment of women, children, criminals, dumb animals, and considering the rights of labor to organize. While at the University Williams had read the magazines and such modern books as he could find. He had come to know something of Turgot's doctrine that a man's most sacred property is his labor, and the plea of Karl Marx, bitter foe of capitalism, for a classless society in which there should be absolute equality among men: "From each according to his abilities, to each according to his needs."

Though young Williams was not committed to any of these doctrines he wished to know about them. At Chapel Hill his spare hours had been given to an academic discussion of the subjects debated in the Phi Society. But he was not content with this superficial knowledge. He wished to go into the core and center of the intellectual life of America and learn for himself something of the great questions agitating the world of thought.

He still clung to the notion that religion is essential to

the well-being of the human family. He was also sure that a minister of the gospel could best aid in spreading abroad the blessings of religion. But the question of his own ability either to preach or to teach constantly perplexed him. If he remained in Gates would he not rust out? In the entire county there was no public library; among the people there was no mental attrition. It took two full days for a State paper to reach the village of Sunbury, where his father's mail was delivered.

He saw no fun in wading, waist-deep, through the Dismal in pursuit of deer and bear, nor did he relish setting steel traps for mink, raccoon, and other smaller varmints. In a word he was lonesome, and he made up his mind to quit his little backwoods school and go off and prepare himself really to teach and preach. He therefore resigned his position and applied for admission to the Yale Divinity School. He chose Yale because Timothy Dwight, a recognized exponent of Bible literature, was teaching there and had reformed and liberalized the school and given it national fame.

As may be imagined, there was a great commotion in the staid, conservative Williams family when Horace made known his intention to give up a certainty for an uncertainty, and to go, as everyone firmly believed, upon a wild-goose chase. "Is the boy plumb crazy?" said the disconsolate father. Nor was the feeling of antagonism softened when Horace announced his purpose to fit himself for the Methodist ministry. As a matter of fact, the Williams family considered him hopeless, and the neighbors called him a crank. But not all the family deserted him; his mother and little Lizzie and one uncle, these three, were steadfast and confident. Mrs. Williams approved and bestowed her blessings upon her beloved son, bidding him go forth and win.

Horace Williams did not leave home or State in bitterness of mind or spirit. At times he may have been critical of the antiquated notions and ways of his old-fashioned neighbors. While at Chapel Hill he may have concluded that the University and the public schools were behind the times and should be improved. But he was never hypercritical. His object in going to Yale was to expand his own horizon so as better to aid in improving the intellectual life of a people he loved so well.

A short while before leaving he had encroached upon his scant hard-earned funds in order to return to Chapel Hill and visit former haunts. It was the Easter Season when he reached the village. Grass, shrubs, flowers, trees, and birds were at their very best. As he strolled through the familiar campus, he listened to the clang of the college bell, rung by the faithful janitor, Wilson Caldwell, peeling forth sines and cosines and reverberating through the length and breadth of the classic groves. Into the Phi Hall he wandered, the scene of so many contests and triumphs, and gazed upon the portraits of his distinguished predecessors.

He met again his teachers, Graves and Grandy in mathematics; Hooper in Greek; Winston in Latin and German; Mangum in moral philosophy; and President Battle, friend of the human family—men who had overcome the great odds of poverty and poor equipment and a hostile, misguided public opinion and were laying the foundations of an institution whose usefulness, under God, was eventually to equal the very greatest University in all the land. Quite a boast, I admit. And yet it should be remembered that from the small, impoverished institution there soon sprang men of the greatest usefulness to State and nation.

During this visit to Alma Mater Horace often called at the home of his little friend, Mary Anderson, now a year older than when he last saw her, and far more winsome. Mary's "Grayma," as she innocently called her grandmother, was the widow of Congressman and Governor Rencher. She was now living in Chapel Hill with her daughter Mrs. Anderson and Mary and dispensing a simple, gracious hospitality. In years to come Horace's dream of happiness was sitting with his Highland Mary by the open fire in the Rencher home, as the elders plied their needles and talked of Scott and Dickens and the village gossip and the firelight played upon them all.

6

YALE, HARVARD, AND GERMANY

Young Horace's first impressions of Yale tended to confirm his fears: His native land was not keeping step in matters educational. Soon after he was assigned to his quarters, his janitor engaged him in conversation and remarked, quite casually, that the Governor of North Carolina was a fine man and much interested in education. Horace could but contrast this sage observation with the scant knowledge of his faithful Chapel Hill janitor, who was unable to read or write.

Nor had he been in New Haven many days before he heard a disturbing, slurring public address. One afternoon as he wandered around the city he noticed a placard on a church bulletin-board saying the pastor would deliver a lecture that evening and would give his impressions of a recent visit to the South. Lonesome and homesick, Horace attended, expecting to hear some news from home. Instead, the South was skinned from New Orleans to Richmond, not omitting Charlotte and Greensboro in his native State.

"My friends," said the orator, "I can tell you in a word, it is a God-forsaken country." This blunt thrust so incensed the young divinity student that he almost rose in his seat to protest.

But there were compensations. If New England was ahead of the South in book-learning she was behind in things of more value—a discovery made by Horace one day while he was walking down Elm Street in company with a brother divinity student.

"Williams," said his companion, "if I get caught in this Hebrew exam, I want you to help me out."

"What do you mean?" Williams inquired.

"Why, there are sinners in New England I must save, and the faculty consider it necessary for me to know Hebrew."

Instantly Horace turned to his companion and, looking him in the face, sternly advised him of the honor system at Chapel Hill.

"Ha, ha!" laughed the easy-going candidate for Holy Orders. "I am not interested in fairy tales."

Williams' ability to see both sides of a matter was bred in the bone. From childhood he had been in the habit of listening to both sides, generally taking the minority view, a trait further developed at Yale University.

Dr. Timothy Dwight gave the young man a new idea of an educated person, one who suspends his judgment and learns to speak the last word. In so doing, he made a permanent contribution to Williams' life. During Horace's first term Dwight gave an exposition of Paul's Epistles to the Galatians, and a stimulating period it proved. The lecturer cautioned the students not to learn the Epistle but to understand it. He then proceeded to recount the early trials and struggles of the apostle until he was finally converted to Christianity and became "a new specimen of a man." The source of this new man was Christ's confidence in the power of truth. To be rooted and grounded in the truth is to be educated, to rise above the group, to transcend the process of the particular. St. Paul saw in the life of Jesus not a partisan process but the process of truth. Paul not only transcends the Jewish process but he transcends Plato and his vital idealism. Paul was the first educated man in all history. His own statement, as written in the last two verses of the eighth chapter of Romans is the finest description of a man in all literature. Paul, as Dwight conceived of him, functioned in the truth, and there is no partisanship in truth. The educated man seeks and exhibits truth. Thus, he will support a political party only in so far as it exhibits truth. This exposition of St. Paul's view amazed the new pupil, who, years afterwards, in commenting upon Dwight's explanation of Paul, said, "I had supposed that a gentleman was a Democrat, that a Christian was a Methodist or a Baptist. To ignore the claim of any particular and seek citizenship in a universal was new. From the start I was fascinated. I accepted every chance to talk with Professor Dwight. . . . To me he was strong and big beyond any man I had known. He was the kind that enlarged my view, that challenged me to another sort of life. St. Paul . . . invited men into a new citizenship. Education is the process of this new citizenship."

The aim of education, as Dwight insisted, is truth; its technique is righteousness; its form is beauty. Instruction of this kind brought light and guidance into young Horace's life. For him Professor Dwight was a teacher, and had given an answer to the question, What is a Christian? In the Yale Divinity School Williams' search after a rational religion was satisfied. For the first time he had been instructed to seek a religion of the spirit and not of the senses—a quest, it must be admitted, rather for philosophy than religion.

Down at Murfreesboro Professor Conrad had hinted at a faith of this broad and liberal kind but had not dared to proclaim his conclusions or follow his convictions to the end. Dwight, unafraid, and in a more favorable atmosphere, did not hesitate to declare his conclusions and to follow his reasoning faculties to their utmost stretch. In one lecture, while he was discussing the verbal Bible and its importance, he asserted, in the simplest manner, that in a hundred thousand cases we do not know what the original was. All the original manuscripts are lost. In one hundred thousand cases the copies do not agree, and because of this disagreement it is difficult, as he insisted, to maintain the theory of verbal inspiration.

Horace Williams in after days declared, "I do not recall ever being so disturbed by a sentence. For the moment the temple had crumbled before me." But before finishing the course the pupil had gone over, bag and baggage, to his teacher. Williams had accepted Dwight's view that a literal interpretation of the Scriptures is impossible.

On a certain occasion at Mount Carmel Church, where students sometimes conducted services for an honorarium, Williams was the leader. His talk created an uproar. His subject was the Epistle to the Hebrews and he began by saying that we do not know its author, and that not one of the manuscripts says anything about Paul's writing it. "I am not alone in thinking Paul did not write the Epistle," the young preacher asserted. "The scholars are agreed on this matter." This bold, unvarnished pronouncement, much too sweeping it must be admitted, brought a summons for the young man before the faculty and he was duly disciplined for heresy.

A valuable thought was implanted in Horace's mind in regard to using a book. "Find a great one and master it," said Dwight. "Waste no time on collateral reading." This advice became the rule of Williams' life.

He read and reread the masters and them only. He purchased such standard works as Shedd's *Theology*, Müller's *Doctrine of Sin*, Dorner on Theology, and Otto Pfleiderer's *The Spiritual Development of St. Paul*. This last treatise greatly impressed the young student and really shaped his religious thought.

In the midst of these arduous labors Horace found little time for recreation, amusements, society, or companionship. At New Haven he was leading a life more secluded than ever before. One evening a classmate invited him to come around with a lot of other boys to partake of a box from home. Williams declined. He could not afford to waste time on parties or get sick from ham and pickles and pound cake.

But frequently he would lay aside books and let his mind wander back to college days at Chapel Hill, a spot very close to his heart, in fact his only home. At night, when northeast gales whistled through the gables and snowflakes were falling thick and fast, he would take pen in hand and talk to his Highland Mary. "Chapel Hill is a delightful place," he wrote. "I always want to go there when the summer comes. The campus, the well, the magnificent oaks still haunt me. The association is pleasant yet and cheers me in many a weary hour. After all, it is a dear old place."

Very soon Horace was begging his child-friend for her photograph and telling her he had said to Greeley, his chum, "She is the brightest woman I ever met." Addressing the little girl, who was now fast growing up, he calls her "my charming friend." "I can't bring myself to believe that you have changed as radically as the description of your photograph would indicate. I prefer the one 'whom to look at was to kiss' as most like yourself. Please send that and thereby throw a charm of the days of yore about this bachelor den."

During his second year at Yale Horace turned out in a full beard and had a picture of himself taken at Niagara Falls. This bewhiskered likeness he forwarded to Mary with the remark that it was much admired since it hid the most of his face. Again he writes to her and chronicles the fact that Nakashuma, a Japanese friend, and Dinsmore, another comrade, agree that her face is beautiful—"so filled with intellect and soul." At the Easter season he wishes for her "A calm and sweet religious day, a day of contemplation and growth of soul."

In a letter suggesting that Chapel Hill must be somewhat monotonous he slyly asks if she would not love to move to a more stimulating atmosphere. In a short while he was sending her beautiful roses and with the flowers a billet-doux: "I should like to look into those large, beauteous eyes tonight. There is in them the affection that stirs and quickens." But his letters were soon manifesting doubts. April, 1886, he writes:

"*My dear Friend,*

"As I returned from recitation this noon your letter and photo were waiting me. This afternoon I have spent looking at you. A friend from New York was invited up to meet you. If it were not against my creed to make people vain you should hear a few things said about the handsome maiden. You will pardon the slight violation for the first remark of his, 'What beautiful eyes!' This is perhaps enough to lift the veil. Women, you know, have a way of getting at things without plodding man's weary way of logic. What makes the crown of the head so white? Surely you're not becoming in the blush and beauty of youth one of the silvered locks! But pardon, please, it may be for aught I know the latest fashion. If such be the fact please don't laugh immoderately over the sweet immense ignorance of this lone bachelor. I mean sweet in immensity. I suppose one should keep posted as to such matters. But, Oh my! this little head can't keep pace with the writer's own theology. And sorely befuddled he'd soon become if flounces, ribbons, bonnets and bangs were added! *Me miserum!*

"I give you very hearty thanks. Your first description was very good—leaving out the actress. You see I did not accept your second edition on the letter 'K.' As soon as I fill with studying the face it is to go into a cute frame with red doors. Then I can open them and have your company while the heart thrills with happiness; but when those choleric spells swoop upon me the doors shall shield you. It seems that you look just a bit solemn. My last impression of you is that of a beaming, winsome lassie.

"Do you like to hold the photo of a friend for a long time and let the tide of memory roll back upon you? I fancy one must be among strangers to get the full of such communion . . . being alone and unknown seem to tune the heart strings for the softest, sweetest harmonies. The joys you have given me now play upon them. If making a wearied traveller through life's labyrinth happy brings you good cheer I charge you now be full of joy.

"Beneath the rose is the thorn. I have frequently remarked to my friends on my constitutional lack of that something which pleases ladies. I have as strong an admiration for a noble woman as any man dare lay claim to. I have made an honest effort to be manly and not to trifle. Woman's love is in many senses a holy thing. To trifle with it is akin to ridiculing Heaven. These things I believe. One may unconsciously fail in giving a daily expression in actions to his beliefs. I may have failed. Then there lies the solution to my problem. But if I may claim a modicum of success, then the solution lies, it appears, in my matter-of-factness, or lack of the poet. Woman's longing is satisfied in the heroic. She loves the dash and *élan*, the bars and banners of combat. The routine of civil life is irksome. The prosaic is to her heart as the chill day is to the flowers. Under the beams of the romantic her deepest nature unfolds, throws out its tendrils, and clings about the riven oak. I hope you are not exhausted by this effusion. Many more pardons and adieux,

"Yours,
"H. H. W."

Evidently the young man had begun to realize that the glorious Mary was not for him. "My powers of adaptation are not very great," he complainingly writes. But he must not give her up until he has seen her face again. He therefore visits Chapel Hill, ostensibly to lecture on Martin Luther but really to see Mary. Returning to Yale and reflecting on his recent visit and the number of beaux who flitted about the dear child, he almost despaired. Sadly he wrote and begged her not to marry. "If you should marry I would lose my very best friend."

As a June commencement came off at Chapel Hill with dancing, banquets, and flirtations, of which he well knew that Mary would be art and part, he grew serious and lonesome. "I am growing old and prosaic," he writes, as he decries the frivolities of the commencement and gently chides her for participating therein. Yet a desire for her happiness is uppermost. Unselfishly, he picks out a husband for her. "I presume you are about recovering from the commencement," he writes. "Of course you had abundance of fun and pleasure. That man who is 'as good as ugly' was at his best, his tongue tuned to dulcet strains and his action the perfect *suaviter in modo*. I think you will find Jule Wood at Edenton. This however is a genuine conjecture, not a vestige of fact-basis only a rational supposition since that is his quondam home. To be sure this information can't be charged with being premature, but I suggest that you send a ticket at once with, of course, the remark that you had just now learned his where-a-bouts." Thus ended the idyllic episode.*

While he was still at Yale, Williams somewhat reluctantly accepted an urgent invitation from Julian S. Carr, the North Carolina philanthropist, to join the faculty of Trinity College (now Duke University), then a small Methodist institution in Randolph County. After a year at that literalistic college, he resigned his job. But during the year he had saved enough money to spend a summer in Germany. There he mingled with the people, and at the universities he studied their system of education and delivered a few lectures. Ever after this rare experience, Hegel's *Logic*, in the original German, was kept close at hand. In after years it lay wide-open upon Williams' desk, to be often read by the midnight lamp.

At Christmas of the following year, he reëntered Yale. It was unfortunate for Williams that in the midst of his studies Dwight was called from the Divinity School to preside over Yale University. Dr. Russell succeeded Dwight,

---

* It is an interesting circumstance that Williams' prophecy came true, for fifty years after it was made Julien Wood and Mary Anderson were married, as appears later.

and Williams was disconsolate. He considered Russell a literalist. Under Russell no broad reaches of thought were possible. Russell preferred to discuss dogma rather than Christ. He reveled in the Decrees of the Synod of Dort.

From the very beginning, Russell and Williams locked horns on the authorship of the Epistle to the Hebrews, Russell maintaining that Paul wrote it and Williams opposing. In the course of the term, Russell required of each member of the class a thesis on this subject. Williams delved into his Pfleiderer and, after much research, prepared and handed in a paper combating Russell's conclusion—a study so thorough and searching as almost to change the professor's opinion.

At the suggestion of a fellow-student, Horace submitted this thesis to the Divinity School of Harvard. It won for its author a Williams Fellowship, carrying a stipend of five hundred dollars.

This new honor elated Williams not a little. But when he proudly wrote home and announced to his father's family, his mother now being dead, that he was soon to become a Fellow of Harvard the usual chilly response came back. "I see no sense in hanging around a college all your life," his brother Herbert wrote. "The thing to do is to come home and go to work."

In due course Williams became a Bachelor of Divinity at Yale and, upon graduating, was one of four out of a class of fifty chosen to deliver an address. His thesis discussed the authenticity of the Pentateuch. Here again he maintained a radical view. He asserted that Moses did not write a word of the Pentateuch, Moses having died before any one of the first five books of the Old Testament was written. A second time he was summoned before the faculty and reprimanded. Of this rebuke, he afterwards declared that he was censored for asserting that to be true which no one nowadays ever thought of denying!

Williams' life at Yale had not been happy, and he quit the institution lonely and puzzled, but full of fight. "I had no friend in the Faculty," he declared. "Professor Russell had a mild wonder about me. The other members of the faculty discounted me." *

In the early fall of 1888 the young Fellow of Harvard, with five hundred unexpected dollars in his pocket, set out for Cambridge and the Harvard Divinity School. Arriving in Cambridge, he entered at once into an atmosphere much to his liking. Professor Everett, Dean of the Divinity School, became his instructor, his guide, and his inspiration. His new experience, as he expressed it, was rich beyond anything he could imagine. Everett, a cousin of Edward Everett, and a quiet, unobtrusive man of the broadest vision and the noblest purpose, was an independent Congregational preacher, a Universalist, in fact; an idealist and a humanitarian, opposing creed and dogma of all kinds, as well as a literal interpretation of the Scriptures and the old-fashioned Hell of fire and brimstone. Under Everett at Harvard Williams picked up where he had left off under Dwight at Yale.

The Dean had a course in comparative religions, the first of its kind in America. In this comprehensive line of thought, Williams was at his best. With all his soul he entered into Everett's concept of a faith that rested on no creed and no dogma, but put Christ in the supreme place and sought truth as its only goal. The Hindu philosophy intrigued him. He read with deep interest the sacred books of the Hindus, their Vedas and Upanishads.

Men of all faiths were among Everett's pupils. George Santayana was a fellow-student with Williams. In his lec-

---

* While a student at Yale, Williams performed a notable service to his native State. He had heard much of John Crowell, Yale, 1883, a good scholar and a successful executive, just the man for president of Trinity College, at that time in a bad way, since Dr. Craven had retired and his successors were not making good. Williams recommended Crowell to the trustees and he was chosen as president. A few years after his election, the college was removed from remote Randolph County to the bustling city of Durham, where Julian Carr donated a site and Washington Duke contributed $85,000 as a starter for the buildings. In the 1920's Trinity became the famous Duke University.

tures, Everett antagonized none, sympathized with all, and confined his teachings to the realm that lies beneath all the divergent creeds.

Two of America's greatest philosophers, William James and Josiah Royce, were also Williams' instructors—Royce, author of *The Philosophy of Loyalty*, and James, author of *The Varieties of Religious Experience*, the first an exponent of idealism, the second wedded to a more practical doctrine —the bread-and-butter philosophy—"Anything that works is religion."

Williams allied himself with Everett and the idealistic group. From the very beginning he took a disrelish for James. He dubbed the pragmatist an experimenter, his feet not planted on the rock of truth but on the sands of trial-and-error.

One day in the class Everett and Williams tackled the obscure subject of spirit and the Christian life. To be a Christian, as the Dean saw it, was to live spiritually, or, in Paul's phrase, to be born again, to become a new creature.

This incident awakened in Williams' memory thoughts almost forgotten and carried him back to his father's old farm in Gates County, when he joined the Methodist church and Tamar, the black family cook, got wind of it and took him on the cross-examination or, as we would say nowadays, put him on the spot. "Tamar was friendly, called me son [I am now quoting Horace]. When we came home from the all-day meeting, the news for aunt Tamar was that I had joined the Church. She called me into the kitchen, a house thirty yards from the dwelling. . . . She wanted to know if I had 'come through.' That meant what St. Paul had called the 'new creature.' . . . Tamar shook her head and said there was nothing to it. Now the amazing thing is that Tamar was correct. I had not seen nor entered upon the new life. She had been a slave. At the close of the war she came to our place and began to work. . . . Each year she bore a child. She was not married."

Williams' course in logic was even more interesting than

the one in religion. Everett was a follower of Hegel, agreeing with him that life is not inexplicable. Life may seem criss-cross and paradoxical, but it is really uniform and certain. In all things there is unity, and to attain unity one must employ the dialectic process. There must be full and diligent investigation followed by the freest discussion. But this is not all of the dialectic process. The most important step comes next, the forming of a concept, a begriff, a blueprint.* In truth, the first fruit of intelligence is the begriff —the absolute standard of right. Never afterwards did Horace Williams doubt that throughout life one increasing purpose runs.

In after years, when Williams himself became a teacher of logic, he used as a textbook Everett's *Science of Thought*. As Everett had done, he encouraged his students to ask any question or indulge in any criticism. "In Dean Everett's classroom," said Williams, "I saw for the first time the value of criticism. Criticism deals with particulars as they exhibit truth. Hence criticism is essential to the educated intelligence."

At length, with full confidence in himself, and equipped to teach his favorite subjects, the young divinity student was packing up to go West and make the Pacific coast his home when an unexpected letter caused a change in his plans. He was called back to his native State.

---

* The word begriff, becoming as it did a part of the campus vocabulary, is handled typographically as an English word throughout.

7

RETURN OF THE NATIVE

THE CALL which came to Horace Williams was of such a kind that he could not turn it down—an invitation from Carolina, his Alma Mater, to fill the chair of philosophy and psychology, a brand-new field of instruction in the Tar Heel University. In Williams' college days a dull, dry book, Bowen's *Logic*, had been taught, but it was formal and boring, abounding throughout in syllogisms, major premises, minor premises, undistributed middles, *petitio principii's*, and a jingle of mnemonic jargon, ending in the ridiculous words *dadisi filapton*. Modern logic, the science of thought, was either unknown or, if known, was a red flag in the face of the orthodox.

Of this condition of affairs Williams was not ignorant when he arrived at Chapel Hill in the fall of 1891 and assumed his new duties. But its real significance, the deep-seated feeling against modern philosophy, even on the part of the intelligentsia, did not dawn upon him until one day in the late afternoon while he was calling on Cornelia Phillips Spencer, college critic, guardian of its morals, daughter of one professor, sister of two others, and mother-in-law of a fourth.

This remarkable personage Williams had known in former days. He recalled her as a stout, resolute woman, with head as big as Harriet Beecher Stowe's, covered with an old-fashioned lace cap. She had a long inquiring nose and keen, penetrating Presbyterian eyes. The very first of her sex to be honored by the University with a Doctorate, she was, as

Zeb Vance put it, not only the smartest woman in North Carolina, but the smartest man also. Such a powerful influence, as Williams well knew, must be placated and won over to the side of philosophy. Therefore, according to plan, the new professor, adorned in what Walter Scott would call hebdomadal finery and soothed as to his mental condition by reflections upon the teachings of the God-intoxicated Spinoza, went over and was calling on Mrs. Spencer and making the obeisance due her.

He found the village Paragon seated on her conspicuous front porch, a kind of eyrie from which her maternal eye could watch over the little community. His reception was cordial but cautious. Presently the conversation turned to the new chair of philosophy, whereupon this is what happened, as Williams afterwards told the story:

"I knew her influence, it was the power of life and death," said Williams. "A paragraph in the Raleigh paper [Josephus Daniels'] saying that the new professor of philosophy was not sound would have ended my career. . . . I entered her presence in full appreciation of the conditions.

"'I don't like what you are doing,' she said.

"'Why, Mrs. Spencer, I am doing my best!'

"'No, you are not. You are the professor of Christian philosophy. I want you to understand that we do not wish any of that Yankee skepticism down here.'"

This body-blow knocked the astonished Professor against the ropes, but for a moment only. He soon rallied.

"Now, Mrs. Spencer," he blandly smiled, "I'll tell you what I'll do. I'll call my course in philosophy Christian philosophy if your son-in-law, Professor Love, will call his course in mathematics Christian math."

"Get out of here with your impudence," roared the great woman whose sense of the ludicrous was no less developed than her other mental qualities. Ever afterwards Mrs. Spencer and Horace Williams were not only near neighbors but the best of friends.

Having passed muster at the hands of the village Cato,

though by the skin of his teeth, the young philosophy professor next had a run-in with the leader of the faculty, his old Latin teacher George T. Winston, whom President Battle characterized as a bold spirit which feared nothing. Winston had just been chosen president of the University and, as Williams humorously related, was anxious that the new professor should start off right. He wished him to teach the plain, practical, hard, horse-sense doctrine of Francis Bacon, and to cut out every vestige of superstition, of the supernatural, and of hair-splitting philosophy. In a word, Winston, according to Williams, agreed with Descartes, "Give me matter and motion and I will make a world."

"Williams," said Winston, in his confident manner, as the two strolled along the grassy banks of the winding brook in Battle Park, "philosophy is not a search after abstract truth. Philosophy is something altogether practical."

Williams vouchsafing no reply, Winston went on. "And, Williams, truth and utility are one."

Williams still remaining mute, Winston continued. "The basis of knowledge is the perseverance of power. Descartes was right. If he could discover something certain and indubitable he could rear on it a whole system of real science."

Now these utterances were rank heresy to Williams, but he continued to hold his peace, and Winston continued to lecture.

"The South needs liberalizing and that's your task. You must teach a common-sense philosophy based on trial-and-error. Give the boys Descartes."

Here Winston paused for a reply and got it. In a detached, far-away, Yogi-like manner, Williams said gently, "That's interesting, Professor Winston. But Descartes is one of the minor prophets."

This unexpected answer put an end to the lecture, and the apostle of utilitarianism and the apostle of idealism broke into a quiet, good-natured chuckle and branched off into a discussion of the more congenial topics then agitating the country—the free silver heresy of W. J. Bryan, the utter fallacy of the McKinley high protective tariff, and the growing laxity of morals among the young.

Notwithstanding the fact that these two innovators did not always see eye to eye, Winston being bold, straightforward, and sarcastic—spelling philosophy "foolosophy"— and Williams the opposite, mysterious, persuasive, inscrutable, they were, in the main, well agreed. If Winston wielded the battle-axe of Richard, Williams flashed the Damascus blade of Saladin. And both were self-sacrificing, abstemious, and devoted to the welfare of their fellows.

The experiences of Horace Williams with Mrs. Spencer and his old Latin teacher opened his eyes to the difficulties he was up against. He discovered that his main task would be to convert the faculty, who saw nothing to his foolosophy! The faculty, indeed, as Williams concluded, consisted of three groups: the fundamentalists or literalists, who hotly maintained that God made the world in six days and rested on the seventh; the classicists, who were more concerned about the ablative absolute and the ethical dative than about the welfare of mankind; and the scientists, who saw nothing to life, as Williams insisted, beyond the test-tube and the blowpipe. In this infertile field he must sow his philosophic seed and pray for a harvest of liberalism.

As he reflected upon the obstacles standing in his way, the new professor concluded that he must be very careful— step on no one's toes, offend no one, be as wise as a serpent and as harmless as a dove. But how was it possible to be discreet and diplomatic and at the same time true to truth? If he concealed his convictions would he be honest with God or himself? At all events, he concluded to unbend, to come out of his intellectual shell and become one of the plain, everyday folk. He therefore regularly attended religious exercises and was soon chosen superintendent of the Methodist Sunday school. He taught a large, enthusiastic, and highly appreciative men's Bible class, and filled the pulpits of Chapel Hill and other places throughout the State.

A short while before he entered upon his duties as professor he had gone to the University to attend the fourth Quarterly Conference of the Methodist Church and had become a minister initiate. In the records of that Conference, the following entry appears: "The license of Reverend H. H. Williams, L. P. [local preacher] is accepted and his character is passed." Under this license, which he had received at Trinity College, he frequently filled pulpits and laid the foundations upon which he proposed to build his philosophy of life. As the basis of that philosophy he placed spirit and not matter, the thought process, not the materialistic process. He did not seek, as most philosophers have done, to solve life's mysteries. His task was to teach men to think. Though he went deep into German philosophy he was not wholly a mystic. Truth, justice, law, righteousness, personality, and like abstractions engaged his thoughts.

The clashes and conflicts of life were to him the movement of the spirit. He was essentially dialectic. He swept away the gloss of exterior matter and inducted truth. To him nature was mind in solution. He did not care so much to understand reality as to live it. He would examine any proposition, no matter how obnoxious or unpopular. He flinched from no conclusion, however offensive to the people, not even Darwin's monstrous doctrine of evolution, which he had accepted and soon promulgated.

One of his early sermons, preached in a country church, is characteristic. He called the discourse "Christianity in Everyday Life." He pronounced Jesus the greatest of all philosophers, a pattern of the perfect man. Jesus, not sectarian but universal. Jesus, the God-man, but not God. Jesus did not ask his disciples to be orthodox and follow the beaten paths. Rather he prayed that "ye may be as I am." Jesus had already stated the master truth of all time, "I and the Father are one." The process of knowledge is the process of truth and when the intelligence presents the truth as reality the emotions respond and the individual enters into the Kingdom of God. Plato had seen this process, in the abstract, and had called the realities, truth, goodness, and beauty. But Plato did not see them as Jesus did. Plato saw them in the abstract, Jesus, in the concrete. The beautiful life cannot be attained by theory, it must be lived, even as Jesus lived it.

"And now," said the Preacher, as he concluded his sermon, "let me assure you that there is a power in human life to rise out of death and live again. When Hebrew civilization failed and was packed up and shipped to Babylon, it seemed to be the end of the Jewish religion. But not so; one man was left and he gave a new vision of Jehovah's plan. 'The Kingdom of God is a clean heart,' said Isaiah.

"This prophet of God moved through the human heart and not through the church. The record of the beautiful life in churches is a dreary story. The church has had no grand vision of civilization in terms of truth. Dogma, doctrine, compromise, expediency, timidity, these cross-currents have blocked the process of civilization. The church has turned away from the thorny path of truth into the easy way of desirability—a course which leads to bankruptcy and death.

"As for me one thing is certain, I must be friendly to truth. Wherever truth beckons I shall follow. Of late years science has reported that evolution holds truth. I must therefore accept evolution as an accomplished fact. My aim shall be to exhibit truth, goodness, and beauty in my life."

The preacher concluded his sermon; the choir sang the long-metre doxology; the benediction was pronounced. Slowly the congregation went their puzzled way out of the church and gathered in the white-oak grove for the usual after-preaching gossip.

"Did you hear that fellow deny the divinity of Jesus?" asked a dyed-in-the-wool Fundamentalist.

"Yes, and did you hear him endorse evolution?" added another member. "I reckon he thinks we're all descended from monkeys," he laughed. "They do say he don't even believe in Hell," sighed a pious, godly, old sister. "Well, one thing is sartin," concluded a venerable brother, who usually adorned the amen corner. "Ef the University holds on to that heathen man he'll shorely bust hit."

8

A GIFT OF THE GODS

BERTHA COLTON, who in 1891 became Mrs. Horace Williams, was born February 5, 1859, in her father's attractive home at Middletown, Connecticut. Her birthplace was about as near the aristocratic Long-Island Sound section as Horace Williams' birthplace was to the Dismal. The rearing of these young people had been as divergent as their local surroundings. Horace, the plowboy of the Dismal, had come up through the arduous school of hard knocks; Bertha had spent her childhood in a prosperous community unscathed by civil war.

At one time Bertha's father, who was an Episcopal clergyman, had been the owner of a considerable estate, but business reverses had swept it all away. His salary was not sufficient to support a family and he therefore coached Yale students deficient in English. In a few years he died and Bertha was left to shift for herself.

The Colton family was living at or near Yale University while Horace was a divinity student there.

Now at one of his evangelical appointments, in Mount Carmel or elsewhere, fate decreed that Bertha should be present and observe the young fellow in his pulpit. His text that day was taken from Paul's Epistle to the Hebrews: "The brightness of His glory and the express image of His person." The earnest young preacher unfolded the idea of Christ, in His life and in His conduct, as the express image of God. He stressed the necessity of a Christ to furnish a model for inquisitive man. He painted a picture of Jesus, the God-man, the only perfect creature, the model to be followed if one would enter St. Augustine's City of God, a city not made with hands, eternal in the heavens.

Bertha was moved by the discourse—so much so that at the conclusion of the services she, together with others, went forward and shook the preacher's hand. The two did not meet again until some time later. Bertha had moved to the city and was teaching art in the Brearly School, the old home at Middletown having gone under the sheriff's hammer and so lost to the family forever. Bertha Colton, the artist, was therefore almost as lonesome and alone in the world and quite as penniless as Horace, the philosopher. The meeting in New York seems to have been quite casual. Their love-making was typically artistic and philosophical and far from the usual intimate and lover-like performances.

"What are you doing tomorrow?" asked Bertha when Horace had called at her New York studio.

"I should be pleased to spend the day with you," replied the Philosopher.

"Agreed," answered the Artist. "Let's go to the Metropolitan Museum." The bargain was struck, and to the art gallery they went.

"Which is the best portrait in this room?" Bertha asked suddenly. Without hesitation Horace pointed to a portrait. Bertha assured him that the critics thought otherwise, but Horace stood by his choice. "I agree with you," she said.

This little ruse on Bertha's part had been carefully studied out. She knew that Horace intended to ask her to marry him. She also knew that she could not be happy with a man who had no appreciation of art. So far as the record discloses this was the extent of their billing and cooing.

On June 10, 1891, they were married, the ceremony taking place at the home of C. J. Havemeyer, sugar king, at Yonkers-on-the-Hudson. The officiating clergyman was none other than Bishop Phillips Brooks. After several weeks spent in the glorious mountains of North Carolina, climbing lofty Mitchell and picturesque Grandfather and visiting in Morganton and Blowing Rock, they reached Chapel Hill, a few days before the opening of the fall term. They were given a warm welcome by faculty and villagers. The president's wife, a New Hampshire girl, had Mrs. Williams out for a six-o'clock tea. The great Cornelia Phillips Spencer called. The old families paid their respects, the Battles, Malletts, Taylors, Mangums, Graveses, Phillipses—scions of stocks which had been connected with the University for a century. Everyone admired the bride. She was so adaptable, so unspoiled. "Why, she's just like a southern lady, not at all Yankeefied," was the comment.

But the public must have been somewhat mistaken as to Bertha's tranquillity. She was lonesome. The contrast between New York and Chapel Hill was too great. She missed the music, the art galleries, the concerts, Coney Island, excursions up the beautiful Hudson. She could not get along with Negro servants. Their slipshod ways and untidiness offended her. Their wastefulness irked her thrifty New England conscience. Not a drop of her blood flowed through the veins of anyone among her new acquaintances, only one of whom had come down from far-away New England.

At length the time came when she should return the many courtesies shown her by her new friends. She consulted Horace as to the form of entertainment she should give. A formal dinner, with a thirty-pound Chatham County bronzed gobbler, as the *pièce de résistance*, was agreed upon. Mrs. Williams herself had prepared it, unwilling that the colored cook, with her heavy hand for pepper and salt and other condiments, should spoil the fine bird.

The guests arrived, a score of the elect. The ladies removed their wraps and soon all were comfortably seated at the hospitable table. A simple soup was served, toasted peanuts, country pickles, figs from Og Tenney's orchard, and scuppernong grapes, from miller McCauley's farm, were passed around. Dinner plates, nicely heated, were brought in and piled one on top of the other at the head of the table, where sat the philosopher, Horace Williams, with an absent-minded smile on his inscrutable face. Opposite him was his beaming wife. At length the supreme moment was reached. The cook shuffled in, bearing a steaming turkey, baked to a toast, lying mountain-high upon its back in a silver platter borrowed for the occasion from Mrs. Sarah Taylor, the village aristocrat. A murmur of admiration ran through the expectant guests.

"Where on earth, Mrs. Williams, did you find that enormous turkey?"

The professor rose, wielding the carving knife and fork, which had also been borrowed from Mrs. Taylor, and acknowledged, with a nod of his dome-like head, the compliment paid his artistic companion. Awkwardly he began to carve. He sliced off a generous piece of the breast for Mrs. Spencer, most notable of the notables, and was inserting the spoon to extract the toothsome dressing of chestnut, sage, onions, spice and other delectables, when it was suddenly discovered, in more ways than one, that the noble bird had not been drawn!

The laughter of the community was not, however, entirely at Mrs. Williams' expense. Her philosophical husband came in for his share. Dearly the people loved to get off one on Horace, even at this early day. "So wise he hadn't a grain of common sense!" Out on his farm near the village he was raising ducks and one day went to his neighbor and friend, the wife of the president of the University, to purchase some fancy duck eggs. "No, Sir Professor," she laughed, "I'll not sell you any of my nice eggs. You haven't sense enough to raise ducks!"

It was also norated around that the professor did not have enough gumption to take care of the mules and cows on his plantation. As to his pasture lands they were so thin that the stock starved to death. In fact, all sorts of stories were afloat, one of them so absurd as to be incredible. Perhaps it was a practical joke pulled off by the village smart-aleck, to add to the gaiety. Anyway this story went the rounds. One morning at the village drugstore Horace's old mule and cart hove to as usual to deliver milk. When the can was emptied and turned up on its side, a large crawfish crawled out upon the floor!

But, for all this ridicule, the queer, absent-minded, philosophical professor was no man's fool, as those who tried to beat him in a trade soon found out.

The Williamses had been married only a few years when they purchased, at a good bargain, a house on the edge of the village in a grove of much beauty consisting of four or five acres. This place was known as the old Hildreth Smith property. Here Hoke Smith, Secretary of the Interior under Wilson, had spent his early days. An incident in his father's life is illustrative of conditions in the South just before the War between the States. Professor Smith, nicknamed Old Tige by the boys, was a northern man and much opposed to war. One day in 1861 when the war mania had seized the University Old Tige took his seat on the small, raised platform to hear the class in French recite. Suddenly there was a loud explosion, and Old Tige was blown almost to the ceiling!

Before Horace Williams entered into possession of the property it had been owned by the Winston family and occupied by them for nearly a score of years. The one-story, stuccoed house was old and misshapen, a rambling, inconvenient affair on the side of a steep incline. At the bottom of the hill was the famous Roaring Fountain, a spring distant two or three hundred yards from the house. From this spring and up that long incline water for the home must be toted. A more inconvenient dwelling would have been hard to find. In truth it must be said of the old place that for the inconvenience of housekeeping it had no parallel except perhaps the habitation of an eastern Yogi. "The Yogi paid close attention to the abode," we read in the ancient books. "The practice of Hatayoga required the Yogi to live alone in a small hermitage, situate in a place free from rocks, water and fire, where he would not be disturbed. The hermitage should have a very small door and should be without any windows. It should be dimly lighted and smeared over with cow dung."

Mrs. Williams made some improvements in the house. On the south side she arranged a study. She likewise changed the vestibule into an inviting studio. But even with these additions the place was so old and poorly arranged that it was a nightmare.

Occasionally she would leave her primitive abode and cross the street to visit with a professor's wife and unbosom herself. "In the name of high heaven," she would laugh, "what could have possessed me to leave the comforts of New York City for the inconveniences of Chapel Hill!" Sometimes she would cheerfully relate how she had discharged her cook and was doing her own work in order to raise enough money to buy a new dress, or some fancy article.

Once she told a neighbor of her lonesome life, especially at night when Horace would be in his study, where the only student's lamp burned, pouring over his philosophy. Presently she would creep into the study and sit very quietly, reading an art book. As she would finish a page, she would turn the next leaf as noislessly as a mouse, but even this disturbed Horace, who would flinch and glance her way. The next page she would turn even more noiselessly. "Its your presence, my dear," the overwrought philosopher would ejaculate, nervous and wholly absorbed in the task of reforming southern thought.

Because of conversations of this kind, some of the neighbors concluded that Horace Williams was mean and stingy and even unkind to his wife. But were they not mistaken? Undoubtedly she loved him and he loved her, that is, they loved one another as much as two people—unemotional, cold-blooded, intellectual—could love. Williams' whole life was a tribute to his mother and his wife. No person could have exalted the marriage estate more highly than he did. "To be associated with a great woman," he once declared, "is indeed the choice gift of the Gods. Somehow the wife lifts the man. She is a living invitation into the higher life.

To be happily married is the basis of success, to be adequately married is a fortune."

Why, then, it may be asked, did Professor Williams not fix up a home and spend his salary for pleasure and for his wife's comfort? The answer is that both of them wished to lay by a competency for old age. She was a thrifty, close-fisted Connecticut Yankee. He was possessed by a poverty-complex, compelling and controlling. They were indeed two of a kind. He recalled the horrors of poverty and the pangs of hunger; she had seen the ravages of debt, sweeping her father to his grave and their elegant home to the auction block.

On one occasion he told her of a professor in the University who had squandered his salary and died leaving a dependent widow and three small children. On a cold December day as he passed by the widow's home he saw her in tears and without food or fuel. He sent her a cord of wood. "And now, my dear," he continued, "here is my quarterly check, five hundred dollars, a heap of money. What shall we do with it? We can spend this money and live on credit, but is this wise? I have observed that each one must pull a load. My plan is that we bear our load while young." Bertha heartily agreed. They then bought two thousand dollars of stock in a prosperous corporation. In a short while they sold the stock and bought real estate. In one of these trades he realized a profit of fifteen hundred dollars. With this check in hand he walked into Mrs. Williams' room and placed it in her lap and said it was hers. She put the entire amount into a dining room suite of mahogany, a wood she dearly loved.

Undoubtedly Bertha Williams was lonely, but so was Ruth, the beloved consort of Boaz, as she sighed for her far-away home. In Bertha's heart there was,

> *The self-same song that found a path*
> *Through the sad heart of Ruth, when, sick for home,*
> *She stood in tears amid the alien corn:*

But there were many compensations. She and her husband were becoming independent. He was a leader on the campus. His study was the resort of perplexed people from far and near, seeking advice, consolation, and guidance. Her studio, with violin and palette and easel and paints, was a delight. She could divert herself with music and art, in which her husband coöperated fully. Indeed, he was never happier than in the praise of her as artist and musician. Her drawings and paintings hung on every wall of the old home. A handsome miniature of herself he kept always in front of him upon the desk.

The walks around her home were inviting, incomparable for variety of soil and scenery, of hill and dale. Not far distant was the bed of an ancient sea with queer deposits of marl and fishbones. A short way out and to the north of the Durham highway was a mineral spring, where she and her friends, and the entire community indeed, would gather in the early morning hours and drink the health-giving waters. She knew and loved every tree and shrub on the old homeplace, the famous Japanese ghinko tree which Dr. Cheshire, father of the Bishop, had planted, the massive oak in front with a swing attached to a dependent limb, the graceful elms, the evergreens, the flowers, and the rank hen's-nest grass, where bob-white whistled at eventide.

No doubt these pastoral surroundings made an appeal to the aesthetical, nature-loving Bertha. Nature never does betray the heart that loves her. And yet she was lonely. Naturally so. The pathway which she and her husband had chosen and were treading was rough and thorny. Away from old friends, away from kindred, with a philosophical husband abstracted and bent over his books, she was quite alone. Oftentimes her childhood days in the beautiful home at Middletown would come to mind.

Walking over to the bookshelf she would take down sister Lucy's charming little idealistic work, *Children of the Old Stone House*, the story of the four Colton sisters, their names disguised and changed. She herself had become Bettina; sister Lucy was Millie; the other sisters were Frankie and Susie. Her papa and mama were called Mr. and Mrs. Faxon. As she turned the pages her eyes would fill with tears. She could see the dear old home, of cream-colored stone, its shapely cupola, two chimneys, immaculately white and jutting above the roof. And then the greenhouse, the croquet ground, well-trimmed hedge, the three terraces, the orchard, the well, so deep and cool, and the gardens of lilies and ferns.

In the chapter called "Pets" she read an account of her early aversion to cats. It seems that sister Millie, when a babe, had fallen from her crib and broken her collar bone, whereupon Papa Faxon required Maggie Maloney, the nurse, to remain in the nursery and watch little Bettina, who had succeeded Millie as the infant—a regulation which the fun-loving Maggie resented, her head being set on a nightly visit to the Jubilee Service. Now before leaving little Bettina in her crib, Maggie manufactured an amazing tale. "When I take this light away," said Maggie in a deep, terrifying voice, "a great big, white cat, its teeth shining, its bristles up, its claws out will appear on the wall up there and the very moment you whimper that cat will drop down on your chest and smother you to death!" Until the nurse returned, Bettina would lie almost without drawing a breath.

Bertha Colton was twenty years old before she overcame her horror of cats, but when she succeeded she did so most effectively. In her Chapel Hill home cats were Bertha Williams' best friends. Every rug had its cat.

9

MENTAL MIDWIFE

HORACE WILLIAMS was fond of a saying of Humboldt's, "What you want in the Nation you must put in the schools." This maxim was improved by Kesler, of Vanderbilt, who added, "And what you want in the schools you must put in the teacher." It is the teacher, therefore, who molds character and turns out real men, not books, nor costly trappings, nor a champion football team.

Measured by this standard, Horace Williams, Old Man Horace as his boys called him, has had few superiors.

From childhood he had a controlling ambition to become a real teacher. Like Socrates he would be a midwife, an accoucheur to young minds giving birth to their ideas. On a certain occasion he was summoned as a witness in a case on trial at Hillsboro, the county seat of Orange, the county in which Chapel Hill is located. To magnify the witness's importance with judge and jury and add weight to his testimony, the examining lawyer asked Horace what was his profession, expecting of course some such high-sounding reply as, "I am the Professor of philosophy in the University of North Carolina." Instead of this pompous answer the witness replied, in the most careless and indifferent manner, "Teacher."

Yet, in those early years, he did not neglect duties outside the classroom. He coöperated with the faculty in developing athletics and was a regular baseball and football fan. He loved to boast of the wicked ball which he served on the tennis court. When President Battle first called on the new professor and asked his views on athletics, he replied that he was heartily in favor of them. "Not football," objected the old-fashioned president. "Yes," was the reply. "That is the best of all."

Soon after Horace's arrival in Chapel Hill he appeared on the main street of the village in a tennis suit, knee-breeches, bare arms, and a striped shirt. The professors and ther wives were shocked. Such lack of dignity was unpardonable. "See that outrageous man!" one lady exclaimed.

So provincial was the University at this time, that a rule was in force forbidding intercollegiate athletic contests. This ordinance localized Chapel Hill and was obnoxious to the students, red-blooded youngsters full of life and adventure. A bunch of the athletic boys called on old Horace and asked his assistance in repealing the narrow rule. Williams coöperated with them and drew up a petition assigning strong reasons why intercollegiate contests should be allowed. The petition was granted, and Chapel Hill was soon playing good ball with colleges North and South.

The new professor's activities extended likewise to the insufficient eating facilities of the University. He took part in establishing a well-furnished mess-hall and was on the faculty committee which saw that the new enterprise func tioned properly. When the profits of the Commons were not plowed back into the department, he protested and resigned from the board of governors.

The honor system made a strong appeal to him. He strove to stimulate an ethical spirit among the students. He would develop and reward leadership in all directions. He therefore joined with Eben Alexander and Edward Kidder Graham, to establish the Golden Fleece. This distinguished order, molded somewhat after Skull and Bones at Yale, was very close to Williams' heart. As he visualized the Golden Fleece it should look far-afield and render adequate service. It should seek to develop leaders, men of more than ordinary ability. "Such men cannot be grown in the mechanical process of education. Somehow we must tap the fountains. In the spirit of this adequate service, in the challenge of this larger life, the Golden Fleece seeks itself."

Horace Williams' chief interest, however, centered in the science of debate. For nearly half a century he was the inspiration of University debating activities. Under his instructions Carolina debaters, grounded in the dialectic method, forged to the front, and soon the strongest colleges bowed before Horace's well-trained logicians. The reason for this development is manifest. Williams' classroom was a free-for-all debating club, the foundation-stone of which was the method of Socrates. If indeed that eccentric old Athenian had chanced to stroll in as the exciting battle was on, he would undoubtedly have felt entirely at home. Horace's classroom was a hot-spot where there was neither ceremony nor formality, and where no quarter was asked or given—everything free and easy, teacher and pupil on a dead level, thrust and parry, the rule.

Horace's philosophy room was one of the most commodious on the Hill. Its walls were adorned with numerous blackboards, four large windows opened out upon a grove of venerable oaks, and twenty or more semi-circular benches, rising one above the other, accommodated scores of students. Before facing his boys he made it a rule to prepare the lectures with great care, oftentimes sitting up till late hours of the night, digesting Hegel's *Logic* in the original German. His habit was to enter the recitation room in advance of the class. As the students—together with the assembled guests, consisting of preachers, teachers, and curiosity seekers—poured into their places, they would observe the Teacher standing with his back towards the door, gazing out of the window into space, a solitary, abstracted figure. After a few moments the noise of trampling feet would cease and silence would prevail. The Teacher would then begin his talk.

A panorama of lightning-like rays of light, homely illustrations, abounding humor, merciless personal criticism and prodding. Possibly the subject would be the category, one of the most basic classes to which objects of thought may be reduced. Other philosophers made use of a number of categories; Horace employed three only, quality, quantity, and relation.

"What do you understand by quality, Mr. Ray?" the professor would softly begin.

"Fineness, Professor. High-grade stuff," Ray would venture.

"No, not fineness. Can you help us, Mr. Broadhurst?"

"Why, it's what the thing is made of, Professor."

"That's some better. Quality is the thing itself, the essence."

Here Old Horace would strike his stride and be off on the categories, quality, quantity, and relation. Quality, being the thing itself, how can it become something else? How can a thing be itself and yet not itself? This is the puzzle which the scientist is unable to solve. "When I ask a chemist what water is, he tells me it's hydrogen and oxygen; that is, water is not water at all but something else. At this point the scientist stops, he goes no further, but philosophy goes beyond this and solves the paradox.

"Quality becomes quantity when it ceases to exist and dies. Out of death comes life. The grain of wheat is sown and in due season dies. Out of its death comes thirty, forty, fifty new grains. Minus three multiplied by minus three gives plus nine. When the death process ends the life process begins.

"In a recent lecture Mr. Bernard raised an interesting question. He said I had been talking a great deal about religion but had not used the word miracle. 'No,' I replied, 'it's my fixed rule not to lecture on a subject until I have achieved a begriff of that subject. I know nothing about miracles.' Now that answer was satisfactory to no one, least of all to myself. I concluded, therefore, to investigate further. I must answer Mr. Bernard's question or my logic must go into bankruptcy.

" 'What is a miracle?' Mr. Bernard asked. Well, it is that which happens when quality and quantity are related, that is, when the impossible happens. Quality is that which maintains its identity in itself. Quality is in itself absolute, just as God is absolute. Under these conditions there can be no relation between quality and quantity, but there is, since relation is the unity in difference, the synthesis of opposites. Miracle, therefore, is the dogma of relation. There can be no relation between quality and quantity, but there is. Quality, the unchangeable, becomes quantity. This is miracle."

At this point Old Horace paused to let his words soak in, whereupon one of the brightest of the boys, Tam Bowie, spoke up and said, "Professor, I don't see a bit of sense in all that." Old Horace, after eyeing the young man in a pitiful manner, walked away to the window and gazed out upon the giant trees, some of them hundreds of years old. After a pause he spoke very softly, as if addressing himself alone, "It's my fault, Mr. Bowie. I should have made the point clearer. You must think the question over and report at the next lecture."

The professor used no textbooks and assigned no lessons. He simply taught or conversed in the Socratic style and expected his boys to absorb his lectures. Oftentimes his examination paper consisted of one question only, "Trace the course." Though Everett's *Science of Thought* was recommended to the class, the Professor did not confine himself to any one field of philosophy. He did not concern himself with such insolvable subjects as the origin of matter or of mind or even of species. Nor did he split hairs with Hobbes and those philosophers who teach that the infant mind is a blank and is operated on only by outside impressions. He dealt with mind and matter as actualities, in much the same way as Dwight of Yale and Everett of Harvard had taught.

At the beginning of the course he would lay the founda-

tion deep and firm, frowning down upon interruptions.*
The concept or begriff was the cornerstone of his logical
process. Logic is the process of intelligence and intelligence
achieves itself in the begriff. Begriff is the way an object is
made. The begriff is the structure of the process as it appears in the object. The structure of the process is the type.
The begriff is more than the type, it is the type as expressing the object and the object as in and of the type.

The process of the begriff is an orderly process. It is the
process of civilization and of constructive growth. That is,
the individual advances upon himself. He is a son, a father,
a citizen, a scholar, a Christian. As perfect obedience is demanded by science to her method and laws, so in the moral
sphere. One cannot express character in violating the Decalog of the moral life. "Thou shalt not lie" is grounded in
the character-process as H_2O is grounded in the water process. Working within the begriff, science has changed man's
attitude to nature. It is not chaos or illusion. It is an orderly world. On the social level there is a similar achievement.

When the individual sees himself in terms of the begriff
he is more than an animal. The begriff becomes his aim, his
center; it incarnates itself in the individual, lifting him into
the sphere of character. The physical loses its importance.
History accepts him as a hero. A few individuals have developed a perfect character, that is, a character beyond the
reach of the physical to crack. Every people that reaches
the level of the begriff has its Daniel, an individual of character beyond the reach of any known force. . . .

It is sometimes objected that there is no such quality as
the absolute or the infinite. It is urged that all things are
relative. And yet, at our very doors we find examples of the
absolute and the infinite. The begriff of water is H_2O, an absolute symbol, the square root of 10 is 3.333—an infinite
series.

---

* The reader will find this line of thought developed in Horace Williams'
Modern Logic, pp. 45 *et seq.*

We have just seen that the begriff of water is H_2O, what is the begriff of God? Since God is truth, the process of truth is the pathway to God. Let us trace this pathway. The starting point is the individual, I, the One. The starting point is self-evident, intuitional. As the apple seed is the starting point of the apple process, so the One is the starting point in the process of knowledge, whose goal is God or Truth.

Logic, as we have seen, is the process of knowledge. Knowledge is on three levels, the static, the dynamic, and the organic. The static is well known to everyone. It is the level reached through the five senses, seeing, hearing, feeling, tasting, and smelling. The lower animals attain this level. The dog, the horse, the cow operate on the static level. But man rises out of the static level into the dynamic or scientific level, where the object is analyzed, dissected, and its parts exposed. Science is the insight into the object. Science is friendly to man. It works for him and brings him vast power. It teaches him patience and obedience. It is the career of the begriff in the sphere of nature. Science is orderly and continuous. The lamb process is always lamb; it is never the dog process. Birds are after their kind, fishes after their kind, and animals after their kind.

Science does not, however, explore the third level of knowledge, the organic. Life is organic. Intelligence seeks itself in truth. The passion for truth is the philosophical impulse. The individual, seeing himself in reality, must be in himself the source of the process of reality, its pathway being the dialectic and the begriff.

"What I am saying to you is this," and the professor would slowly conclude his fundamental lecture. "The facts are necessary. They come first and must be analyzed. We then must lose the facts and obtain the laws illustrated in the facts. This gives us mastery of the facts. But we must go further. The facts must find themselves in some unity. The law must be seen as the life of this unity. And so we reach the stage of vision—of insight into the nature of truth—that is, in an organic unity. That day a fire is kindled in a soul that will not burn out."

Now there was nothing new or original in this metaphysical discourse. It was but the groping after God through the intellect, the teachings of the Yale Divinity School founded on Immanuel Kant's synthesis of the concepts. What was it, then, that swept generations of young people off their feet and worked a miracle? It was not only the novelty of the thing, it was Horace Williams himself: his magnetism and personality, his rich well-modulated voice, his earnestness and sincerity, his conviction and confidence—those intangible qualities characterized by Demosthenes as action—it was this that so stirred the emotions of the young men in his classes that one of them, Ralph Harper, afterwards a clergyman of the first rank, was moved to declare, "I did not anticipate Heaven for I knew I was already there."

In those early days the South had not been stirred intellectually. The strange, new philosophy which Horace Williams was bringing was therefore taken very seriously. And there were the usual growing pains. Deep was calling unto deep. The campus at Chapel Hill was stirred to the center. Horace's boys were busying themselves with begriffe and concepts. Concepts were formed of poverty and progress, of war and peace, of society and crime, of orthodoxy and unorthodoxy, of anything and everything.

One day after a lecture on concepts and begriffe, George Connor, a scholar and a great joker, raised a laugh. Pointing toward Old Horace, who had left the classroom and was on his way home, George whispered, "See here, fellows, I've made a discovery. That word begriff is a misprint; it isn't begriff at all—it's giraffe. And darn my buttons, if I don't intend to tell Old Horace so!" But George never dared to.

10

THE REACH AND THE GRASP

AT YALE and Harvard, Horace Williams' hours had been useful in one respect only and that was in the field of religion and logic, the most beautiful and the most useful of all studies, as he devoutly declared. He prized very highly the educational system of New England and the way in which every community and every individual took part in public affairs. But at Yale and Harvard he made no study of government or the sciences. The pursuit of abstract knowledge, this and this only, engaged his thoughts.

After his arrival at the University he continued in the same course. The upheaval which he proposed to start was to be ethical and intellectual, not social or political. He would attempt to reconstruct southern thought. He would substitute the objective for the subjective; in the place of the personal he would put the impersonal. At Chapel Hill he took no direct or active part in the social or political activities of town or state.

His job was with fundamentals, with the thought-process of the people. If he could pass along his own ideas and sufficiently impress the youth of the land, he would thereby improve the fountain-head, and the stream would be purer and more wholesome. Somewhat after this fashion he put the case: "Give me ten real leaders upon this campus and I will dominate its thought." He did not propose to pull down the strong but to make them stronger and thereby to pull up the weak.

"If I can save one thoroughbred, the rest may go," was a

favorite saying of his. In a word, Socrates-like, he worked from the top down and not from the bottom up.

Throughout the South, as he well knew, there was much room for improvement. In parts of his own State the school term was only three months. School attendance was voluntary, and the one-teacher schoolhouses were dreary and bare. There were no public libraries, and the newspapers were local, partisan, and uninteresting. Roads were well-nigh impassable. Epidemics of diphtheria and typhoid were frequent. The death rate east of the Roanoke River, where huge doses of cholagogue were taken nightly to overcome ague and fever, was so high that no one could get insurance in a reputable life company. Agriculture lagged and was confined to the one-crop system, usually the cultivation of cotton. Industry was in its infancy, money scarce, country life humdrum. Things generally were out at the heel.

Such bad conditions demanded attention. Who should undertake the job? Williams concluded that he was the man to help in the liberalizing of his State. Not directly, but indirectly, not as an active participant in affairs, but as the Warwick of youth, to mold their minds, to educate them, and to turn out leaders who would make a new land.

Down in Georgia industrial and humanitarian leaders had already appeared. Such men as John B. Gordon, Henry W. Grady, Clark Howell, and Joel Chandler Harris were making of Georgia the empire State south of the Potomac River. In North Carolina, however, the social, industrial, and educational awakening had not yet taken place. Life was at a low ebb, existence on a small scale. The tax rate was low and taxes were grudgingly paid. Though the State possessed advantages of soil, climate, water-power, and healthfulness, unexcelled, no effort had been made to develop its industries or to advertise its advantages. The governor of the state was usually but a glorified brigadier, a stuffed shirt to lend dignity to state occasions, and never more than a moderator. The chief topic of discussion was politics, how to hold down the nigger, and how to keep the little brown jug full and always handy, and at the same time be a good prohibitionist. The State's slogan was of a piece with the general mediocrity. "What did the Governor of North Carolina say to the Governor of South Carolina?"

Happily these conditions presently were to change. Aycock, McIver, Joyner, Alderman, and Walter Page were already at work and, together with industrial leaders, greatly aided by the Populist revolt and the emergence of the University of North Carolina, were soon to remake an old Commonwealth. In this glorious awakening what part was the professor of philosophy to play? Would he take the stump, canvass the State, go to the legislature, make the laws, coöperate with various social and educational groups in active work, or would he stick to his last and become the gadfly, the Socrates of Chapel Hill, stimulating the youth and sticking pins into stuffed shirts? Would he endeavor to bring the liberal, and therefore much execrated, notions of Channing and Emerson from Boston to North Carolina, at that time rated as the tail-end of illiteracy?

As we have seen he chose the latter course and, as he concluded, the nobler one. He would be a teacher, a provoker of thought, and follow in the foolsteps of Socrates, wagering all he possessed of brains, place or influence in the task. He would give himself to his boys.

While a student at Harvard he was constantly hearing of a simple, self-effacing individual, Garman by name, who was teaching philosophy at the small college of Amherst, not a great way from Cambridge, and who was so molding the character of his boys as to create a spirit of loyalty to Alma Mater and to truth which was beginning to enrich American life. Garman's classroom was indeed a laboratory of experimental thinking and his course in logic was the pride of every Amherst alumnus.

Now Amherst was but a small college, not much larger than the University of North Carolina. Why might he not become another Garman, or even a Dwight or an Everett, and kindle a flame of knowledge to lighten his native land, as teachers elsewhere were doing? In all ages, as he often claimed for his profession, it had been the teacher, the seer, the prophet—the Isaiah, the Jeremiah, the Buddha, the Socrates—who had moved mankind upward. The age of Pericles was just such an era. The spirit of that golden age was not the clash of arms, nor the fortitude of the people, nor the beauty of the temples. The glory that was Greece was the Teacher. What period can compare with the age of Pericles, the *fons et origo* of modern civilization, the day of the Teacher, when Anaxagorus taught Archelaus and Archelaus taught Socrates and Socrates taught Plato and Plato taught Aristotle and Aristotle taught Theophrastus and Alexander the Great?

Undoubtedly there had been useful teachers in Williams' native State, but they were teachers of the "greats" only—Latin, Greek, and Mathematics. But, all the way from Boston to Galveston, there was not a chair of modern logic. In North Carolina, which was a typical southern State, the Binghams, the Horners, the Lovejoys had conducted excellent classical academies. And yet it may be doubted if a single teacher of them all had ever run across the magical word begriff or knew that it was Socrates who established the concept, or begriff, as basal to knowledge, or that the solution of problems is the achievement of the begriff, or that the begriff had been raised to the dignity of ontology—in a word, that the begriff is the basis of everything, the key to all knowledge, the blueprint of eternity.

It was this kind of pure knowledge that Horace Williams proposed to impart. As Emerson in his "Divinity School Address" had proclaimed an intellectual Declaration of Independence to New England, so would the new professor of philosophy set free the people of his native State. Now when Horace entered upon this seemingly impossible task he surely had his nerve about him or else he was taking long chances. Daily he was striving to demonstrate to his students something which he was teaching to be an impossibility, that is, the reconciliation of irreconcilables. He proposed to intervene and shave old Shaggypate. He would cut off the whiskers of superstition and orthodoxy. Not as did Sibli Bagarag, the barber of Meredith's incomparable allegory, with the aid of Noorna (science) alone, not with the sword of Aklis, but with the sword of the spirit and the power of truth.

By what stretch of the imagination did Horace Williams reach the conclusion that he could transpose the ultra-liberal views of cold, unemotional, intellectual Yale and Harvard to the warm-hearted self-satisfied, fun-loving land of plantation barons and fox-hunting squires? At all events, such was his purpose, and fortunately his surroundings were not altogether unfavorable. Battle, the genial and beloved University president, who had literally raised the venerable institution from the grave and had conducted its affairs as no one else could have done for fifteen years, had retired. Winston had been chosen to succeed him. Of necessity, Battle had been conciliatory. Winston was aggressive. Under the new policy the University was moving forward. Appropriations were increased, the number of students had risen from two hundred to five hundred. Valuable additions to the faculty were made and necessary equipment was supplied.

When Winston was inaugurated, he spoke words which greatly encouraged the new philosophy professor. He acclaimed the honor system; he showed the money value of education; he likewise stressed the idea that the University was in no sense a machine or a factory but a vital organism; and he urged that the University campus should be extended to the boundaries of the State.

Walter Page's address on this inaugural occasion likewise delighted Professor Williams. After Page had portrayed the difficulties of the past and the hope of the future and had exhorted a wise settlement of the relations between the races, he turned to the new president and begged him to remember that there was but one courage, and that is the courage of truth, because there is but one victory, and that is the victory of truth, which is the invincible voice of God.

"To every mendicant tradition that asks favor of you," said Page, "to every narrow ecclesiastical prejudice that shall demand tribute; most of all to the colossal inertia that you inherit, in whatever form they come, in whatever guise they present themselves—to them all say with kindness, but with firmness

> '*Go honored, hence, go home,*
> *Night's childless children: here your day is done,*
> *Pass with the stars and leave us*
>   *With the sun.*' "

This was new and strange doctrine, coming from a southern college chapel. Indeed it was startling! Hitherto such addresses had won popular favor by the propagation of platitudes, by the saying of undisputed things in a solemn way, and by not even speaking disrespectfully of the equator! Page's address was a departure, and Williams took courage. The two men were indeed kindred spirits and had often conversed together of southern affairs. He and Page were traveling in the same direction. Along the paths outlined by Page he would train his thoroughbreds to tread. He would put them in every community of North Carolina, and, as far as possible, throughout the South, to leaven the lump or ignorance. He and his boys should work a miracle. No difficulties should deter. The Fundamentalists should be conciliated; these sincere, devout people should be handled tenderly. They should be won over by the glorification of Christ, the very center of hope and civilization, and by acclaiming truth, goodness, and beauty as the goal. No quarter should be shown the materialists or the scientists who saw nothing in life but corruptible matter. These stubborn, self-sufficient, half-baked investigators should be laughed out of court! The classicists and the dilettantes were a small, innocuous group. They should be ignored.

A colossal undertaking, that of Horace Williams, it

must be admitted. No lesser task than the transmogrification of a people—

Ah, but a man's reach should exceed his grasp,
Or what's a heaven for?

Surely if little David, with no armor save the mantle of righteousness and with no weapon but a pebble and a sling, could slay the giant Goliath, Horace and his boys might go forth and slay the giant Ignorance.

11

BEGRIFF IN ACTION

PROFESSOR WILLIAMS loved to call himself an Hegelian. But it must be understood that while he taught the philosophy of Hegel he practiced the methods of Socrates. In substance he was Hegelian, but in form he was Socratic. With Hegel he was wedded to the idea of absolute truth, which must be attained by the dialectic process, by cross-questioning, by conflict, and by the use of concepts. But in the method of teaching this philosophy Williams followed Socrates.

Of Hegel we read that he was a timid person, small and insignificant in appearance. While lecturing he always sat with his head bowed and with a snuff box on his desk in easy reach. His long, insipid lectures were written out and, as he would laboriously read, each sentence would be interrupted by a cough. Horace was the opposite of all this. Tall, erect, raw-boned, confident, defiant, he had a mission in life and all Hell could not head him off. In the classroom he always stood. His lectures were delivered extempore and with a punch. Oftentimes he would leave abstract, metaphysical subjects and deal with the homely happenings of village, state, and nation.

After the manner of Socrates he would wander around the streets and play the gadfly, prodding and teaching people whether they liked it or not. He would stop a dignified member of the faculty in front of the postoffice and ask him the most embarrassing questions. He was particularly fond of showing up the Ph.D.'s—"experimenters, men whose intelligences were trained but not educated." "Your Ph.D. can tell you precisely how many hairs there are on the left hind leg of a dog and which hair is in the exact center."

The scientific method of trial-and-error bored him. No scholar moved on that level, he would quietly remark. The scholar investigates, assembles the facts, and draws a conclusion. The scholar does not experiment. The scholar knows.

Pickard's livery stables and the village drugstore were his hanging-out places. There he would run up against the saucy, corn-field denizens of the village, Og Tenney, Tom Lloyd, George Pickard, and others—strong-minded men, standing firm in their shoes and not over-educated. In these rugged surroundings he would try out his philosophy, gather the village gossip, swap yarns, cows, horses, anything and everything, and get down to real life. Thus armed with new and original thoughts he would betake himself to the classroom and begin an interesting hour. "Professor Williams," Bully Bernard would perhaps saucily break in, as the lecture began, "I have caught on to you. You don't lecture, you just tell us what's going on in town."

"That's interesting, Mr. Bernard. So you have made that discovery, have you? I was afraid you would not catch on to my plan."

After the laugh would be over Old Horace would proceed to put the begriff to work, making a kind of experiment station, an intellectual laboratory, of the classroom. In a solemn, self-depreciatory manner he would give his idea of what a real teacher should be. The teacher deals with the life of intelligence. The real teacher puts the begriff to work. He insists that a blueprint is necessary. Without a concept or a chart to guide, man is but a vessel afloat upon an uncharted sea. As in the world of nature, so in the world of spirit, there is orderliness and a definite goal. Unit and universe are round. Seed are sown, death follows, and then comes life; this is the nature process. It is also the process of philosophy: affirmation, negation, synthesis.

Perhaps he would then spring numerous homely illustrations upon the class to exemplify the magical concept.

"Mr. Jacocks," he would ask, "what is the most important part of an ox-cart?"

"The wheels, Professor," Jacocks would glibly reply.

"No, not the wheels."

"Then, Professor, it must be the body," Adams would venture.

"No, not the body."

"Is it the ox, Professor?" Thompson would timidly inquire.

"No, not the ox. It's the concept of a cart, the blueprint. After the blueprint has been made, any jackleg can do the rest. The blueprint is immortal; it lasts forever. The cart soon wears out. Euclid is a concept of geometry. Euclid is stable, firm, invariable. Euclid is more real than matter, more enduring than stone or iron. Science changes; the concept never changes."

"Professor," said W. J. Brogden one day, as the subject of the validity of concepts was under perpetual discussion, "you are always talking about the concept, but have never given us your concept of God."

"That's a fair question, Mr. Brogden, and many philosophers have tried to answer it. Spinoza tried and explored the absolute. Kant tried and illustrated the process of intelligence. Then came Jesus and answered your question, harmonizing the discord. 'God is Truth,' said Jesus. 'I in Thee and Thou in Me that we may all be one.' If religion is to be in and of life, then the dedicated life is the fit expression of religion."

"But, Professor," Bynum added, "I want you to show God to us, not philosophize about God. Show Him to us."

"Mr. Bynum, your question places you in the sensory class. On that level the horse and the dog move. Man has risen out of the realm of the senses. Spiritual things are spiritually discerned. Intelligent man has a standard, the brute has instinct only."

"Now, sir," broke in Hughes, a candidate for the Episcopal ministry, "all that's fine, but it's not practical. I charge that you plow and harrow but you don't sow."

"Your remark is interesting, very interesting, Mr. Hughes. But do you think I should control your actions, put you in a strait jacket? I furnish you with a kit of tools. It's your part to use them."

"But, Professor," broke in John Umstead, one of the crack debaters, "we boys don't always know how to use those tools. You mix us up. Take that big idea of yours that dualism is wrong and monotheism right. How do you reconcile that idea of unity with the parable of the sheep and the goats, the sheep on the right-hand side and the goats on the left?"

"Do you know goats, Mr. Umstead?"

"Oh, yes sir. Out on Flat River, where we live, we raise a lot of goats, and sheep, too."

"Well, Mr. Umstead, which is the smarter, a sheep or a goat?"

"Why, a sheep, sir."

"Are you sure of that, Mr. Umstead? I know goats and I know sheep. When a Mississippi flood came some months ago every sheep in the low grounds drowned, but the goats had more sense. They climbed on top of the floating houses and ate shingles all the way to New Orleans, where they got off in safety."

"Well now, Professor Williams," said Harper, who like Hughes was preparing for the ministry, "there's something I've wanted to ask you all this session. Do you really believe in an ever-living, an ever-present, God?"

"Yes, Mr. Harper, I believe in God." Then, after a pause, "Do you believe in God, Mr. Harper?"

"Why, certainly I do, Professor. In my home I was taught that God is all-powerful and can do anything he wishes to do, and I believe it, too."

"Do you think God could cook breakfast with a snowball?"

A knock-out blow of this kind would put an end to all questionings and the class would subside into silence. Old Horace would then use the remainder of the hour to amplify the morning's round-table, sometimes recounting an incident in the life of one of the Masters. One day he told a story of Epictetus, the slave of Epaphroditus, born during the first century, A.D.

Epictetus was asked how a man might convince himself that every single act of his was under the eye of God. He answered by desiring to know if his questioner held that all things are bound together in one. The answer was in the affirmative. The next question was—"Are all things on earth and in heaven continuous and in unison with each other?" Again the reply was in the affirmative. "If, then," said Epictetus, "all things that grow, nay, our own bodies are thus bound up with the whole, is this not still truer of our souls? And if our souls are bound up and in contact with God, as being very parts and fragments plucked from Himself, shall he not feel every movement of theirs as though it were His own, and belonging to His own nature?"

"Professor Williams," said Rondthaler, one morning, in a rather dejected manner, "they say you flunk boys just for the fun of the thing. Is that so?"

"Not exactly, Mr. Rondthaler. But you raise an interesting question. I rarely give an A and never an A in a boy's first quarter. To do so would be to spoil him."

"But, Professor," interposed Wilson, one of the brightest students on the Hill, "we boys want to get to be Phi Beta Kappas and if you flunk us we can't do this."

"I expected you to say that, Mr. Wilson. Striving for Phi Beta Kappa and for other college honors has its bad features. That idea has ruined many of my boys. If a boy's heart is set on some college honor and not on improving his mind, I do not wish him in my class. My aim is to set a standard so high that it will be an honor to pass my course. Flunking a boy puts him on his mettle and often leads to victory."

"But, Professor," Carmichael inquired, most sympathetically, "don't your severe methods raise up a lot of enemies?"

"Yes, Mr. Carmichael," the professor answered, "I have enemies, but I should doubt my own integrity if I had no enemies. Out of conflict comes truth. Truth is to be found at the end of a rocky road."

"While you are speaking of truth, Professor," said Russell, "I should like to ask if you think a lie is ever justifiable."

"No, Mr. Russell, I do not think a lie is justifiable under any circumstances whatsoever. If there were to be one exception to the rule of truth there might be a dozen exceptions. Such a variable rule would be no rule at all."

"Mr. Graham, would you tell a lie to save the life of your mother?"

"Well, now, Professor, that's a hard question, and I'll have to think it over."

"Well, sure thing, I would," hotly broke in Miss Penn. "I'd tell a dozen lies to save the life of my mother."

"No, you are mistaken. If you did and someone asked me if you were truthful, what would I say? Had Socrates deviated one jot from truth he might have saved his life. Had Jesus stayed away from Jerusalem he would have lived. But how much poorer the world would be without the example of Socrates and of Jesus. The great of the earth lose themselves in a great cause—the quest of the absolute."

After a reflective pause Tillett asked, "Professor Williams, after all, do you really consider anything settled and above dispute?"

"Mr. Tillett, your question requires a double answer. If you mean to ask whether I, Williams the individual, think anything settled, my answer is 'Yes.' Truth is settled but the world disagrees with this and puts truth itself in dispute. Expediency seems to be the rule and in its justification an old saying is quoted, 'Circumstances alter cases.' There was never a more hurtful or a more fallacious saying. On this level a lie becomes truth; on this level crimes are justified, wickedness enthroned, and disorder prevails."

"Professor," interrupted Robinson, "we boys are beginning to dub you an individualist, almost a solipsist!" As the class coughed a derisive cough, Robinson concluded, "Are we correct?"

"You use such big words, Mr. Robinson, I can't follow you."

"Well, I'll cut out solipsist and ask how you can be an individualist, fly in the face of public opinion, and not do violence to Geist, a principle you talk so much about?"

"I am glad you raise that question, Mr. Robinson. It shows thought. Geist is useful; it is growth. Geist reveals the consciousness no longer as critical and antagonistic but as the indwelling spirit of the community, but beyond Geist is Aufklärung when the mind gradually emancipates itself from conventions and superstitions and substitutes the moral view of the world. This moral law gives place to God when the spirit knows itself as spirit. The vice of our day is mass psychology, mass activity—quantity without quality. Even the Supreme Court of the United States has fallen into this heresy. They seem to hold that a judge should have no convictions, no standards. A judge should be a good clerk, a first-class statistician, he should poll the people, count them one by one, tabulate the results, ascertain what they want and decide accordingly! What the end of this half-baked method will be, unless there is a return to honesty, is plain, a house built upon the sand has but a frail foundation."

"I judge from what you are saying, Professor," spoke out Ross, "that you advocate free speech, free thought, and free action, under all circumstances and regardless of consequences?"

"Yes, Mr. Ross, I do."

"Do you contend that even the Bible may be discussed and criticized and dissected?"

"Undoubtedly. If the Bible cannot stand criticism, it should go. Truth is impregnable."

"Then you oppose the recent censorship of college publications by the faculty?"

"Undoubtedly. Let me tell you a little story along this line. Mr. Stacy was once editor of the magazine and wrote a piece for his paper. The president of the University sent for him and ordered its suppression. Stacy was perplexed and came to my study to ask advice. I was shocked at the president's action, and so informed Mr. Stacy.

"'Shall I submit?' Stacy eagerly inquired. 'Never!' said I. You go to the president's office and say this to him, 'Mr. President, do you still insist on suppressing my article? Do you stand by your decision that it shall not appear in the next magazine?' He will undoubtedly answer, 'Yes, Mr. Stacy, the article is obnoxious to the faculty and shall not be published.' 'Very well, Mr. President,' you will quietly reply, as you pick up your hat to leave the room, 'this matter between us shall be threshed out in the public press.' The editor followed my advice and shortly came back to my study, quite happy. 'It worked, Professor,' he said."

At different times John J. Parker and W. P. Stacy were students of Horace's, Parker afterwards becoming the second United States Circuit Judge North Carolina can boast of, and a model judge to boot, and Stacy becoming the great Chief Justice of the Supreme Court of the State. While Stacy was a student, George Washington University challenged Carolina for a debate. The query suggested was, Resolved that the principal of Labor Unions is inimical to the best interests of the laboring class. At a preliminary meeting of the debating squad the matter had been considered and the affirmative of the question chosen—that is, the class decided that labor unions should be put out of business. This decision was duly reported to the philosophy class by Stacy, who was one of the debaters.

"What do you think of our decision, Professor?" said he.

"It's all wrong, Mr. Stacy."

"Why, Professor, the economists advised us. They told us there was but one side to the question. They called our attention to the cost of strikes, to the loss of time, and to the bad feeling engendered. They insisted that we should stress concord and brotherly love between master and servant, and further that—"

"Yes," wearily the philosopher sighed. "I'm not surprised at the economists. They are over-educated. Does it hurt religion to organize the church? Did it damage social life when the state was organized? Education was not damaged when this University was organized. Is labor to be segregated, set off by itself, picked upon?"

"Is that the question?" Stacy gasped.

"Yes, when you have formed a begriff of the matter."

"Then we take the negative," said Stacy.

An interesting episode followed. At the next commencement Stacy was one of the speakers. He enlarged his thesis, used the same analysis, and won the Willie P. Mangum medal for oratory.

One morning when the village of Chapel Hill was holding an election to authorize bonds for roads and to borrow money with which to move forward in population and in wealth, if not in ethics, Professor Williams entered the classroom with a smile on his usually imperturbable countenance. He had just withstood public opinion and voted against the bond issue, the crowd standing around the polls and scowling at him.

"Young men and young women," he quietly began, "I am just back from the voting place and this I tell you. There has seldom been a better example of crude thinking than is going on down the street at this moment. A few of the leaders started a racket for good roads. They made no investigation of the subject, they had no blueprint. Orators took the stump. The press followed; the faculty, even conservative men like Dr. Mims, went wild; people, like sheep followed the tinkling of the leader's bell. I raised my voice against this folly. I inquired what material would be used in building the roads, what would be the cost per mile, and which highways would be reconstructed. I was ridiculed, brushed aside as little better than a simpleton. A few moments ago I cast my ballot against the bonding of our town for this foolish enterprise. The mob which surrounded the polls was almost ready to tear me to pieces. Let time judge between me and the misguided populace." *

"Professor Williams," said Teague, one of the best debaters in the class, "may I ask you a question?"

"Yes, Mr. Teague, if it's to the point."

"Mr. Williams, if you continue to defy public opinion, are you not afraid of losing your job?"

"No, Mr. Teague, I am afraid of nothing except offending God. In the Christian process there is no compromise. This means war, reform, infinite restlessness. But, as Christian, one must get a begriff of reality and devote himself wholly to that begriff. As Christian, one ceases to be natural-minded; he becomes spiritually minded. If teaching the Truth, and living the Truth, Mr. Teague, shall cost me my job, or my head, so be it. I can do no other."

Thus daily was Horace Williams proclaiming sentiments of the loftiest. Did his conduct always square with his teachings?

---

* Bonds were issued, many thousands of them. Roads, thin and unscientific, were hastily thrown up, and the next July freshet washed them into the Haw River.

12

STRUGGLE AND CONFLICT

As session followed session, and class after class was taught by Old Horace, wild rumors began to float around and spread from the ocean to the mountains. Students would write to their parents and tell them astounding stories of Horace's strange sayings and his political and religious vagaries; during their vacations they would gather in public places and boast of their new concept of life. The newspapers began to inquire if public funds should be used to hire a professor to teach atheism at Chapel Hill.

The Fundamentalists were deeply stirred; they resented the idea that the Bible, or any jot or tittle of it from Genesis to Revelations, was untrue. But neither warnings nor threats swerved the professor of philosophy from his course. In the classroom and in his study, on the streets, the lecture platform, and before select groups, he candidly expressed himself, standing firmly upon the principles of correct thinking, common sense, and individualism. Never, however, did he rant or scold, or become personal or vindictive.

When a religious journal would attack him or a preacher from the pulpit call him an atheist and take him as a horrible example of anti-Christ, he would show no resentment and make no harsh reply. His strength lay in a studied understatement. The people who abused him were not bad, he would say, they were uninformed and uneducated. The way to meet such attacks, as he concluded, was to show the authors the error of their ways. So numerous grew the complaints that his old boys, now scattered throughout the State, urged him to make reply.

With much reluctance he consented and went forth and spoke before curious audiences in the larger cities, never referring to the attacks on himself or calling any names, but quietly outlining his philosophy and elaborating his religious convictions. "I welcome criticism," he would begin. "Free discussion is necessary. Conflict is not wholly bad." These ideas he would then proceed to elaborate. Life is an antagonistic process. In the lion process the lamb is killed and eaten. The lamb disappears. The lion lives as he kills.

The process of intelligence is not so; it is more like the wheat process. The grain of wheat as it sprouts does not destroy the grain form. In the process it will reappear in twenty new grains. But the moments in the wheat process do not coöperate. The moments of the intelligence process do coöperate. . . . God and man are related. The One, the I, is the unending struggle between two selves. The struggle cannot be finished. The Christian life, in its structure, is a triumph and a disappointment, a success and a failure. As physical life has its spring, its summer, its winter, over and over, so the Christian life is an infinite hope and an infinite disappointment. The Christian process is an imperial achievement: It has gone to the corners of the earth and found a foothold. For two thousand years the continuity is unbroken. It will never die. . . .

When Saul had found the solution for his problem he became Paul. The discovery made the Pauline theology. The Christian process is a process in truth. It is the process of the perfect individual; the absolute God; the synthesis of these moments. There can be no compromise here. Christianity is the living truth, the synthesis of the absolute process as absolute, the individual process as individual, in the truth. The first step is to translate the content of truth into terms of the process of intelligence, to categorize the process. The first step in building a bridge is to know what the project is. If one is to be a Christian, he must know what it is to be. This was the work done by St. Paul. He does the kind of service for Christianty that Galileo did for science.

The relation of which we are speaking is vital. "In Him, we live and move and have our being," says St. Paul. Faith is the relation that guarantees to the individual his salvation, that is, his ultimate value as individual in the absolute process of ultimate reality. The process of the individual in the process of reality is the goal.

At the conclusion of this deep metaphysical discourse the old philosopher would raise his long bony arms, as a signal for the audience to rise, and in a rich mellow voice would say, "May the God of Truth endow his earthly creatures with the spirit of wisdom and righteousness, so that at last we may all enter into those mansions not made with hands eternal in the Heavens."

Discourses of this nature had their effect. Horace's boys and the liberals were delighted; good Bible Christians were softened; but Fundamentalists and die-hards were unconvinced and resentful. "He's a slick brother and will bear watching," they would shake their heads and say.

When Winston accepted the presidency of the Texas University and left Chapel Hill, Alderman succeeded him. This change in administration was irksome to Williams. He considered the new president a photographic, surface character, an accomplished orator, picturesque and handsome, but without depth. Despite the difference in outlook between the two there was no breach. Very soon, however, a lack of cordiality was manifested. A celebration in Memorial Hall to honor Carolina's victory in debate over Georgia was held. Bowie and Broadhurst were the heroes of the occasion and had been trained to a nicety by Horace Williams, indoctrinated into his pet hobby of the begriff and the concept, by use of the dialectic method, thereby penetrating to the principle involved and cutting out the collateral, the extraneous, and the incidental.

Upon this joyous occasion an enthusiastic crowd of students had gathered, and Alderman and Williams had been chosen as the roustificators. Alderman spoke first and in his ornate, flowing captivating manner. His central thought was the dignity of labor, the exaltation of work. "Buck the line," he exclaimed. "Without labor there can be no reward." Amidst enthusiastic clapping of hands the speaker resumed his seat, having swept along the entire audience except one man. Old Horace was not only unmoved, but resentful, almost mad. President Alderman had reflected upon his teachings; moreover he had totally missed the point. In winning the debate labor had been a secondary consideration. The thought process had won.

Slowly rising to his feet and looking the crowd over Horace, in a voice filled with resentment, but thoroughly restrained, made bold to reply. "I beg to differ from our distinguished President," he quietly began. "Work is a material process. Work did not win this debate. My boys moved on a higher level than work. They planted themselves on the plane of principle and of character. Each of them as an individual, grounded in principle, moved forward to the attainment of truth. Let us not descend to the valley. Let us stand on the heights. The individual grounded in principle always wins."

Williams resumed his seat and Alderman was visibly nettled. He had been rebuked by his subordinate. "Yes, indeed," said he in reply, "the learned Professor of Philosophy may be correct. His begriff and his concept, his one among the many, and his individualism may be all he claims for them. But let me say this, I have known the individual to be a fool."

This incident points a moral. Horace Williams was not diplomatic. He was blunt-spoken and often offensive. Just as Socrates used to do, he would do—fling discretion to the winds and seize upon some public occasion to make an opponent appear ridiculous.

Alderman was perhaps the most accomplished university president the South has ever brought forth. In the languages he was deeply versed, and as a public speaker he was in the highest class, along with Choate and Depew, if not their superior. But he was deficient in the natural sciences, in mathematics, and in sociology. While superintendent of public schools and professor of pedagogy he had canvassed the State for universal public education and had rendered invaluable service to the people. During the short period of three years that he was president of the University he opened its doors to women and accomplished other fine things. With might and main he strove to give a certain degree of style to Chapel Hill, to tone it up. Hence his nickname, Tony. His tendencies were altogether aristocratic. He could not fit in with the homely democratic ideas which characterize the popular Chapel Hill University. When called to the city of New Orleans as president of Tulane he therefore quickly accepted.

Francis Venable succeeded Alderman and again Williams was disappointed. He considered Venable a rule-of-thumb man, a scientist and nothing more. A fine type of the hated Ph.D.'s, a group which stopped in the particular and never penetrated the sphere of the spirit. One day when the new President called Williams to an eleven-o'clock conference and Williams arrived on time to find not the president but a note directing him to call again at four, the professor of philosophy got on his dignity and at the hour of four was astride his saddle horse reviewing his farming operations.

F. P. Venable was, beyond all doubt, the most learned chemist Carolina has had. Moreover, he placed the University on a scholarly and a scientific basis. He was one of the most useful and laborious executives in the line of great presidents. In his administration, however, Williams sensed danger ahead. He feared that Carolina would become so scientific that philosophy, aesthetics, and fundamental thinking would be crowded out. This tendency he set himself to combat, at all costs and without let-up.

During the past two administrations the University had grown in numbers but little. As yet, it had failed to touch the heart of the people or to show its value to the State at large. Moreover the fight with denominational colleges was still raging. Many strong professors, however, had been added to the faculty, some of whom were Williams' friends. Others were indifferent to him. Many were resentful because of his slurs at science and his ridicule of college government.

Some of the new members of the faculty had bought lots and built homes just across the street from the Williams' place and were strictly up-to-date in their sanitary arrangements. They had no cow, no pig, no horse, and no chickens. They screened their window, swatted the flies, and poisoned the breeding places. Now in these sanitary precautions Horace Williams did not coöperate. He proposed to live precisely as he had lived when a boy down on his father's farm in Gates County. He kept animals, a "mess" of them, a cow, two horses, and numerous chickens. His back lot was a wilderness of tumble-down cow sheds, unscreened horse stables, and antebellum slave quarters, a breeding place for flies, mosquitoes, and other insects and, from the beginning of time, a source of friction between neighbors. Very soon these conditions were to flare up into serious antagonism between the professor of philosophy and his more coöperative, but less individualistic compeers.

Already, indeed, neighborhood gossip was busy, specially among the ladies. "An old hypocrite," they would sneer, "always prating about uncovering the human soul, he'd better be covering up his cow dung! Mean, stingy! Buying up Negro houses and charging unreasonable rents. In the classroom a saint and on the streets a devil! Well, one thing is certain—the stingy old thing can't take it with him."

Such was the talk of some of those who disliked the individualistic philosopher. But there were others and many of them, including neighbors, who overlooked his oddities and held him in a respect which amounted almost to admiration. Let us not pass a hasty judgment upon these charges of stinginess and avarice. The question as to how Horace

Williams finally disposed of a fortune laboriously built up by thrift, self-sacrifice, and economy remains to be answered.

With the passage of time Williams became in theory more religious but in practice less so. Though he would sometimes accompany his wife to her church or she would go with him to the Methodist church he ceased to be superintendent of the Sunday school and to teach the Bible class. Long before this time he had abandoned the idea of becoming a minister. In truth, he was turning more and more to the doctrine of Channing and Emerson, as taught by his preceptors, Dwight at Yale and Everett at Harvard, with this difference, however: he considered Jesus the image of God Himself. Religion he looked upon not as creed or dogma but as spirit.

His wife had become his good angel; John Stuart Mill was not more indebted to Mrs. Mill than Williams to Mrs. Williams. She had learned to prepare choice dishes to tempt his failing digestive organs. She had come better to understand Negro servants. She played soft music when he was overwrought. She stimulated him to go forward, breathing a new spirit into him. She insisted that there was no height which he could not attain. Their only sorrow was the lack of children.

Frequently Mrs. Williams would arrange an afternoon tea in her studio and serve the simplest refreshments with no tobacco in any form and no intoxicants of any kind. These social affairs delighted her husband. In the midst of the prattle and social gossip he would awkwardly stride in and make foolish, banal observations and then retire. He had no small talk.

Her husband's study was the object of Mrs. Williams' best thought and attention. This den or study was of ample dimensions, being some twenty-eight or thirty feet long by twenty feet wide. Four large windows looked out upon a wealth of oaks and elms. The fireplace was closed up, a King heater, burning pine knots, serving as a heating plant.

Bookshelves full of books devoted to philosophy and printed in German circled the room. Above the shelves there were numerous paintings done by her own hand, the Madonna and Babe, classical reproductions, and homely scenes and characters of the village. Two of these paintings are notable. One of them is of an humble patriarchal Negro man with a shaggy beard, of benign countenance and patient aspect. The other represents an elderly country woman, the salt of the earth, with furrowed cheeks, and wearing a fly bonnet.

The thoughtful wife, having purchased a table large and handsome, had placed it in the center of the den. Around the table were a dozen or more plain, ordinary chairs, two of them rockers. A cheap davenport stood to the right of an outside door through which visitors might enter without passing through other portions of the dwelling. The most conspicuous article in the den was a handsome miniature of Mrs. Williams which always confronted Horace as he sat in his old-fashioned swivel chair and pursued his studies by the light of a student's lamp.

As the years came and went, the study of Horace Williams became not only historic but an institution. In this philosophical den his classes would sometimes assemble and recite. Every Tuesday evening from 7:30 to 9:00 o'clock, for a half-century, a seminar would be held around that famous table, and difficult questions would be debated, such as causation, original sin, individuality, the One and the many, space, time and deity, freedom and responsibility, the concept of atom. At one of the seminars Ann Forbes Liddell (afterwards head of the Philosophy Department of the Women's College of Florida) read an illuminating paper which touched the very heart of Williams' philosophy. Many of these theses were published in pamphlet form and circulated.

This study of Horace Williams, however, served a deeper purpose than as a mere recitation room. To this inspiring spot came disheartened students, village preachers, perplexed people from far and near, from Raleigh, Durham, Hillsboro, Oxford, Pittsboro, and Greensboro, seeking advice and encouragement, gropers in the dark, children crying in the night and with no language but a cry. Invariably the visitors would go away encouraged, stimulated, and edified, having been assured that they, as children of God, would find an abiding place in the Father's House. The philosopher had confirmed his belief in immortality, had said that the Christian is a new type of individual, and that the change of center from flesh to spirit might be illustrated by a change in life when animals pass out of water and find themselves on land.

Professor Williams' study was indeed the Mecca of old Horatians when they returned to the Hill, to live over again happy college days. With many of his boys he had kept up a correspondence. Some of them he had visited, all of them he bore in his heart, their triumphs were his triumphs, their sorrows his sorrows.

Despite Old Horace's caustic tongue and merciless criticism of economists, scientists, and other rule-of-thumb men, as he called them, his relations with many of the faculty and villagers continued cordial. At all athletic gatherings he was one of the chief speakers. In Memorial Hall, upon commencement occasions, he offered prayer. His reading of the Bible was unsurpassed. Who of his auditors will ever forget his rendition of the first chapter of Romans, notably verse 14; and of the Epistle to the Galatians, Chapter One, notably the 18th verse (Moffatt's translation). A sympathetic reader with a deep spiritual voice, without self-consciousness, bombast, or theatricals and with due attention to the value of the cæsural pause, he moved on the level of the spirit, not of the flesh. When the seniors received their diplomas he spoke unforgettable words of encouragement and admonition. On one occasion when a meeting was held in honor of Charles Baskerville, a great chemist under Venable, Professor Williams was one of the speakers.

At a dozen or more homes in the neighborhood Mrs.

Williams would often call and sit a while, and indulge in neighborhood gossip, her conversation almost always turning to her husband. How he suffered from poor digestion and how she must feed him almost as a babe. Every morning she would walk to the village postoffice and to the stores and markets, and when she made purchases, she would pay cash and, true to New England breeding, take the articles along home contrary to an ancient, lordly, southern custom. "If the nigger wasn't made to wait on white folks, what was he made for?"

In her strolls about the village Mrs. Williams would be often joined by her friends Mrs. Bain or Mrs. Pratt or Mrs. Stacy or Mrs. MacNider or Mrs. Daggett or Mrs. Van Hecke. Occasionally her husband would join the party and joke Mrs. Daggett about her numerous progeny. He was fond of the prattle of children; their innocence and artless ways pleased him. In the late afternoons he would saddle and mount his horse and gallop, with grace and dignity, out to his farms which lay just across Bolin's Creek and a mile or more from the village. Hardly a day came without this visit to his beloved hobby, a plantation which his brother, Paul, superintended for several years. During one year Horace's favorite sister, Lizzie, came to Chapel Hill and was a welcome guest in the Williams' home.

Thus, day by day, strove and struggled Horace Williams, gadfly of the village, his chief pleasure the consciousness of difficulties overcome, his aim to develop a race of superior men, his hope hundreds of boys, loyal and devoted, scattered throughout the State and in many parts of the South—a rare individual, solitary and isolated, but driven forward by an uncontrollable impulse, by an inexorable fate. "I must, I must, I must," held him thrall.

13

THE GOOD TEACHER

Garrick's well-known couplet characterizing his friend Goldsmith,

> *Here lies Nolly Goldsmith for shortness called Noll
> Who wrote like an angel and talked like poor Poll,*

is in no wise applicable to Horace Williams. In the classroom or on the platform he was unexcelled, whereas at his desk and with his pen he was dull and lifeless.

Even this commendation of his platform performances, however, must be somewhat modified. Only when speaking on a favorite topic did he rise to the heights. Addressing a picnic party or any other gathering where platitudes were in order he was as flat and thin as a May shad in spawning season. But let him tackle some great theme which engrossed him, such as education or religion or philosophy, and rarely was sweeter music ever heard. As a speaker he used no artifices. He was neither theatrical nor conventional. He never ranted or indulged in artificialities. His spirit spoke, not his body.

He spurned the elocution voice, and in later years the radio voice, mechanical, overtrained, emphasizing the wrong word to catch the ear of the groundling though it might make the judicious grieve. Superlatives and generalities he avoided. Adjectives, adverbs, interjections, these hindrances to the orderly flow of thought, he rarely employed. Like the rugged Homer he used short, robust, rock-ribbed, nouns and verbs.

His excellence as a speaker must be attributed to the training which he got as a debater and an essay writer while a student at the University and as a member of the Phi debating society. My friend Gladys Hall Coates has made a comprehensive synopsis of the intellectual and sociological activities of this society and of the Chapel Hill community covering more than one hundred continuous years and including the subjects debated, essays written, college politics discussed, and village gossip in all its varying moods. This study is indeed a mirror of community life and is unique. Its value as source material to some future historian, a Macaulay or a John Richard Green, may not be overestimated.

As I glance through this document, now lying open before me, I am struck with the part Williams played in the activities of his day. Not only at Chapel Hill but throughout the State. There is scarcely an issue of the *Alumni Review*, the *University Magazine*, *The Hellenian* or the *Yackety Yack* without some reference to Old Horace, either by way of praise or censure. The *Daily Tar Heel* often featured his eccentricities and whimsicalities, but usually wound up with high praise of his honesty, fearlessness, and broad view of college life.

The far-sighted man was commended, on the one hand, for espousing the side of the underdog, for enlarging the electorate, advocating the election of officers by the student body, and taking this privilege from the few; for extolling the honor system and contending that the student body was capable of self-government. So superior was the University debating team under his dialectic training that, at a great annual alumni banquet, he was heralded, amidst applause, as "the apostle of debate." On one occasion when he spoke at the Y.M.C.A. and called for twenty men to join him in the resolve that gambling should have no place in this student community, the auditorium was crowded to the doors. On all occasions he frowned upon strong drink and upon dissipation of any kind. So much for the good things spoken of him, but what of the bad?

Contributors to the college periodicals sometimes attacked him because he flunked students without cause. They likewise asserted that his conduct did not square with his teaching. He should coöperate more and teach less. He was an old fossil, a twentieth-century Socrates. To give point to these criticisms it was charged in the village drugstores that he drove hard bargains. On one occasion he loaned the sum of eighty dollars to John Caldwell, one of the thrifty Negroes of the community and took a note and mortgage for a hundred dollars. Insinuations of this kind, it must be admitted, were unfortunately true. When Horace came face to face with a trader, someone on equal terms with himself, he was as rough as a cow's tongue. Memories of a destitute childhood and dread of a dependent old age haunted him. Moreover he wanted to show that he was a great business man and not a fool-philosopher! This he did on a noted occasion.

There were two rival banks in the village and Old Horace had stock in one of them. He made an examination of his bank and formed a concept. He arrived at the conclusion that the village could not support two banks and that his bank was the weaker and would not survive. He therefore sold his stock to a member of the rival bank, at a handsome profit. The wise ones of the community laughed and said Old Horace had made a fool of himself again. But a few months afterward when the bank failed and its stock became worthless, they changed their minds.

Occasionally an anonymous contributor, who perhaps had been flunked, would write a letter to one of the college publications and characterize Old Horace as a shallow fellow, a mere braggart. "Why isn't he humble?" they would ask. "Why does he claim to know it all?" Now it must be said that these attacks but added to his popularity and swelled the attendance at his lectures. Surely a man so much talked about must be worth while. Besides, what difference did it make, this darting of arrows at the sun? Were not the students, almost to a man, backing him up? Undoubtedly they were, and so were the trustees, a hundred of them, chosen by the legislature because they were strong, influential, and independent.

As might be expected, Old Horace's fame was not confined to the village of Chapel Hill. The entire State was aware of him, some for him and some against him. As a speaker he was eagerly sought after. Unfortunately he never wrote out his lectures and there were no shorthand reporters to take them down. Only one, so far as I can discover, is extant. It was published by his friend and faculty associate, N. W. Walker.

The subject of this lecture was "The Good Teacher." The occasion was a meeting of the teachers of the State at Chapel Hill during a flourishing session of the Summer School. When it was announced that Old Horace was to be on the platform, expectation ran high. Hundreds of teachers from ocean to mountains, and some from adjoining states, crowded the hall and filled the galleries. It had been whispered around that the speaker had something on his mind and was going to tell it. Perhaps he would state his religious convictions and reply to his critics.

Quietly and smoothly he began: "I should like to say in the beginning that I wish you teachers would dismiss from your mind any feeling that you may have that you are to listen to a lecture. My invitation this evening is that we study together the subject which I think must be of deepest interest to each one in this hall, 'The Good Teacher,' and I must begin with a little bit of pessimism. It seems to me that frankly we have to admit that things are not quite what we should like them to be."

Here he paused to let his words sink in, and after a few seconds resumed. He said he wished to ask the teachers what we do when we educate a man. He then went on to say that he had asked this question of a good friend of his, a professor of science. "What do you suppose was his answer? His answer was, 'We make him efficient.' Then he looked at me, something in my face suggesting that he should complete his definition, and added, 'I mean efficient along the right lines.' Well, that was an interesting statement! An educated man is an efficient man, is he? I think not.

"I asked another friend, likewise a professor of science, 'What do you do when you educate a man?' 'We give him the ability to think,' he answered. 'Well, you do! Please educate me.' 'Well, now,' he rejoined, 'is not that what we do when we educate a man?' 'No,' I replied, 'It is not what I do.'

"I asked another man, also a professor of science, the same question. He said you stir up in the student the spirit of inquiry, you give him the capacity to know the truth if perchance he should happen to find it. The man who has the spirit of research, as he said, is the educated man. Now such answers as these may exhibit the low ebb of our educational system. Is there anybody in the hall tonight, who can put these three answers together and find out what we do when we educate a man? If so I wish he would come around tomorrow and tell me. It is quite too much for me!"

At this point the lecturer paused for quite a while and seemed to be forgetful of the fact that an audience was hanging on his words. At length he resumed and asked if superficial teaching had not lowered the standard of intellectuality in the State. At this hour is there a great doctor or physician or lawyer or preacher in the entire State? If there were any biggest lawyer or other man somebody would have found him. He could not hide himself under a bushel.

Have we, then, ceased to grow men of true State proportions? If this is the fact I think the subject which I invite you to study with me is a timely subject. But, in advance, let us inquire if this situation is our fault. Not entirely, I conclude. Three influences have contributed to it. The first is the terrible civil war when thousands of our best young men were killed, men of imagination, of courage and of daring spirit, leaving behind the prudent, prosaic, cautious men, good fellows, but limited by their nature. In the second place war left us very poor; there was neither time nor money to spare for education. Hence very few men gave themselves the discipline they would otherwise have enjoyed.

But more important than these is our teaching, our pedagogy. Our methods of teaching are a curiosity. Let me tell you a funny thing about our work here in the University. When a student comes here and expresses his purpose to specialize in English we welcome him and tell him the requirements. And what do you suppose they are? Well, English is a language, and if a man is to teach a language it would seem logical that he study the best of all languages, which undoubtedly is the Greek. To require a knowledge of Greek therefore would seem a logical thing. Not so; the student may do as he pleases about Greek. But he must study a science. In the name of common sense why must a man who makes the teaching of language his profession be compelled to study a science?

The answer is simple. The men who teach science in the University outnumber the men who teach language. On the whole, I am driven to the conclusion that we do not believe in education. We are emotional. We are partizans of a theory. We have a scheme and this scheme must prevail. One day it is vocational training, the next day it is scientific. The third day it is classical. Education—the full, free, profound development of the individual, is not an article of our faith. Education is not fundamental in our living. Education is an instrument of social preferment or of official success or material profits. The passion for truth, the persisting effort to reach it, full confidence that it can be attained, submission to its sway, these are rare qualities.

I wish to be frank. Let us see our task. The picture I am drawing seems to me underdrawn rather than overdrawn.

Is there a way out? I think there is. I have already said we do not believe in education. We will take a little church education, or a little university education, but education pure and simple, never! This situation makes a man visionary, or materialistic, or skeptical. In the face of it what is the Good Teacher to do? Let me try to answer this question. The French have a fine phrase—*la grande passion*. The Good Teacher has this grand passion. His one desire is to see the truth prevail in the lives of men and to see the lives of men illustrating the truth everywhere. If you have not this passion, I cannot see why you teach school. I think you should not try it. You will not endure the strain upon your patience, your temper, your health. But if you have this passion, then I ask you to consider with me the method of its work.

I think it is unfortunate that we use the word knowledge in the singular. I think the word should be knowledges. It is a mistake to try to put all the activities of the mind into one word. They do not fit. There is knowledge, and there is knowledge, and there is knowledge, three sorts of knowledge, because the mind works in three ways. Every human mind functions in three ways and no human mind has ever been able to translate these three ways into one. I want you to take that statement and consider it.

In my class room I always say over three different times a thing which is interesting. One day a student of mine noted this and said that it bored him. "Well," I said, "it bores me." But it is this way: in the class there are bright students, those of medium intellect, and dull ones. The Good Teacher and his class are a company and they must go along together. The Good Teacher, therefore, goes over the subject three different times. Did you ever try to measure molasses with a yardstick? Try it sometime and you will appreciate the teacher's difficulty. You will lose your molasses, ruin your yardstick, and get no results. It is nothing against the molasses, it is nothing against the yardstick, though you get the best yardstick in Chapel Hill. They simply won't get together. It is not the proper way. Did you ever try to measure a silk dress with a quart pot? That cannot be done. Did you ever stop to wonder why it is that a good merchant has a yardstick, a quart pot, and a pair of balances? It takes all of these to do business; he cannot carry on his business without this equipment. It is in the nature of business.

So is it with the mind. One mind is a quart pot, another a yardstick, still another a pair of balances. Of course these are not the proper terms but I simply want to bring out the differences. If the mind works as quart pots and yardsticks it is not your fault or my fault. We are made that way.

Now, let us see if we cannot discover what are the three ways in which the mind works. The first we call the perceptual process, the second we call the scientific or conceptual, and the third mysticism, inspiration, the power of vision.

Amidst the closest attention the speaker continued:

"The perceptual mind depends upon the senses. It works only when the object stands off by itself. Let me give you a simple illustration. Some day when you are in High Point, drop in the law office of Barnhardt and introduce yourself. He is a good friend of mine. One day after the class he came to me and complained that there was one trouble with my philosophy. 'Well,' asked I, 'what is that?' He said, 'We can't pray with it.' I replied, 'That is a pretty serious trouble. Why can't you pray with it?' Then he said, 'I cannot pray unless I can see God.' I think that was a very remarkable statement. He had to see his God if he prayed. Now that is the perceptual mind. If you talk about God as a spirit, or as a principle or as truth some people will condemn you. They cannot pray with that philosophy. Now let me ask those people one question, 'Can you see a principle, did anyone ever see the truth?' No, indeed, truth does not yield itself to the perceptual process. Nor does God. Good pious Catholics have this perceptual mind. They see God in their ceremonials. They are made that way. Their religion has comforted the world for hundreds of years.

"Take another case of the perceptual mind. In my student days I had a friend who spent three years without joining the fraternity. In his junior year, however, he did join and next day met me and said, 'Well, I joined a fraternity last night, and what do you think about it?' 'All right,' I said, 'Go ahead.' Then he said, 'I don't believe fraternity men can afford to associate with non-fraternity men.' 'Jim,' I answered, 'I didn't think you were that big a fool.'

"Did any of you teachers ever have a very aristocratic feeling? Did you ever feel that you were away up, and could not have any dealings with the Samaritans, awfully common people? Well, sensible folks have a line on you, all right. You are simply using the perceptual process in your social life. That is all there is to aristocracy. Now philosophy has given a name to the perceptual mind. We call it static. And it abounds in human history, in politics, and in social life. Enough for the static mind.

"Let us now take our fact of the static mind to the scientist, the high priest of knowledge. He knows. Let us ask him about it. We take a specimen of water and he and I go into the laboratory together and when he gets through I say to him, 'Well, have you got any knowledge?' He answers, 'Yes, water is hydrogen and oxygen.' 'How is that?' I say. 'I thought water was water, is there no such thing as water?' 'No,' the scientist answers. 'Water is never water, it is hydrogen and oxygen.' 'All right, Mr. Scientist, what is hydrogen and oxygen?' 'Why they are elements,' he answers. 'Why I thought it was hydrogen and oxygen. What are elements?' 'Go to the professor of physics,' the scientist laughs. I go to the physicist and he says it is not hydrogen and oxygen, it is motion. Everything is motion. 'Well, Mr. Physicist, I want to know what motion is.' 'Why, motion is the manifestation of life,' he says. 'Then what is life?' I inquire. 'Well, now, you mustn't ask that question. If you do, you are in danger of getting into metaphysics and away from science, and when one gets away from the path of science he is lost. The notion that the world is still and fixed is an illusion. The world is in a perfect whirl. Nothing is fixed. Everything unsettled.'"

This, continued the speaker, is scientific knowledge; this is all the knowledge that science can give. The world of fixed facts is gone. Confusion reigns. Science has knocked the bottom out of everything. Frankly, now, you know, I am taking my life into my hands when I say this: We have to be scientific here to be respectable. Everything is scientific. Scientific history, scientific language, scientific mathematics. If there is anything that science does do, it is to stand us on our heads. Everything is something else. All is one vast relation—water to hydrogen and oxygen, hydrogen and oxygen to motion, motion to life, and life? Well, now you must not ask that question. It is unscientific. Now it gives me no pleasure to say all this because I have some good friends who are scientists and I will catch it tomorrow. Nevertheless, I repeat, science has set us on our heads, and the bottom is out of things. We have no truth. We have vast relations.

Now, I want to say another thing that I do not expect anybody to accept. We are the most unhappy people in the world. I mean by that the scientific folks, what we call our folks—the German, the Frenchmen, the Englishmen, and the Americans. We are profoundly unhappy and I believe science is the cause of it. Things fixed, things definite, things profound have slipped away from us and we are eternally chasing something else. I would not discredit science. I think it has done us a vast service. But I also think science has done us a vast damage, because it has materialized our lives.

As I have said, science has done us a vast service. Efficiency is the great output of science, the reality [*sic*], the man who can do something. At this point however, science fails us. Science goes no further. It tells us that man is the product of environment, but it never tells us what the man is. Science speaks in terms of heredity or environment, or in results of man's achievement. Both of these are awfully interesting, but neither is the man himself. If this hasty sketch is fairly correct, and I think it is, we have two types of teachers, the perceptual and the conceptual. We see the strength of each of these and we see the limitations of each. Now it seems to me that many a teacher limits himself to one of these.

If my analysis is correct you see at once that the good teacher cannot be simply the scientist, he cannot be simply mathematical. The man who works only with facts, important as they are, cannot be a good teacher. The man who works only with relations, important as they are, cannot be a good teacher.

There is a third power of the mind, a third capacity, a third demand of human life. And I care not how you call it. Some people speak of it in terms of revelation, others in terms of method. But tonight I care not what name you give it, the truth is the same. The third power of the mind has to do with Soul, with Spirit, with God, with Truth. The great Augustine broke forth in this way, "Speak to my Soul, Oh God, speak so I may hear and live."

"The most remarkable letter that has come back to us in recent years was from a young lawyer in Charlotte. He said, 'I have no fault to find with my college course, I have no fault to find with my profession, but Professor, I want God.' I think that was a very remarkable statement. His college course was satisfactory, his work at the bar was satisfying, but there was one thing he wanted. And I want to say tonight that this is a deep demand in human life. No man escapes it. It is the ancient and great call of human life. And I want to say another thing: We, as teachers, as individuals, and as intelligent beings are under obligation to meet and satisfy this elemental requirement of man. And tonight I shall endeavor to answer the universal yearning: 'I want God.'"

Quietly and impressively the speaker drew near his conclusion:

The mind has the power to perceive and the power to understand. The perceptual powers give us facts, the conceptual powers separate them into relations and find the laws illustrated in these relations. This process completes itself in a concept. The object or the fact is lost and concept takes its place. For example, take a cat into a laboratory and ask for knowledge of it. When the operator is through with his work, the cat is gone forever. He tells us he has found certain laws illustrated, certain characteristics of the type—and this is all. We go home without our cat.

But the power to think rises higher, it is the power of vision, the power to see unity. To think is to bring the fact of the static process and the law of the dynamic process back into vital unity. To think is to see unity, that is, principle incarnated in facts. Thinking is thus an infinite process. As we think, the range and depth of our unity change. Every man has the power to think, though men differ in the range of this power. The greatest sentence ever written is the first sentence in Genesis.

Teachers, after this meeting is over go to your rooms and read the first verse of Genesis, "In the beginning God created the heavens and the earth." Look up that word God in the Hebrew. God, the Creator, the great first Cause, God, a Spirit. Another fact is discovered from the Hebrew. This word God is plural and not singular. Herein we have the first reference to the Trinity, a plurality of persons in the divine nature: Herein we find a complete concept of Christian thought.

If man has the three powers, which I have enumerated, then the task of the Teacher is clear. The facts are necessary, they come first. The Teacher must then analyze these facts. Next, we lose the facts and obtain the laws illustrated in the facts. This gives us mastery of the facts. But the work of the teacher, the good teacher, is not yet finished. The facts must find themselves in some unity. The laws must be seen as the life of this unity. And so we reach the stage of vision—of insight into the nature of truth—that is, in an organic Unity. This analysis I submit is the answer to the letter, "I want God."

I think it is a necessary thing that a man should now and then leave the valley and climb to the top of some mountain. Let him go high and stand there and see the largeness, the unity, the infinity of things. So the Good Teacher, afire with the grand passion, ascends into the high places of his subject, leading his students into some master vision, inspiring them with the zeal of a Paul to press toward the mark for the prize of the high calling of God in Christ Jesus.

After the courageous old philosopher had concluded his lecture, and hundreds of voices had echoed Luther's stirring words, "A Mighty Fortress is our God," and the audience had been dismissed, the teachers, aglow with new and ennobling ideas gathered about and were profuse in their words of commendation. "Oh, Professor, you have confounded your critics. You have not pulled God down, you have raised man up."

But, even so, the Fundamentalists were unconvinced. "He's a slick brother and will bear watching," was still the cry. In truth, old-fashioned church members were lying in wait for Brother Williams. They were going to smoke him out. They proposed to ask him some searching questions at the very first opportune moment.

"Professor Williams, how do you stand on the Bible. Is it true or false?"

"What say you of Jesus? Is he the only son of God?"

"Do you subscribe to the doctrine of the atonement?"

"Do you doubt the resurrection of Christ from the grave?"

"Do you believe in original sin?"

These, and like questions, were being prepared, and the professor of philosophy must some day answer them, answer categorically, yes or no. If he failed so to do he must be branded as a corrupter of youth, a destroyer of faith, a downright heretic, and the University must get rid of him. Would his boys and the trustees back him up or would they fail him?

14

MY BOYS

PERHAPS Horace's nearest approach to familiarity was when he was referring to his students. "My Boys" he (most affectionately for him) called them. One and all, Horace's boys were the objects of his solicitude. When students they had been the material out of which he was striving to exalt the human race and create a better civilization. In after years when they left his classroom and went forth, whether to Maine, Texas, or California, or to China or Japan, they never ceased to be other than My Boys to their rough, erratic old school teacher.

When Johnson, a true Horatian, was leaving the Hill to open a school of his own, he called on his old master for a final word of advice. "Remember, Mr. Johnson," was the admonition, "your boys come before your system." In a word, as Paul Green has said, Horace Williams implanted in his boys a great idea, the glory and dignity of being an individual.

Neither office nor place nor power nor honors made any appeal to the stubborn, solipsistic old philosopher. Diogenes-like, he was everlastingly wandering around in broad daylight holding a lantern in his hand and searching for a man. Not a specialist, not a Ph.D., not a Phi Beta Kappa, not a titled creature, not even a judge or a colonel, but a thinker. "Know thyself," Socrates dingdonged into his pupils. "The individual is absolute in himself," Williams proclaimed. "The individual is pivotal in civilization, a link in the process of ultimate truth."

True to his individualistic tendencies, Professor Williams did not organize his boys. Though they coöperated they were not incorporated, nor had they any officers or agencies of any kind. Each student was an ultimate unit, a law unto himself, a consumer of his own smoke, a *Ding an sich*. First and last Horace must have taught three or four thousand young men and women, but they went forth from his classroom just as they had entered, free as the casing air, tagged with no tag, labeled with no label, with no hook in their noses and no collar around their necks. The rock on which his philosophy rested was the dignity of self, the One among the many, the I, the individual. The I, the One, is the ultimate unit. All else but the I is the non-I, all else but the One is the non-One. When the One disappears, all else disappears with it. Originality is the desideratum.

The ultimate unit is the individual. The individual will seize some expression of existence, get a begriff of it and find himself in and of this begriff. The individual must be in himself reality. This consciousness of reality as individual and as reaching into the plan of God becomes the steadying purpose of history. A sense of vast value comes into individual existence. The process of individual existence has a ground in itself. Its end is to coöperate in the absolute process of reality. This has made Christian civilization irresistible.

Having thus elaborated his pet hobby of the One among the many and of the inviolability of the individual the Good Teacher, one morning, turned to the class to experiment with them and ascertain how deep, if at all, his thoughts had sunk in.

"Mr. Battle," he asked, "have you a concept of the individual?"

"Well, I hope so, Professor."

"Now, Mr. Battle, what is this I hold in my hand?"

"Why, a stick, Professor."

"Nothing but a stick, Mr. Battle?"

"No, Sir, unless you refer to your hand."

"So that is all you realize, just a stick?"

"Why, certainly, Professor. What else is there but the stick?"

"Mr. Battle, it's the non-stick. If there were no non-stick, would there be a stick?" The class chuckled.

"Mr. Winslow, I suppose you have seen a bung-hole in a barrel, haven't you?"

"Certainly, Professor."

"Did you see nothing but the bung hole?"

"The bung hole and the barrel, Professor."

"So that was all you saw, was it?"

"Of course, Professor, I saw nothing but what I was looking at."

"Did you realize that the hole could not be there if there had been no non-hole?" The class chuckled again.

"Miss Denham, I am sure you have eaten a doughnut?"

"Many a one, Professor."

"Did they all have round holes through them?"

"All I ever saw did, Sir."

"Now, Miss Denham, could you have seen the hole in the doughnut if there had been no non-hole?"

"I suppose not, Professor, but what has that got to do with the individual?"

"That's a good question and I'm glad you asked it. The individual, just as the stick or the hole in the barrel stands alone, apart, and opposed to all else besides. The individual, in the process of reality, is a continual struggle, an endless strife. We come into life crying, we go out groaning."

"Professor Williams," broke in Couch, a thoughtful student, "I don't see any sense in all that. What good can it do us? I know that up is down and down is up and that minus three multiplied by minus three gives plus nine and this side of the street is the other side of the street, but what of it? I came into your class because I was told you solve the problems of life: progress and poverty, society and crime. I adhere to the absolute, but what I want is something workable."

During this arraignment, Old Horace's face was a study. Slowly and careless-like he sidled off to his window and looked out into space. After the young man had finished speaking he wandered back and calmly answered him. "Mr. Couch," he said, "I fear you are in the wrong room. You should be in the School of Commerce under Dean Carroll. You are inclined to be particularistic. You deal in the accessories, not in principle. Some day Mr. Couch, you will emerge from the particular into the universal. You will discover that principle governs the accessories. The tail, Mr. Couch, follows the hide."

The professor then resumed. The individual being in the process of reality, is true to himself. The real individual cannot lie, or cheat, or steal. He maintains his quality. He enlarges himself, he becomes quantity, but he retains quality. Quality becoming quantity and yet remaining quality is miracle. The individual may develop. He may become president, he may visit Paris, he may be tempted, but he will never yield. His quality remains. The I abides.

"Mr. Jones, you are on the ball team. Now suppose the game was with Duke and the score tied, two-two, in the last inning. You were on second base and a Texas leaguer was knocked out to center and you saw the umpire was not looking and you could make homeplate and win the game but only by cutting the third base, would you cut the base?"

"That's up to the Ump, Professor," Jones laughed and the class laughed with him.

"No, Mr. Jones, you would repudiate the run and lose the game. You would turn to the grandstand and say, 'That run doesn't count, I cut the third base.' You would be true to truth, Mr. Jones."

"The other day, I was greatly shocked when I heard that a student-assistant in one of our women's dormitories had reported a girl for coming in late, though she herself had been late, an hour before. She sought to justify her conduct by saying that there was no harm in violating a rule, the harm was in being caught. On that level civilization will finally go to pieces."

Dignifying and honoring the individual as he did, Horace could never indulge in the ordinary familiarities of the campus. No matter how young or insignificant the students might be, he invariably put a handle to their names when addressing them. It was Miss Smith or Mr. Jones and never Mary or Tom.

The old philosopher's manifestation of interest in his boys was as paradoxical as his dialectic process. Even as the she-bear will sometimes hug her cub to death in an excess of affection, so old Horace would occasionally crush the very life out of an aspiring student, no matter how much he thought of him. He graded regardless of consequences. Numerous examples of this peculiarity still linger. In his day, Rondthaler was a crack pupil in philosophy. Old Horace flunked him. Horne was equally gifted. He flunked Horne. Robinson was a ripe scholar. He, too, fell by the wayside. So also did Wagstaff, Wilson, and others, who afterward became distinguished as teachers, lawyers, and publicists.

The professor wished no student below a junior to enter his classes. Woe betide the luckless freshman or sophomore who ventured into Horace Williams' ruthless beargarden. During one term, thirteen sophomores made bold to take the course in philosophy. At the end of the term, every one of them was flunked except one, a bright young fellow named Peace who skinned through with a measly D. So ruthless in his gradings was the Old Teacher that the boys likened him to God Almighty. "Whom he loveth he chasteneth," they would laugh and cuss.

Indeed the eccentric man had an original theory that early success would bring on complacency and self-satisfaction, deadly attributes of any student. He, therefore, proceeded to stir up the boy, to arouse his curiosity, to make him think, to ruffle his feathers, and finally to excite his wrath. And he was not over-scrupulous in the accomplishment of his purpose, oftentimes dealing in apparent trivialities.

"Mr. Ray," he would say, "suppose someone were to call you a liar, and you knocked him down, what would you say caused the blow?"

"The ugly word lie, of course, Professor," answered the spirited Southerner.

"Are you sure of that, Mr. Ray? Have you made a begriff of the situation?"

"Well, let someone call me a liar and see what will happen."

"Precisely, Mr. Ray. You'd knock him down, but would you do this because of the insult or because you are a high-strung Southerner?"

"What say you, Mr. Everett? Did Mr. Ray strike because he was insulted or because of his warm Southern blood?"

"Well, Professor, I guess it was some of both."

"Do you agree, Mr. Smith?"

"No, Sir, I say it was not the insult, but the Southern blood, which caused the blow. If the incident had happened in Boston or in other cold climates there would have been no fight."

"What does the class say? Let's poll them and see," said the professor.

"Those favoring the lie as the immediate cause, hold up your hands. One, two, three, four—fifteen in all. Those opposed, raise your hands. Twenty-five in all. Thus we have formed a concept or begriff of the situation. This we must do on all occasions and under all circumstances."

A few days before one of the June commencements Umstead called at Horace's home and boastfully informed him that he had been chosen to debate a given query and had selected the negative side.

"Well, Mr. Umstead," the critic quietly replied, "you've chosen the wrong side. You had just as well surrender in advance. You can't win."

At commencement, when the negative had won and Old Horace met the victorious debater and his father on the campus, he complacently remarked, "Congratulations, Mr. Umstead, but your son didn't win that debate. I won it. I made him mad and he went to work and won!" And how the professor did laugh at his own little joke!

On a certain occasion, Hassell of the philosophy class, marched down to Horace's study and proudly declaimed his commencement oration. When he had finished, not a word was spoken. Finally the disappointed youngster broke the silence. "Professor," he said, "what do you think of my speech?"

"Why, I didn't hear a word of your speech, Mr. Hassell."

"Didn't I speak loud enough, Professor?"

"Oh, yes, I suppose so, but, Mr. Hassell, I was thinking of my pigs."

"Why, Professor, you surely do hurt my feelings."

"Now, Mr. Hassell, a speech that can't keep one's mind off his pigs isn't much speech. I advise you to write that speech over again."

On a certain Sunday evening, Francis Bradshaw conducted a green, confiding divinity student to Horace's den, where the following interview took place. "Prof," said the candidate for orders, "I'm going to be a preacher of religion and I want your help." Old Horace eyed the youngster a moment and then quietly asked, "What is your idea of religion?"

"Well, Prof, I don't exactly know that."

"How are you going to teach a thing when you don't know what it is?" Plead as the bewildered youngster would, he could not get the Professor to tell him what religion is. "Think it over and report," Horace snarled.

Next day, on class, old Horace related the incident and said each one must work out his own problems. "But," he added in a soft, remote voice, "as Tamar, our old black nurse and cook put it, 'You must come through,' first.

Absolute reality is experienced within the individual in religion."

At one commencement the senior class sent a committee down to the Professor's home to invite him to make the prayer. "Why do you want me to pray?" Old Horace curiously queried. Instantly the committeeman smelt a mouse. He knew that if he said, "Why Professor, we always have prayers at commencement," his mission would be a failure. So he said, "Professor Williams, our class is all at sea. We need encouragement. We know that you have a message for us and are the only man that has." The ruse worked. The prayer at commencement was a gem and awoke the highest aspirations of an appreciative audience.

Somewhat in confirmation of the statement that Professor Williams was impartial in his grading and was wedded to the idea that a high mark would spoil a freshman, is the following incident. The closest friends that Horace ever had were the Ralph Harpers, now of upper New York, whom he sometimes visited in their delightful home and with whom he carried on a spirited correspondence. In a letter from Harper to Williams, the fact was mentioned that the eldest son, Ralph, a freshman, had just received an A in philosophy. Friend Horace replied that the news was very distressing to him. No freshman should ever get an A. He cannot stand the praise. "I give an A to no student in his first year," he wrote. "Rarely do I give an A to anyone."

By this statement Professor Williams did not imply that he would absolutely throw a good student, but would condition him on an intermediate paper in order to make him get down off of his high horse and go to work. The case of Rondthaler, already referred to, who was flunked but graduated with the highest honors and is now president of one of the oldest and best women's colleges in the land, is interesting. When related on the campus it still creates a laugh.

In the class one morning, the professor was dealing with the three levels of intelligence, the sensory, the scientific, and the spiritual and, in order to clinch the point, turned to Rondthaler and asked, "Mr. Rondthaler, do you think a horse can appreciate a sunset?"

"Now Professor," was the rather short reply, "not being a horse I am not able to answer your question."

The class broke into a loud laugh, of course, and tradition has it that this answer flunked the young man, but the rumor lacks authentication.

Horace had little patience with mediocrity or with the memorizer. "The parrot approach," he would say. Unless a student was original he stood little chance of winning honors under Williams.

On the whole it must be admitted that no teacher of his day exerted a wider influence or had more loyal and appreciative boys than Horace Williams, a fact attested even by students such as Craig, Connor, Graves, and others, who did not fully enter into his philosophical concepts.

Scarcely a boy left the classroom without carrying away some lasting thought, big or little.

"He taught me to think," said Lee.

"I brought away this thought," added Spike Saunders. "Do not accept anything as true merely because it is stated. Investigate!"

"His dialectic process was an eye-opener to me," said Bryant.

"He freed my mind of moss," declared Phillips Russell.

"He communicated his own alertness, his originality, his power to think," declared Tom Wolfe. "First came Socrates, then Plato, next Hegel. After Hegel—well, it didn't matter, for after Hegel we had *him*. He was our own Old Man."

Garland Porter, a diligent, strong-minded young fellow, was a Horatian through and through. He was likewise the first president of the student body to be elected by the entire campus. Porter was partial to the accomplished Mary Yellott, a Phi Beta Kappa student. Therefore when his friend Mary got a low mark in philosophy Porter challenged Old Horace.

"Professor," he complained, "you have not treated Mary Yellott right on her last paper."

"How so, Mr. Porter?"

"Why, I have read that paper through and through and Mary made a perfect analysis of your work. She didn't miss a single step."

"True, Mr. Porter," Old Horace drawled. "She didn't and that's why I gave her a 2. Her paper was too perfect; it was nothing but what I had taught her."

The truth of the matter is that the diligent young woman had not questioned a single step of Old Horace's nor had she added anything of her own to the subject. This, according to Horace's harsh standard, was fatal. It may be said, in passing, that a like rule obtains at Oxford University.

Despite Old Horace's peculiarities, or perhaps in consequence of them, he continued to fascinate the students. A brilliant, original boy was Vermont Connecticut Royster. Upon entering the University such a genius naturally gravitated to Old Horace's class and soon fell for him, despite warnings from his orthodox family, "Beware of that atheist, Horace Williams!"

In the memory of his grateful pupil, George McCoy, there lingers a thought implanted by the Good Teacher: "Now I want to tell you something," said Old Horace to the class. "I am an old man now. I had nine years of college preparation and there isn't a thing to preparation except what we master and understand. One may read thousands of pages and it will all come out in the wash except what he understands. What good does it do to read of a big dinner that some one else has eaten? Well, that is what many of you are doing, reading of the experience of somebody else as if that could nourish your intelligence. Take my advice, young men, and don't graduate till you have understood something. Work out something for yourself."

Horace's students, as McCoy concludes, were not disciples of a school of thought. They were members of the Tribe of Horace, and distinguished from others.

In a popular address by George Herbert Palmer, entitled "The Ideal Teacher," an amusing incident is related. Two years after a young fellow had graduated from Harvard he knocked at Dr. Palmer's door and said he could not pass through Cambridge without thanking him for his work on Locke, Berkeley, and Hume. Pleased to be assured that his methods were justified and unwilling to drop a subject so agreeable, Palmer asked the visitor if he could tell precisely where the value of the course lay. "Certainly," was the answer. "It all centered in a single remark of Locke's. Locke said we ought to have clear and distinct ideas. I don't think I got anything else out of the course."

This compliment was so doubtful that Professor Palmer was inclined to think the fellow foolish, so to mistake a bit of commonplace for gospel truth. "Why did he not listen to some of the profound things I was saying? But on reflection I saw that he was right and I wrong. That trivial saying had come to him at a critical moment as a word of power, while the deep matters which interested me, and which I had been offering him so confidently day by day, being unsuited to him, had passed him by. He had not heard them."

As with Palmer, so with Williams. But if such were the impressions of some students who took philosophy as a pastime, or a part of the course, or to see Old Horace in action, what shall be said of that larger group who took philosophy seriously and who based their lifework on Horace Williams' dialectic process: a majority of our State Supreme Court, a dominating number of our University trustees and of the legislature and many molders of public thought?

Let one of this number, United States Circuit Judge, John J. Parker, answer this question: "He was the greatest intellectual and spiritual force in our State. He visualized philosophy as the synthesis of all knowledge. A great teacher, a great philosopher, a great man, he took us by the hand in the dewy and liquid morn of youth and led us up to heights which we could not have reached without him."

15

HORACE ON THE BIBLE

AFTER SERVING as President of the University for nearly twenty laborious years Venable resigned and became dean of the Department of Chemistry. He was succeeded by Ed Kidder Graham, of the class of 1898. Now Ed was the most farseeing, philosophical student Horace ever taught. He was indeed the apple of the professor's eye, and yet, once upon a time, old Horace had almost flunked him, turned him down flat, just as he did Ed's classmate, Archibald Henderson, afterwards to become the authoritative biographer of Shaw and dean of mathematics in our University.

And this is the story of that flunking as told by the inimitable Henderson: "Ed Graham and I were deeply interested in the first course under old Horace, which was called Philosophy One. Although we both were green and gullible, we had intelligence not markedly inferior to the average run of college students; and I am sure we did well on class. When we took our first examination, we were greatly perturbed in spirit, but on comparing notes, after the exam, we found a certain comfort in the discovery that our answers were similar, that we thought very much alike about the questions Horace had asked on the examination. Before the time had come to post the grade, we became greatly concerned about the matter, and decided to interview Professor Williams in company and keep up each other's courage, for neither of us dared to tackle him alone.

"In answer to our rather tremulous inquiry, he looked at

us with a look of sadness and said, mournfully, 'Young gentlemen, you have disappointed me greatly. Your papers clearly show that you have not learned to think and to reason. I have been compelled to give you each a D.' Now this was the lowest grade in the class and we felt, each of us, that we deserved a much higher grade, and were convinced that one of Horace's principles was that people learned through suffering, sorrow, and tribulation."

One of Horace's tenets was discipline, discipline, and again discipline. The best discipline for a beginner is to give him a poor mark when he really deserves a good one. "My interests carried me away from philosophy into mathematics and broadly scientific studies," Henderson continued, "but at our next examination Ed and I both received high grades. That was my last classroom experience with Horace; but Ed Graham went on to great triumphs and became a star performer under Professor Williams. But Horace would not give Ed the highest in Bradley's Logic, because he averred that Ed's paper broke down in the middle and no one could logically bridge over the hiatus between the first half and the last.

"Poor Ed, I fear, was still undergoing the heavy hand of the Horatian discipline in later years through the defiant individualism and impolitic public utterances of Williams." So much for Archibald Henderson.

The coming of Graham to the presidency was gratifying to Williams. Now at last, he imagined, the ideal would have its innings and science be forced to take a back seat. How far this expectation was realized I reserve for a future chapter. At all events Old Horace felt that he had a friend at court and might speak his mind freely and without censure, expounding the idealistic philosophy of the best thinkers of the past. Many obstacles, however, were in the way.

Despite the loyalty of his boys and of most of the other students, and also of a great majority of the trustees, public opposition grew with the growing years. The rank and file held the professor responsible for all the new-fangled notions which emanated from Chapel Hill. The doctrine of evolution, which, at this time, was taken as a matter of course by such learned scientists as H. van P. Wilson, Coker, MacNider, Bell, and others, including all whims and fancies, however heretical or unorthodox, were laid at Horace's door.

North Carolinians were willing to forgive Horace's political vagaries but not his religious. They remembered that after the war many of their wisest brethren had refused to ally themselves with what they called the secession Democracy and had become Republicans, leading their party to many a victory in county and congressional districts and occasionally in the State.* But these were orthodox; Horace was not—a vice which sent him to coventry, according to the Fundamentalists. So bitter was the feeling against an unorthodox person that his death-bed was watched, on occasion, to discover how he faced the hereafter!

The suspicion which at first attached to Professor Williams is well voiced by the opinion of Josephus Daniels, editor of *The News and Observer*, the only newspaper in all the land owned by one person, himself sole stockholder, director, editor, and proprietor! And thus sayeth Josephus: "Horace Williams accepts nothing as settled, his orthodoxy is giving place to such doubts as to lessen his value as an apostle of evangelical religion. He examines everything and leaves his pupils in doubt so that they question, if they do not deny, the truths of orthodox Christianity. He reopens doctrines which the leaders of Christianity have long decreed are so well established as to call for acceptance."

Now, half a century ago, these old-fashioned notions of

---

* No greater names adorn the scroll of the State than those of such Republican judges as Buxton, Brooks, Rodman, Bynum, Boyden, Pearson, Douglas, Furches, Faircloth, Settle, Reade, Cook, Montgomery, Dick, Robinson, Moore, Timberlake, Thomas, Starbuck, Cloud, Pritchard and others. No families have served the State better than the Dockerys, Moreheads, Youngs, Duncans, Folks, Linneys, Yorks, Dukes, Holtons, Hargroves, Briggs, Grissoms, Seawells, Caldwells, Bullocks, Peaces, Winsteads, Walsers, Merritts, Reynolds, McIvers, Prices, Jenkins, and many others, most of whom had been Old Line Whigs before the war.

Daniels were not at all exceptional. We Southerners were strictly orthodox and took the Bible literally. The Catholics might have their Pope; we Protestants had our Bible.

An incident may further illustrate the simple childlike faith of that day. In the early 1900's the Baptist State Convention met in the city of Raleigh where I then resided, and so large was the attendance that public houses would not accommodate the delegates. We housekeepers, therefore, threw open our doors, and my home was honored by the presence of five or six interesting people, among others that brave biologist and thoughtful Christian W. L. Poteat, and also Henry F. Cope, of Chicago, General Secretary of the Religious Educational Board of the United States; N. Y. Gulley, a law teacher of great wisdom; Professor Brewer, head of the Religious Department of Wake Forest College; and last, but not least, C. M. Cooke, one of the drollest and best beloved of Tar Heels. All of them Baptists, true and tried to the very bottom of the pond!

One evening after supper we had all gathered in my sitting-room before a grate of glowing coals, and the talk naturally turned to things religious and to a universal belief in God.

"Why, even the savage Indians have such belief," said Dr. Poteat.

"Precisely," said Cope. "And call it Manitou—spirit."

"Gentlemen, gentlemen!" I protested. "Why invoke the practices of savages to bolster up our holy religion? Why reason by analogy instead of directly?"

"Explain yourself, Judge," Dr. Cope remarked, in some surprise.

"Why, this," I said. "You never call in secondary evidence, if primary evidence is at hand."

"Now, Cousin Bob," drawled Captain Cooke, in his dry way, "you are always drappin' into law!"

"Seriously," said I, "why go outside the Bible for proof of God? Doesn't the Bible tell us there is a God?"

"Which Bible?" Cope dryly asked, no doubt having in mind the Koran and the Upanishads.

To say that this remark left me cold is aptly to describe my condition. There I was a sinner, and outside the pale, taking up for the Christian Bible and these learned men of the cloth attacking it! What was to become of the world!

What, then, was Horace Williams' offense and why was he suspected and on everyone's tongue? Undoubtedly it was his liberal interpretation of the Bible, a concept which he had brought down with him from Yale and Harvard. Let us sit under him in the classroom, for a hour or two, as he deals with this subject. It may be that we will get a new light on the misunderstood man.

It is the beginning of the fall term and the class is to take up the subject of comparative religions. A gentle rain has recently fallen and each tiny dewdrop is a pearl. The leaves are gloriously purpling. The historic campus is a scene of beauty, so tranquil, so soothing that one can hear the still, sad music of humanity. The class, consisting of fifty or sixty eager men and women and not a few visitors, including the beloved Parson Moss, enters. At the window, oblivious of the chatter of voices and clatter of feet, stands the teacher, toying with the tassels of the window shade. Presently he turns from his musing and approaches his accustomed place. His greetings are short and to the point; he merely says he hopes the session may be pleasant and profitable. "During the coming term we propose to study together the subject of the Christian religion and to compare it with the ancient religions which we have heretofore considered."

At this point the old philosopher paused and reached down for a well-worn, dog-eared book lying open on his desk—the King James Bible. Deliberately he picks it up and begins to read, "In the beginning—*God*." Here he stops. The words "created the heaven and the earth," are not read. "In the beginning—God"—no more. What a depth of meaning the old philosopher has managed to put into those first three little words, the first in the Bible. God, the beginning. God, the ending. God in all, God over all, God for all, God the Eternal Spirit! The class is entranced, motionless. They have caught the inspiration of the Master.

"In the beginning God," the profoundest truth ever uttered, the basis of the Christian religion, the essence of monotheism, the cornerstone of truth and unity. "Before Abraham was I am." God, everywhere and in all things, permeating life, pulsing in the sap of the giant oak and the graceful willow, roaring in the ocean storm, flashing in the lightning, beautiful in the rose, manifest in the life of truth, goodness, and beauty. Not a God of this church or that church, but a God of all, Jew and Gentile, of saint and sinner.

"Thou shalt have no other Gods before me." This is the first and greatest of the commandments, a truth shaping the destiny of men, urging on the trend of civilization, the challenge of monotheism. God a unifying force, above all, including all, and in all. Let us examine this commandment. It speaks of other Gods. Does monotheism mean abolishing all the other gods? If so, we come back to the Hindu idea again. We particularize. No, we should not abolish the other gods. As it takes variety to give meaning to unity, so it takes many to give meaning to one. This is the dialectic process working in and through all things. The ocean exists because of the drops of water which compose it, but woe to the drop which sets itself up as the whole ocean. Our problem is not one of destruction but one of relation.

"Professor," interrupted the gentle Reid, a divinity student, "I would not interrupt, but you seem to consider God simply as a force, or a spirit, and not a person."

"Mr. Reid, I expected that question. It is the usual objection to a reasonable concept of God. Mr. Reid, get your history professor to tell you of an incident in the legislature of 1875. Thorn, a legislator, was on trial for denying that there is a God, and Mr. Platt Walker, another member, was prosecuting. Now it so happened that Mr. Walker was in love with President Battle's handsome daughter, Nellie, who was in the crowded gallery, watching the excited scene below. 'Mr. Thorn,' said Prosecutor Walker, 'have you not published in this pamphlet that you do not believe God is a person?'

"'Yes sir, I have.'

"'Have you not gone further and uttered the following libellous words, "God is a Spirit, without body, parts or passion."'

"'Yes, I used those words.'

"'And you still stick to it?'

"'I do, sir.'

"'That is the case for the people,' said the confident Walker.

"'Does the accused wish to make a statement?' asked the presiding officer.

"'No, but I would like to ask Mr. Walker a question or two.'

"'That is your privilege, sir.'

"'Mr. Walker do you happen to belong to any church?'

"'I do, sir. I am proud to be a member, though an unworthy one, of the Protestant Episcopal Church of America, and orthodox, through and through, sir,' waving his hand to the gallery where sat his lady love.

"'Now, Mr. Walker, will you be good enough to examine the book I hand you and say what it is?'

"'Why, the Book of Common Prayer of my church.'

"'So far so good, Mr. Walker. And will you now oblige us by reading a portion of Article I of the Articles of Religion of your church?'

"Very timidly and gingerly Walker took the book and falteringly read, 'There is but one living and true God, everlasting, without body, parts, or passions.' This blunder ended the case of atheism against Thorn and the incident may show the loose way of thinking on the subject of God and the Bible.

"What, then, is this wonderful Book? It is a collection of manuscripts, written by wise men a long time ago. And how shall we interpret it, literally or in its spirit, as is usual with written documents? Professor Manning of our Law School tells me there are five approaches to a writing: words, context, subject matter, effects and consequences and its spirit. No one of these justifies a literal interpretation.

"The words were originally Arabic. They have been translated through many languages and there are a thousand differences in these translations because the original manuscripts are lost. Martin Luther, as you will remember, rejected three or four of the books. Not only are the words uncertain, but the context and subject matter are alien to us and quite unintelligible. East is East and West is West.

"Moreover, to interpret the Bible literally has led to the bloody doctrines of infant damnation, of a Hell of fire and brimstone, and of the thought that the saint in heaven would be so much sublimated that he will enjoy the burning of the sinner in Hell!

"What then is the spirit of the Bible? It is love, unity. God is love. Though I give my body to be burned and have not love, I am nothing. I and my father are one. The Kingdom of Heaven is within you. These are key texts. With them to guide we will not quibble about side issues, such as infant or adult baptism, whether in a river, a basin, or no baptism at all as the wise Quakers insist. We will not contend for this church or that church. We will base our lives on the rock of truth.

"Matter is temporal, spirit eternal. Matter, form and shadow; spirit, from everlasting to everlasting. The thought of infant damnation or a Hell of fire and brimstone does not square with the spirit of the Bible. The teaching that we are born in sin is an insult to our mother.

"Mr. Osborne, do you believe in that doctrine of original sin?"

"Well, Professor, doesn't the Bible teach it?"

"No, Mr. Osborne, not when rightly interpreted. Born in corruption does not square with the idea of a loving Father."

"Professor," broke in Kenan, a favorite of his teacher, "Tommy Hume says for you to come in his classroom some day and see his bad boys cut up and you'll change your mind on that subject!"

"Well, let's see how the class reacts. Mr. McMullen, is human nature born black with white spots or white with black spots?"

"Well, Professor, you've got me there, but I'll say some of us are born one way and some the other."

"Mr. Huske, you are going to be a preacher, what's your view?"

"Now, Professor, doesn't that raise the question of the Fall of Man? I remember Newman said that even if the Bible had not told of the Fall he would have known it from observation, so many fallen folks in the world and everyone striving to get back to the Father's house."

"Professor," spoke up Jenkins, "I want to add my feeble voice to your thoughts. Literalness, I feel, is deadly to religion. I'm writing a paper on this subject and I find all material religions are particularistic, they have force as their God, such things as air, water or fire, and they propitiate their gods by bribes and sacrifices. The Christian religion, I think, goes beyond this. Christ became one with beauty."

"You are right, Mr. Jenkins. Plato and Christ found something not only beautiful but true in religion and the process they employed was very simple. They insisted that the intelligence in itself can find and exhibit truth. Unfortunately this fundamental idea has been repudiated by the church. The church insists that God is a revelation. This is a great mistake. That God is truth is not revelation, it is innate, primary.

"'The letter killeth but the spirit giveth life,' young gentlemen."

"Excuse me, Professor," said Spears, a diligent law student, "but a Latin phrase occurs to me, *Qui haeret in litera haeret in cortice,* 'Who sticks in the letter, sticks in the bark.'"

"You are right, Mr. Spears. If it be true that God is unity then the pure heart must be a part of the unity; hence the basis for the doctrine of the identity of God and man. Mr. Gwynn, will you tell us what you get out of the morning lesson?"

"Why, Professor, I almost conclude you are a Quaker. You're so full of the idea of spirit."

"Not a bad observation, Mr. Gwynn. And it's this way, Mr. Gwynn, the Catholic gets to Heaven through the institution; the Episcopalian gets there by being a perfect gentleman; the Methodist and the Quaker by the route of feeling."

"See here, Professor," rose up an indignant Baptist named Jones, a large, dignified youngster who was treasurer of the local Baptist church, "You've left out the Baptists. How do we get to Heaven?"

While Jones was proposing his questions Old Horace moved over to the window as usual and the boys knew he was going to make a kill.

"Mr. Jones," he drily remarked, "I expected you to ask that question. Why, Mr. Jones, the Baptists are the religious obstructionists!"

As the boys broke into a laugh, and Jones collapsed, Charley Maddry, a stalwart Baptist, with a head full of sense, came to the rescue.

"Now, Professor," said Maddry, "they do say that you are so individualistic you'd be a Baptist yourself but you are afraid to pass through Jordan!"

Well, anyway, there were fifty or sixty of Old Horace's boys, alert, eager, curious, and determined to find God if by searching they might haply do so. Yet they were all, teacher and pupils alike, under suspicion, attacked in the press, thundered at from pulpits, and ridiculed upon a hundred stumps.

In a later chapter I tell of my own experience in Horace's classroom. Under the inspiration of his philosophy I wrote a thesis and called it, "The Noose of Darwin and the Neck of Orthodoxy." In this paper I sought to advance the Kingdom of God by means of the intellectual process, though I well knew that the usual and the better approach was intuitional and through the feelings. I attacked the weak spots in Darwin and insisted that Man was as superior to the brute as spirit is to matter. I likewise called attention to emergent evolution, whereby the spirit entered the body of Man and distinguished him from the brute. "Yet," I wrote, "how ennobling the concept of evolution: the atom, the indwelling spirit, the struggle, the ascending scale, millions upon millions of intervening years, Man and his plaything world, death another name for life and back again to God."

This thesis was so well thought of by the class and by Professor Mims that it was forwarded to the *American Mercury*. Editor Mencken returned the manuscript, after high praise, but declared that his readers were not interested in religious matters. "They are already signed up for Hell," he wrote. The article may be found in Odum's *Social Forces*.

The storm created by this innocent paper and others prepared by Horace's boys, has rarely been equalled. Throughout the State the preachers busied themselves with Professor Williams and his unorthodox pronouncements. Among other critics was Dr. McCorkle, a pious Fundamentalist. The good Doctor not only expressed himself through the newspapers but issued sundry pamphlets in which he called for Horace Williams' scalp and said of me that I was no better than a Chinaman and should betake myself to that Godless land!

16

AND SO IT GOES

"OF TWO contradictions, one is false!" "No! Of two contradictions, both are true!"

Such sage observations one could hear, bandied to and fro across the campus at almost any commencement. Some former philosophy student returning to the Hill, would thus gaily salute his old teacher and get the pat reply.

Then, around the old Well and about the Davie Poplar or on the steps of the ancient South Building, or under the shade of a spreading oak, whose branches had sheltered them in youth, the Horatians would gather and talk of the good old days, when a contested debate was as popular as football is today and when undistributed middles, paradox and antinomy were the ruling topics—a day also when the faculty were bedeviled well-nigh out of their wits, freshmen blacked till they knew their place, and an occasional cow hauled up and stored away in the college belfry there to low and bellow a mournful call for help, as dignified professors and laughing boys crossed the campus to early morning chapel.

Professor Williams had rounded out almost a quarter-century of teaching logic, which he often spelt with a k, when his old pupil and aptest scholar, was elected president of the University. Ed Graham's administration, though cut short by his early death, inaugurated the golden age of organic thought, destined to spread throughout the Old North State and the South.

Before Graham's time the static, the dynamic, and the scientific methods had each accomplished much good. But there is a higher level, as we have seen, and that is integration, which is everywhere present controlling and directing and process of differentiation. The two seem, at first sight, to be utterly hostile but they are merely two forms of the same process. To be a whole everything must have parts.

In the large study of history, as Horace Williams contended, nothing is lost. Philosophy, politics and religion gather up what was vital in the systems they leave behind. Christianity contains the transfigured forms of the world's religion. The complete philosophy has within itself the life of all previous systems. History reconciles the claims of conflicting parties and shows how none of them have contended wholly in vain. This, it will be seen, is but another way of characterizing Williams' concept of truth: unity in structure difference.

The approach to truth, to quote the jargon of the books, is affirmation, negation, and the negation of negation, resulting in an affirmation higher, fuller, and more complete than the first since it involves and retains all the results of the previous negations. This metaphysical riddle delighted Old Horace, who loved the clash and conflict of dialecticism and reveled in the paradox. And though there was nothing new in all this, the teacher drove home to the pupils, with a tremendous drive, the value of the concept and begriff resulting in the cardinal principle of unity which pervades all nature and all life.

In the classroom he startled and shocked the pupils to shake them out of their complacent, conventional minds. Dialecticism, heated debates, endless disputes, wise and foolish discussions, and a relentless "chawing of the rag"—these were the breath of his nostrils. So far did he carry his love of intellectual conflict that he really enjoyed the attacks upon his orthodoxy and welcomed criticism whether from politicians, preachers, or professors.

Of this strange, paradoxical character an estimate by Dr. Mims, at one time a fellow member of the faculty, is interesting. Said Mims, "He has for thirty years set more boys to thinking than any other man in the State and afforded more targets for heresy hunters."

An educated citizenry Williams considered the hope of the world, and the only hope. But this education must be the real article, not spurious or perfunctory. Trial-and-error he held to be a fatal method as he did the mere act of memorizing. "Water boys," he would call the debaters indulging in quotations from the masters who had sunk the well. There is no such thing as one intelligence understanding for another, he insisted. The teacher is the sunshine, the student must do the growing. Thoughts of this nature greatly agitated him. Many a night he rolled and tossed on his sleepless bed, as he contemplated the future of the hapless human family, unless they were taught to think. He came to believe that shallow thinking was the curse of the hour. To cure this evil he began to evolve a remedy.

The thought that gripped him was this: *The establishment at the University of North Carolina of a School of Thought.*

He concurred with Everett, his Harvard teacher. Thought is a science, the science of sciences, and more substantial, and more easy to organize, than business or industry. The thought-process is the key to knowledge; it is primary, whereas experimentation is secondary.

If students in schools and colleges were taught how to think, the problems of life would vanish. Labor and capital would agree, war give place to peace, religion supplant irreligion. If he had his way, no student, in college or university, should be allowed to graduate until he had learned to think for himself, to think, not in terms of this subject or that, but universally.

It is hardly necessary to say of Horace Williams that he had now become a character in every sense of that word, with all its implications and variations. The man had news-value. His birthdays were heralded forth in the press. Bob Madry, University press agent, would interview his old teacher and get his opinion on controverted subjects agitating state and nation. And he never failed to get something different, something startling. When the preachers ran dry of thoughts they came to his classroom to refresh themselves. His very critics would sometimes take a seat in the back row and watch the professor's antics.

One of these critics was the clear-cut, incisive Louis Wilson, Carolina librarian and later Dean of the Graduate School of Library Science at the University of Chicago. Dr. Wilson was a near neighbor of Horace's, and the fleas and odors from Horace's horse stables and cow lot had pestered him and his family. But Old Horace's fame had spread abroad and he was such a favorite of the students and his debating squad was winning so many contests, that the Doctor concluded to sit in on the classes and see for himself what it was all about.

"I went into his classes," said Wilson, "and I brought away with me three ideas I shall never forget. They were the following: First of all, thoughts should be continuous, that is, connected up; second, the debater should search for and discover a broad general principle; this he should elaborate, avoiding side issues; third, there should be a personal approach to the subject accompanied by action, action, action."

Williams' classroom was so diverse and kaleidoscopic that it had become a genuine curiosity. Today would be given over to a discussion of ethical matters, presented with dignity and power. Tomorrow might degenerate into a mere cut of wits. But no matter whether the teacher was serious or ridiculous, he was always in pursuit of the absolute. Beyond the ethical and political sphere, as he insisted, rises the world of absolute spirit in art, religion, and philosophy. In such an atmosphere of sense and nonsense the effect upon a pupil depended upon his natural bent and his outlook. If he were willing to wait and take a long view, he came to regard philosophy as more valuable than all his other studies put together. If, on the contrary, he was quick on the trigger, sniffing the battle from afar, or if scientifically minded, he would shun philosophy or, after entering the class, soon drop out. This statement must be added: if the pupil had quit the class midterm he might have been an agnostic, but at the end he would have found God.

Visitors to Horace's classroom came away with impressions diametrically opposite, depending upon circumstances. If the discussion happened to be light and trivial they would conclude that the instruction was elementary. If, however, Hegel's intricate system was up for discussion and Horace's famous *Sein, Wesen,* and *Begriff*—and his head-splitting concept that truth lies in thought, for nothing can be but what can be thought, and, since Being *is* and Non-being is not, Being is One—the visitor would throw up his hands, and cry out, "I give it up! Old Horace is too deep for me!"

In the village of Chapel Hill there lived at this time a Presbyterian preacher, affectionately called Parson Moss. The pipe-smoking, lean-faced Parson was almost as solemn-visaged as Sam Weller and quite as droll. No preacher has ever impressed town and gown as did W. D. Moss, whom Tom Wolfe has painted in that human epic, *The Web and the Rock,* under the title of Preacher Reed. Parson's delight was Horace Williams. Horace in the classroom, Horace in his study, Horace on the street—in fact, so much Horace that the public declared that when the Old Philosopher took snuff the Parson sneezed.

On a famous Sunday morning, the day after Carolina had defeated Duke at a game of football, Parson entered the pulpit and took as his text the 20th verse of the sixth chapter of Joshua, a lively account of how the children of Israel, with a blast of trumpets, blew down the walls of Jericho and overcame their enemies. Now, said the Parson, the little story which I have just read to you might be an account of the game of football which we played yesterday with Duke University. The priest blowing with the trumpet is Scrubby Rives with his big megaphone leading the cheers for Carolina. The shouting of the people is the 'Split-Carolina' or 'Yackety Yack' for the team and captain. The falling of the wall at the sound of the trumpet is the crumpling of Duke's defense. The entrance of the people and the capture of the city is the licking of Duke by Carolina and the parade and triumphant march down the main street of Chapel Hill by the students of Carolina who are there for the game."

The Parson had another sermon which though somewhat trivial, was built on the Horace Williams pattern and created a sensation. Its theme was the Prophet Jonah. According to the Parson, Jonah was a fine type of the Fundamentalist, one whose eyes are shut and whose mouth is open. "I have no doubt," said the Parson, "that if Jonah were living today he would be a Fundamental Baptist with his immersion and close communion; he might be a Fundamental Presbyterian with his catechism. Perhaps he might even be a Fundamental Catholic with his Mass."

Anyhow, according to the Parson, Jonah was appointed by his Bishop to take charge of a modernist church at Ninevah. But Jonah refused to go. Like all Fundamentalists he was opposed to change. He flew in the face of his Bishop and set sail for Tarshish, a moss-back Fundamentalist community. But his efforts to get away from trouble, as usual, brought on more trouble. A storm overtook his ship, seasickness swept him off his legs, he begged to be thrown overboard, a big fish swallowed him. In the fish's belly, another name for Hell, he came to himself at last, and saw life as spirit, not form.

"You know the rest of the story, how the fish committed Jonah to dry land, how after a time he reached Ninevah, where his old habits overtook him and he continued to preach the Fundamentalist doctrine of total depravity and eternal damnation!

"My friends, life is bigger than Jonah conceived. Fundamentalist Judea was wrong; open-hearted Ninevah right. Life is unity: Life is beauty. We are our brothers' keepers. Save us from the Jonahs, say I."

What the Fundamentalists undertook to do to the Parson because of his free interpretation of the text is reserved for a future chapter.

Now, on the campus at this time there was a vigorous-minded youngster, of whom the Parson was fond. His name was Robert House, and his chief philosophical interest was ethical. The Parson, therefore, induced his young friend to go along with him and sit in the ethics class. And this is what Dr. House, when some twenty years later he had become Dean of Administration in the University, said of the incident. "I got much joy out of the discussion in the classroom and out of the Parson's comments. On one occasion, as I well recall, Parson turned to me and whispered, 'unity is the secret of the whole thing.'"

But this pleasant picture had another side, as pictures generally have. Some students were doubtful of Horace's method. A few laughed and called him a crank. The college papers were filled with jibes. They cartooned the erratic professor. They put him under the microscope. In one issue of a student publication appeared two columns by an irate student—a fierce blast demanding more psychology and less Williamsology. "The Professor's course is totally non-understandable," the student charged. "The wayfaring man is completely befuddled. To pass Horace Williams' course is a 'thing in itself' and very hard to do." In a few days a reply appeared charging that the attack was a mere grouch, the student having been flunked and now exhibiting his sore toe.

But neither praise nor censure provoked a word of reply from Old Horace or deflected him from his course. On he went, pillorying the Ph.D.'s, criticising politics, religion, and the shallow educational methods of the day. Nor did he let up, for a single instant, in his ridiculous methods of putting over his thoughts in the classroom. "Eccentric, outré, bizarre," as Archibald Henderson paints him, he had now developed strange personal peculiarities and eccentricities, such as an outlandish drawl, winding a piece of string around his nose, toying with the electric cord, acting like a half-witted yokel when he was being most intelligent, and humiliating his students with a sort of refined cruelty. "But unfailingly interesting and arresting. Old Horace never bored you. You couldn't go to sleep on his classes!"

"Miss Denham," the old professor drawled, one day as the class was considering the effect of Christianity upon civilization, "how do you define progress?"

"Why, Professor, I'd say progress is advance along proper lines."

"Do you think the world is growing better or worse, Miss Denham."

"Better, Professor, much better."

"So you think, do you, Miss Denham?" And then, after a pause, "Do you think, Miss Denham, you are better than your mother?"

On another occasion, the subject under discussion being the relative value of a concept and its results, for example the concept of an ox-cart is more important than the mechanical part, to which the entire class had agreed, the teacher propounded this question. "Do you agree to that proposition, Miss Kennette?"

"Yes, Professor, I think the idea superior to the mechanical."

"Now, Miss Kennette, if you were to make a cake and use your neighbor's recipe, it would be her cake, would it?"

During another lecture Old Horace was harping on his well-worn theory that intimations of immortality may be found in the emergence of a plus out of two minuses, this being his old illustration of minus three multiplied by minus three producing plus nine. In his desire to implant this idea firmly in the minds of the dullest student the Professor reached in his pocket and pulled out a spool wound around with tape—this performance being highly dramatic and mysterious.

"In my hand, young gentlemen," he suavely began, "I hold a spool of tape. Now I negate it." Slowly and deliberately he unwinds the tape. "What am I doing, Mr. Weil?"

"Unwinding, I guess, Professor."

"Nothing else?"

"Nothing that I can discover."

"Why, I am negating the object, destroying it. At this point I cease to negate." Here the Professor stopped unwinding. "I now cut the tape." This he does. "In a word, I negate the negating process and thereby create a new object, a well defined article, a piece of tape two feet long and an inch wide." With much satisfaction he then exhibits his experiment to the class.

"Mr. Shore," the professor said one morning, "this side of the street is that side of the street to the man on the other side of the street, how is that?"

"Why, Professor, that sounds like Kant to me."

"That reminds me, Professor," broke in Worth, a student from the Cape Fear. "A Bladen County boy, from the Tory Hole, took your course and got so much fed up on logic that he concluded to try it out on his home folks. 'Dad,' he said, one day at the dinner table, 'you think there are only two chickens in that dish, but there are really three.'

"'How so, son?'

"'Well, here is one chicken and there is another. One and two make three, don't they?'

"'Yes, I suppose so, son, and I'll take this chicken and your Mammy'll take that one and you may have the third!'"

As the class tittered approval of the hit, Old Horace proceeded as though nothing had happened. "The idea is this," he said, "the point of view controls. Last summer, I was up in the Blue Ridge Mountains and puzzled a handsome young woman sitting near me on the porch by telling her that the chair she thought she was in she was not occupying at all. "The chair I am sitting in," I explained to her, "is that chair to you just as the chair you are sitting in is that chair to me. So this chair and that chair are the same chair."

Next morning's *Tar Heel* played up the incident and wound up an article with the query, "Well, what chair was that lassie sitting in, anyhow?"

But badinage of this kind was interspersed with words of comfort addressed to confiding souls, who loved truth and walked therein as those whose feet are resolutely set straight toward the morning. Writing his tender-minded friend, Lilla Vass Shepherd, the old philosopher said, "It has been my purpose to eliminate the personal and seize the moments of reality as they are. Only this process leads into paths where the Truth blazes with light."

An incorrigible youngster in Horace's class was Oscar Coffin, from the backwoods of the Uharie Mountains. Oscar was fond of placing torpedoes under Horace's aesthetical arks. One day Horace was going on as usual, exalting spirit, or Geist. "God is Truth," he declared, "eternal, everlasting, without limits or exceptions."

Now Oscar had stood this kind of talk as long as he could, when he perked up and said, "Why, Professor, you talk idealism, but you practice the opposite."

"How is that, Mr. Coffin?"

"It's this way, Professor. You win debates, but you are careful to pick the judges. They do say, Professor, that you are as good at picking a jury as lawyer Jim Pugh down in Raleigh."

As the class enjoyed Old Horace's discomfiture, he sidled off to the window and turned his back to them. Presently he resumed. "Yes, Mr. Coffin, I do select debate judges and do it carefully. Let me illustrate. A debate had been scheduled. One of our debaters came and showed me the judges' names, hand-picked against us. I said, 'Refuse to go on. Demand an impartial jury. He took my advice, another committee was chosen, and he won. Mr. Coffin, do you imagine I am going to let my boys be led like sheep to the slaughter?"

"No, Professor, I'll swear you ain't!"

The class roared with laughter at the professor's expense and he continued with the lecture on the individual and his inviolability. "Mr. Haywood," he said, "do you accept the doctrine of the One and the many—the integrity of the individual?"

"I think so, Professor, and if I understand the doctrine it simply means to be yourself."

"Yes, and a little more, Mr. Haywood. One is one because it is one of many ones, many is many because made up of many ones."

"Mr. Gray, what did Socrates imply by his famous remark 'Know thyself'?"

"Why, get acquainted with yourself, Professor."

"Not exactly that, Mr. Gray. Socrates, being a philosopher in action, insisted that you must know yourself as a part of reality."

"Mr. Rights, have you a clear concept of the difference between Kant's notion of the paradox and Hegel's?"

"Yes, Professor, I'd say Kant did not try to solve the clashes of life, he left them alone. Hegel tackled them."

"How did he do this, Mr. Rights?"

"Really, Professor, just now I can't recall."

"Mr. Rights, Kant conceived of the conflicts of life as real and insolvable, he named four major antinomies. Then came Hegel and differed from Kant. What was Hegel's view, Mr. Bahnson?"

"Why Hegel concluded that Kant's conflicts were imaginary and not real."

"Precisely. Hegel saw life as a continuous whole, without gaps. Unity pervades all things. From the same stem arise good and evil. Continuity and discreetness are essential elements of the same thing. Each one of us is essentially a paradox—an antinomy."

The college press, as well as the philosophy classroom, was full of the whims and oddities of Old Horace—he himself being the chief paradox of all. In a certain issue of the *University Magazine* a disillusioned student of Horace's, who should have been in the School of Commerce instead of the School of Thought, wrote a diatribe in which he dubbed Old Horace one of the "duds and dudheads!" The humorous publication, *Yackety Yack*, was never happier than when picking on the philosophy professor.

In one issue it depicted Old Horace as a thin, cadaverous, bespectacled individual, hands folded in front, a head all forehead, a small chin, standing with his feet far apart and gazing abstractedly in a show-window. The skit was called, "The Power of Logic." It told that a new merchant had come to Chapel Hill to establish a trade in hides and had worked out a sign which he thought would attract customers. He bored an auger hole through the door-post and stuck a calf's tail into it with the tufted end outside. Presently a sad-faced person approached and gazed at the sign. The merchant watched the stranger a minute and then stepped out and addressed him.

"Good morning, sir," he said.

"Morning," answered the other, without taking his eyes off the sign.

"Want to buy leather?" asked the merchant.

"No."

"Got any hides to sell?" "No."

"Are you a farmer?" "No." "Merchant?" "No." "Lawyer?" "No." "Doctor?" "No."

"What are you, then?"

"A philosopher, and I've been standing here an hour trying to figure out how that calf got through that auger hole!"

Another *Yackety Yack* cartoon went the rounds and set the campus in a roar. The lampoon was entitled, "How It Looked to Hi." Old Hi Plunkett was the hayseed farmer disgusted because his neighbor Jack Beasley had sent his son Lem off to Chapel Hill under that terrible fellow Horace Williams. Hi was bent on going up himself to the University to spy out the land. If the philosophy professor was as bad as he was painted, Old Hi had made up his mind to keep his son, Sam, away from Chapel Hill.

Accordingly Old Man Hiram put on his Sunday best, with a tall, slick beaver stuck on the back of his head, a pair of huge spectacles on his enormous nose, a Jim Swinger coat on his back, and long straggy whiskers on his chin, and saddled Moll, his mule, and set out for Chapel Hill. As he entered the campus and drew near the Alumni Building, he heard a lot of laughing and went in "expectin' ez how I'd git amused a little."

"The room was full of boys, and up in front a mournful lookin' man wuz a-leanin' 'gainst a table a-talkin' to 'em." The mournful man never paused when Hi came in and in about two minutes everybody had forgotten he was there. "The mournful man was a-lookin' out uv the winder, and didn't seem to be talking about anything in particular, or tew anybody in speshul." Everything was now so mournful that Hi concluded somebody must be dead, "but after a bit the mournful man kinder perked up like, an' sez, seze,

" 'Mister Day, why don't a cat hev wings?'

" 'Fur the luv of heck,' thinks Old Hi to himself, 'he might ez well ask, Why don't a duck hev horns.'

Just then a smart little fellow on the front seat, staring up at the mournful man, answered and said, "Because uv a category, seze."

At this point the mournful man looked out of the window again and said something that Old Hi didn't catch and everybody laughed.

"An' so it goes," says the mournful man. And after a bit he left the window and came back and started afresh.

" 'Mister Parker,' seze, 'which come first, the hen or the egg?'

As nobody seemed able to answer this question, it wasn't long before the mournful man turned around and said,

" 'Mister Logan, why can't you wear your right glove on your left han'?'

"Wuss an wuss!" thinks Hi. "He'll be ravin' 'fore long.

"One of the boys spoke up in a mighty convincing way and said somethin' which I didn't just ketch, and then the

Teacher glanced kind of quick-like over the crowd an' sez, seze:

"'Mister Tillett, do you agree with Mister Logan?'

"Some of the fellows on the back row nudged another fellow who was asleep, and all of a sudden he woke up and hollered out—'Yes—sir, Professer.' At this point the mournful man switched off and began to talk about an 800-pound hog out on his farm and from that he got off to ducks.

"'Mister Hannah,' seze, 'why do a duck hev web feet?'"

Old Hi could stand it no longer, he whispered in the ear of a little fellow sitting next to him and said, "Becase he hez tew swim, ye tarnal idjut."

This last question cooked the goose for Old Hi. He went back home and the next morning, "I tuk my son Sam over tew the big clearin' an' set him tew plowin' a furrer. An' he's plowin' yit, fer my mind, it's done made up!"

This little comedy was preceded by the following Chaucerian lines:

> *Psychologie, of alle my worke,*
> *It's tuffe as helle, the worste of foes:*
> *But stille I knowe I must not shirke*
> *What Horace says: "And soe it goes."* *

Thus the years in Old Horace's classroom came and went, sense and non-sense clashing, paradox, the dialectic and the antinomy permeating the course and Horace the most noted paradox of all. The philosopher often contradicted one morning's dogmatic statement by an equally dogmatic utterance of the next, but such minor aberrations had no effect upon the astronomical progression of a mind which brought its wandering planets under one central law.

"Mr. Graham," remarked the professor one day early in the century, addressing a quiet, unobtrusive young student,

---

* This humorous skit comes from the pen of Quincy Sharp Mills, of the Class of 1907, an editorial writer of *New York Evening Sun*. A gallant youth, killed on July 26, 1918, in an attack on the German line. His life was published by Putnam's Sons.

"do you agree with Socrates that virtue is knowledge, vice ignorance?"

"Yes, Professor, I agree with Socrates and I go further. I say we overestimate people's knowledge and underestimate their judgment."

"I have often heard your cousin, Ed Graham, express that thought."

In later years this thoughtful young man had become president of the University and a factor in world affairs. One day he gave an estimate of his old philosophy teacher. "Horace Williams has made more University students intellectually conscious than any other professor in the history of the University." So declared Frank Porter Graham.

17

DEEP CALLING UNTO DEEP

"WHEN I LEARNED that Jesus was probably not a Methodist," said Horace Williams in his cryptic fashion, "it was a jar." This statement is significant; it shows a development from the local to the universal, from the particular to the general, from diversity to unity. In the search for that which Old Horace called the ultimate unit he had stumbled upon Jesus, the one perfect Man, the pattern of truth, goodness, and beauty. Two thousand years earlier St. Paul had travelled the same road and made the same discovery.

Let us now inquire what Williams considered the connecting link of the individual with this ultimate unit. Beyond all question it is faith. Faith is the source of the life of the individual as ultimate reality, William proclaimed. As the plant has its life in the process of nature, so the individual has his life-as-reality in the process of reality. This relation is vital. "I am the vine, ye are the branches," said Jesus. "In him we live and move and have our being," adds St. Paul—a thought which conveys the idea of growth. Paley's simile of the watch must, therefore, be replaced by the simile of a flower. The universe is not a machine but an organism with an indwelling principle of life. It was not made; it has grown.

But what thought Horace Williams of Jesus? After he had made the startling discovery that Jesus was probably not a Methodist and that the Bible could not be interpreted literally, did he cease to honor and revere the Son of Man?

No. If possible his devotion to this ultimate unit, this everlasting Spirit, grew and enlarged. It is not an exaggeration to say that neither Spinoza, the God-intoxicated, nor St. Francis, the saintliest of saints, held Jesus in higher adoration.

That the illiterate son of a carpenter, the offspring of an humble middle-class family, born in a stable midst sheep and oxen and asses, born too in a small despised conquered country, that this obscure individual should have started the world afresh, given a new date to the calendar, set on foot a universal religion, supplanted force with love, reversed all former thought-processes and developed into the greatest Teacher, the most perfect creature, the one and only Philosopher, casting into the junk-heap Socrates and Plato and Aristotle and even the beloved Hegel, this to Horace Williams was miracle enough for anyone, however skeptical!

"I was thrilled one day," declares Williams, "to find in Hegel the definite statement that his philosophy was the exposition of the life of Jesus." Thenceforth, as he concludes, "my education took a long step, I caught a vision of the beautiful life, a life which all should live since it is the process of reality."

Now this concept of Christianity was but the thought of St. Basil, who declared that Christianity was nothing more than the imitation of Jesus Christ; and of the great St. Augustine, who likewise asserted that Christ came upon the earth there to be an example of a perfect life.

Not the corporeal body of Jesus but the glorified body rose from the grave and entered into Paradise, not three days later but at once. In this conclusion, as will be remembered, Weiss, the devout theologian, concurs in his *History of Primitive Christianity.* In that stimulating work it is said that a majority of devout Christians, at the present time, do not believe in a resurrection of the flesh on the last day. These broad, liberal, unpopular, if not despised, views of Christianity Horace Williams firmly held. But let this be added. The Old Philosopher literally repudiated and contemned the belittling suggestions of Ernest Renan, professing to be a follower of Jesus, but asserting that He worked spurious miracles in order to teach his doctrines. Such a view was repulsive to Horace Williams, and he would have none of it.

Old Horace was not only a student of philosophy but of psychology also. He knew the power of mind over matter, the extraordinary supremacy of the spiritual forces of the world over the material. He realized that Jesus was a teacher above all else and that healing and the casting out of devils were mere incidents of his ministry. Did Jesus not caution his disciples to tell no man? Did he not rebuke those who urged him to show them a sign, and others who failed to understand that his kingdom was a spiritual kingdom and not a worldly one? In this connection Williams often referred to a sermon of Phillips Brooks, in which the great preacher, in imitation of the prophet Jeremiah, uttered a prophetic warning and called attention to the disastrous tendencies of the church. He declared that if his church planted itself upon the unhistorical doctrine of apostolical succession it would degenerate into a fantastic sect.

Though Horace Williams was fond of few modern books, he made an exception in favor of Allen's *Life of Bishop Brooks*. It gave him great satisfaction to read what Brooks had characterized as the suicidal tendencies of the church, these being: the suicide of Dogma; the suicide of Corruption; the suicide of Formalism.

It may be asked, if Horace Williams entertained such liberal views as these, what place did Jesus have in his religion? If Jesus is not the Savior of mankind, why not get along without this hypothesis, as a skeptical astronomer, characterizing God, once proposed? The answer which Williams would doubtless have given is this. Jesus is the image of God. Jesus is the blueprint, the begriff of God. What would one know of God if there had never been a Jesus? Not only is Jesus the express image of God, but God is the express image of Jesus. The religious process is as necessary to the spiritual man as the nature process is to the natural man.

The goal of the pure in heart therefore should be Jesus. He is the standard, and by standard is implied quality, that which is in itself absolute. There is a standard for the insect, and this standard does not vary. There is a standard for the animal; it does not vary. There is a standard for intelligence; why should it vary? The vice of our age is materialism. The world is on a mechanized basis. In such an age there can be no spiritual, such an age would justify itself by denying the spiritual.

This dilute concept of Christianity Horace Williams formed and adhered to in spite of himself. Orthodox he greatly preferred to have been, but could not become. With mind and soul he had sought to be an obedient son of the church. In early life he entered the Methodist ministry. That endeavor had become abortive. In later life his mind was turning to the Catholic church, whose orderliness intrigued him. The whole-hearted obedience of its members he likened to the orderliness of the heavenly bodies. In First Clement he read that all nature, the cosmos above and below, is a complete revelation of peace and order. The beautiful development of the idea begins with the heavens which revolve in an orderly manner; then day and night, sun, moon and the chorus of stars, the earth and the world beneath, the sea and the ocean, in turn; the seasons, the winds and wells, finally the animals, even the smallest of them, all of which meet together in concord and peace. Therefore there must also be order in the Christian church.

While living in northern cities he had seen thousands of devout Catholics, crowding their churches to attend a five o'clock mass, though snow might be falling and a cutting northeastern gale sweeping the land. This phenomenon, so opposed to the ease-loving nature of the carnal man, interested the old philosopher and he sought to solve it and form a begriff of the situation.

Not far from his home in Chapel Hill lived Robert Wettach, now Dean of the Law School, and his wife Alpha, a woman of unshakable faith, steeped in the mysteries of the Catholic church. He determined to consult Alpha Wettach and ask her to show him how to connect with her brand of absorbing religion. Sometimes at the meat market, at other times at the Wettach home, the two would converse together. In the most earnest manner the old philosopher would implore her to teach him to enter into the mysteries of her church. Once he asked her to put in writing the way by which he might attain unto sanctity. Alas, as she said, this was an impossibility. Religion is a personal matter. You either have it or you don't have it. The wind bloweth where it listeth. One must have faith. Ah, that word faith! It was the stumbling block. What part did his intellectual process play in the faith process? A question Dr. Johnson once answered when he growled and said to Boswell, "Sir, we would all be Catholics but for an obstinate rationalism."

An obstinate rationalism! That was the rub. Should he cast aside his reason and rely on faith alone? When he witnessed the externalities of the Catholic church, genuflexions, incense, and the like, he was unable to see how they were related to vital matters.

"Why, they are mere adjuncts," his friend would explain.

"Agreed. But why shall I confess to a priest?"

"But another aid to holiness."

"Well, well, the Immaculate Conception, the Infallibility of the Pope, the Seven Sacraments, are they likewise non-essential?"

"No, indeed, they are fundamental."

"So I feared and my mind simply does not connect up."

"Professor Williams, can your mind connect up with God? Do you know what electricity is or gravitation?"

"No. But a thousand impulses and my whole being tell me of God and truth—not of an infallible Pope or of physical miracles."

"Ah, Professor, what you need is faith."

"There you have hit it, but shall I exercise faith contrary to reason? Must not reason precede faith?"

"Really, Professor, you are past redemption!"

And so the discussion would wind up in a laugh.

Now this searching after God was not an emotional impulse. Far from that: it was an intellectual experiment. Old Horace had no fear of Hell. He did not wish to get religion or to save his soul alive. Religion, he already had. What he was driving at was a check-up on his intellectual process to see if there were flaws in it. Was feeling and emotion the gateway to glory? as he once imagined. Or was the intellectual path he was now treading the right road?

Fortunately, as we have seen, the old philosopher concluded Jesus had resolved his questionings. Jesus had declared that truth and God are identical. The Apostle Paul had likewise taken truth as his key-word. Defining truth, Paul had declared that it is the objective revelation of God, the knowledge of God. Truth is the self-manifestation of God as made known in the Gospel. Because truth is the valid revelation of God, there is no other gospel.

Though this conviction of Williams had an intellectual character, it also had a religious basis. As the Apostle to the Gentiles had insisted, so did Horace Williams: The thought-system of the Gospel is so flawlessly fitted together that he considered it a moral deformity if one would not bow to the the truth but would give obedience to a lie.*

If happiness be harmony with one's environment Horace Williams should now have been happy. Everything was coming his way; his efforts to liberate thought were becoming fruitful. His classes were crowded with students, whose papers dealt in a satisfactory manner with his thought-processes. In every campus poll he was voted the most popular and the most useful professor on the Hill.

* Horace Williams' religious views I respect. Much of Spinoza I see in him. But neither the geometric god of Plato nor the intellectual god of Hegel and Williams seems to me to be adequate. At page 292 the divergence in our views appears.

A clear-cut picture of him would appear in nearly all distinguished University groups. He held a strong grip on boys and trustees. He was in demand as a lecturer. On commencement occasions he was in the forefront, whether as preacher or lecturer. His debaters continued to win-out over all comers. Oftentimes he and Professor Bernard would perform the most unusual feats; they would coach the debaters, entering into the preliminary contests with them. They would accompany Carolina debaters into one of the Society halls and there debate the proposed query, showing no mercy to their juvenile opponents.

In no sense would this be a shadow-boxing contest. The professors would badger the boys with every conceivable argument. They would carefully plan attack or defense. The first speaker would be instructed to assemble the facts, omitting none of them; the next speaker would draw the conclusion, make a begriff. In this manner duplication was avoided and a logical sequence arranged.

Occasionally some members of the faculty would seek to curtail the rights of the students to govern themselves. Horace Williams was uniformly a stout advocate for the boys. Self-government and the honor system he regarded as essential to genuine manhood.

In this bright picture however there was a blur. Many members of the faculty and the Fundamentalist element throughout the State continued hostile to Professor Williams. The grievance of the faculty was, for the most part, a real one. The professor would not coöperate. He was an individualist, and not only critical but sarcastic.

In this fight on Old Horace the extremes had met. The Fundamentalist and the scientist were well agreed. The one considered him an atheist; the other, an ignoramus. But neither social, religious, nor scientific combinations could irritate or move the stubborn old philosopher. God was with him, and God and he formed a majority. His course was clear. The Man of Galilee had pointed the way.

Horace Williams once declared that the most marvellous

phenomenon in all history is Jesus. It was the career of this great Teacher which he was now seeking to illustrate. Not an easy task, an impossible one but for the sympathy, the love, and the untiring attentions of a devoted wife and the comforts of a quiet, well-ordered home.

It is quite true that when Horace and Bertha were first married they were unacquainted with domestic problems and unequal to the restraints of married life; they were in fact mere babes in the woods. But time had worked wonders. Bertha had made the unsightly dwelling more comfortable and homelike. In all things she had subordinated herself to him. He, on his part, had come to realize the blessing of a real companion. Though he was saving and frugal she understood and appreciated the high motive behind this self-sacrifice, and so did her devoted sister, Lucy Wells, who now resided in Wilmington, Delaware. These two women were not only sisters but friends. They often visited each other and exchanged inmost thoughts. On one occasion when Bertha was visiting Lucy she confided in her and said, "Horace's idea of saving money has behind it a future hope of a deep expression of love and loyalty to me."

Lucy Wells held Horace Williams in high esteem. Oftentimes in a literary group she would quote him to friends saying, "My brother-in-law, Horace Williams, says so-and-so." That would put an end to further discussion. In after days when the shadows were lengthening, Mrs. Wells reverted to the pleasure of Bertha's visits and to the affection manifested for her by her husband. "Horace Williams was generosity itself," she declared, "sending Bertha frequent checks for pleasure and for her amusement. I can see her face shine as she opened a special delivery letter enclosing an unexpected, extra $100 to spend on her beloved New York."

The Colton family were friends of Bishop Phillips Brooks of Boston. The Rev. Mr. Colton and his children lived in the cultural atmosphere of the great Bishop. Their early home in Connecticut was one of rare charm. In Mrs.

Wells' little book, *Children of the Old Stone House*, she draws, as we have seen, a lively picture of the early days of the Colton family. The old stone house is now the property of a Greek Letter fraternity at Wesleyan College, and is still mysterious and full of traditions.

Reared in the mystical atmosphere of the old stone house Bertha Colton, a bride, had brought down to Chapel Hill memories and associations which neither time nor space could eradicate. To the end of her life she was a mystic, leading a dream existence, saying and doing things alien to the simple, practical ways and customs of Chapel Hill.

On a certain occasion she was undertaking to paint a portrait of one of the handsomest young women of the village. But her muse went back on her and refused to coöperate. Try as she might, she could not execute the painting. At length, at the appointed day, the young woman called around to get the painting and was conducted into the studio. Laughing, Mrs. Williams pointed to the easel and cried out, "Oh, Eleanor, my dear, I just could not paint you. I tried and I tried but failed. So I blotted it all out and have painted a snow scene!"

Calling on a neighboring spinster, fitted in every way for the estate of matrimony, she suddenly burst forth, "Oh, my dear, you are so lovely! You need a man."

"Why, Mrs. Williams! You surely don't mean it?"

"Indeed I do, and I pray every night for a nice husband for you."

Bertha Colton brought with her from Connecticut the proverbial New England habit of promptness. She was true to form. At one of her five-o'clock teas, some of the guests arrived fifteen minutes late. She left them smiling, astounded, and sitting—uninvited—in the unheated studio!

On another occasion she was doing-over one of her rooms and papering the walls. A neighbor called. Mrs. Williams asked her in to pass on the job. "Do see how I have preserved my color scheme. Why my paper matches Mr. Williams' eyes!"

The sublimated, ethical spirit of his wife did find some response, though slight, in the cold, intellectual nature of the old philosopher. He too was inclined to mysticism. He would follow the gleam. Almost he could hear voices. In the classroom, when he depicted the Standard, the life of the Spirit, the City of God, his face would shine and a feeling, deep and full, animate all hearts. Alas, his faith was intellectual, while Bertha's was from the heart. The one philosophized about Jesus; the other lived Jesus.

It was the life of Bertha that steadied him. Daily he realized his obligation to her and often endeavored to express it—as the dedication of his first book manifests. In thorough-going words, though somewhat lacking in poetic diction and lover-like afflatus, he wrote,

To
Bertha Colton Williams
Who in a companionship of Thirty Years
Met every expectation

18

CONFOUNDING HIS ADVERSARIES

As TIME passed and Professor Williams' strange ideas circulated through every nook and corner of the conservative old Commonwealth and were discussed in churches and hamlets from Currituck to Cherokee, mutterings, deep and ominous were heard. Heresy hunters, Fundamentalists and shifty politicians got busy. "The heretic-professor must go," was the cry. This man was overturning sacred traditions and corrupting the youth.

Judge Tom Shaw, a conscientious, Christian-literalist, took up the good work. The Judge removed his son from the University and its contaminating influences! In a charge to a country grand jury, his Honor likewise inveighed against the atheism rampant at Chapel Hill. "More than half the students in that godless college," he declared, "are infidels." His Honor reminded the grand jury that the Constitution had denounced atheism; he instructed them to go to the bottom of this matter. "I charge you to present any public official who denies the being of Almighty God."

This attack, as everyone realized, was not so much upon the University as against Horace Williams with his unorthodox and transcendental views. No sooner had Judge Shaw's charge reached the public than Old Horace's boys accepted the challenge. "Make good your charge, Judge Shaw, or resign," Tobe Connor, a fearless Horatian, thundered in an open letter to the people.

Judge Walter Neal, a man of more push than wisdom, became chairman of a select committee of one hundred prominent churchmen whose job was to rid the State of professors and textbooks teaching the evolution heresy. Brother Turlington, a successful political theorist wedded to prohibition and a literal Bible, joined the crusaders. As in the adjoining State of Tennessee so in Tar Heelia, the first guns were being unlimbered in a determined campaign which later culminated in the ridiculous Scopes "monkey trial," Clarence Darrow and W. J. Bryan locking horns and the silver-tongued orator losing his life, leaving his Fundamentalist brethren heart-broken.

In this religious crusade there were the usual preliminary skirmishes. Dr. McCorkle continued his newspaper attacks. Religious conventions and synods passed condemnatory resolutions. The religious press fulminated. Political weather-cocks jumped on the band-wagon. The innocent public went into a state of religious hysteria, as was their wont. The home mission committee of the synod requested Orange Presbytery to investigate Parson Moss, whose humorous Jonah-sermon and constant ridicule of Fundamentalism had been bruited around to the scandal of the orthodox.

A few years earlier, when the Parson came into Orange Presbytery, he had been examined by a committee composed of Dr. Anderson and Dr. Clark and had been duly admitted. On that occasion, as the Parson afterwards confided to Old Horace and me one evening as we sat in the Williams study, he had been asked if he believed Jesus was the Son of God and had answered, Yes. "But," laughed the Parson, "I had a narrow escape. If I had been asked, Do you believe Jesus is the only Son of God, I would have said, No—all of us are the Sons of God."

Undoubtedly the effort to investigate the Parson was a part of a comprehensive, well-meaning religious movement then sweeping the South. Since the relationship between Parson Moss and Old Horace was well understood, the Parson's unfrocking would have been a decisive blow to Williams' prestige. But when the request to investigate was put in the hands of Dr. Craig, the wise old clerk of the Presbytery, he tore up the paper and refused to put the motion. In his effort to forestall the ill-advised movement, as the story runs, Brother Craig was so flustered that he spat a mouthful of tobacco juice into the hot air register, mistaking it for the cuspidor!

The religious outburst of the early 1900's may seem at first blush to have been exceptional and quite out of place in the twentieth century. But, when rightly considered, it was true to form. Roughly speaking, the mind of the South of 1890 was the mind of the South of 1790. During those hundred years there had been little change in the religion of the southern people—the religion of their fathers was still their own. Beyond question, the customs, manners, and mores of a people are stronger than the laws.

Now the public opinion which Horace Williams was up against had all the elements of strength. Walter Page had characterized it as ecclesiastical narrowness; Horace Williams called it orthodoxy. But by whatever name called, it was a doughty antagonist.

Because of the fixity of religious thought, therefore, Horace Williams was not at all surprised at the strength of the Fundamentalist movement. Oftentimes he would declare that the greater the religious zeal of a ruler the greater his persecution, quoting the revocation of the Edict of Nantes. This wise law had blessed the people of France, and given them religious freedom for a hundred years, though godless kings and their gaudy mistresses had sat upon the throne. But just so soon as an over-zealous, orthodox queen began to wield her influence, the Edict was revoked.

Notwithstanding the vigor and honesty of the religious movement, Williams determined to go forth and do battle in the cause of free thought and free speech. "When the Fundamentalist movement swept over Tennessee, I was disturbed," the old philosopher declared. He knew that if the heresy won out in Tennessee it would overrun North Carolina and then sweep the entire South—a deplorable situation! But if this reaction did come, if the clock of time were set back, whose fault would it be? With his usual candor he admitted that it would be his fault, and his alone. As the head of the philosophy department it was his duty to guide the State. The Fundamentalist movement at bottom was a philosophical problem, a problem which he should solve. This the University demanded of him and thousands of his loyal boys expected.

And yet a thorny path lay in front of him. "For twenty-five years I was the center of a storm," he declared in 1936. "Had the Board of Trustees been men of a well-known type my career would have been brief and unhappy. I know they were often tempted. But we all loved the University. With their support the battle was won and my work was a daily joy." But how and where should the campaign to correct erroneous impressions and enlighten the people begin?

After a conference with his boys, who were now known as the Young Turks of the New University, Charlotte was chosen as the battleground. And a fitting terrain it was! Charlotte, called by General Cornwallis, the Hornets' Nest of the Revolution. Charlotte, the home of Fundamentalism and of Modernism. Charlotte, where lived exponents of the Right, the Left, and the Center. Charlotte, paradox of paradoxes. The preliminaries leading up to the first gun of the campaign were fitting and adequate. Charlotte's great, independent newspaper, the *Observer*, which Williams read for half a century, played up the meeting, calling attention to a striking address which the professor had delivered two years before and which had been pronounced by those who were fortunate enough to hear it a discourse full of profound thought and inspiration.

The Convention Hall of the Y.M.C.A. was chosen as the place of meeting and Sunday afternoon at four o'clock on May 5, 1917, as the time. The sponsors of the movement were the Mecklenburg University Alumni, one of whom was President Ed Kidder Graham. One day in advance of the meeting Professor Williams arrived in the city and became the guest of his close friend, Dr. Otho Ross. A few hours before the lecture Ross's telephone rang. He picked up the receiver and discovered that his friend and fellow practitioner, Dr. I. W. Faison, was speaking.

"Otho, who is this fellow Williams that is going to speak at the meeting this afternoon?"

"Why, Dr. Faison, that is Horace Williams, for many years professor of philosophy at the University of North Carolina."

"Well, is he that heretic I've been hearing so much about all these years?"

"Now, Dr. Faison, I was a student of Professor Williams' and I think he is the best Christian in North Carolina, and so do all of his old boys."

"Yes, I know what you fellows think, but I know what I think, too. He is the very fellow I'm talking about, and you tell him I want him to answer me three questions, first, the Immaculate Conception, second, the inspiration of the Scriptures, and third, Immortality."

"Dr. Faison, Professor Williams is a guest in my home and is sitting right here in my living room at this moment. I hardly feel like asking him questions that might be embarrassing."

"Well, if you don't ask him I'm going to ask him just as soon as he finishes speaking."

Long before the hour appointed for the meeting the hall was filled, Fundamentalists and Modernists in about equal numbers. The speaker entered and took a seat at the table. In came Dr Faison with his three knock-out questions and took his seat at the same table, immediately handing over his questionnaire to Old Horace—an incident which added to the excitement. In full force the orthodox members of the Second Presbyterian Church, and of other churches, had turned out to back up their champion, Dr. Faison, a forceful man with firm religious convictions. But the Modernists were also on hand, headed by Parker, Tillett, Shore, Ross, Jones, Ranson, and many others, devoted to their old teacher.

Circuit Judge Parker, afterwards appointed to the Supreme Bench of the United States, but unfortunately rejected by the Senate, introduced the speaker. Slowly and deliberately the Old Philosopher rose and moved to the front. Quietly and with dignity he began, unfolding his favorite theme, the growth, the development of civilization until it reaches the goal of truth.

"My good friend, Dr. Poteat, president of Wake Forest College and a noted educator, has recently declared that when religion and science conflict, science always wins."

At this point the speaker paused and made a study of his audience to get their reaction. Intently, every eye was turned his way. What would come next? their upturned faces seemed to ask. The speaker resumed. "With your permission, my friends, I propose to consider with you Dr. Poteat's statement and see if it is sound." Already the Old Philosopher had caught the audience, many of whom had formed a preconception of a pompous, wordy professor dealing in syllogisms and other abstractions. On the contrary, there stood before them a serious-looking man, very simple in manner, desperately in earnest, yet thoroughly objective and restrained, and with a voice of musical beauty and deep emotion.

"My subject as you have been told by my friend Judge Parker is the Law of Progress. What do we mean by progress? Does progress imply populous cities, scientific research, overcrowded and poorly coördinated schools? Is quantity progress? If not, what is progress? The answer is this, The religion of a people is the measure of their progress. And what do we mean when we use the word religion? Why, religion is the right relation of man to God. A proper unfolding of this subject carries one over a wide field, but the route is continuous and unified." At this point the Old Man had struck his gait, and was on familiar ground, the well-known idea of Hegel that life is process, growth, continuity.

After pointing out the progress of the arts and sciences in the improvement of civilization, the speaker turned to the spiritual side of progress. The individual is the unit, the starting point in progress. The individual should develop out of a Christian home, presided over by a godly mother, the guide of his young days, the inspiration of his life. From the level of the animal the individual develops on and up through the scientific process into the realm of the spirit. The mistake of the scientists is that they stop with analysis. They are content with the test tube and the blow pipe. The Christian goes beyond the scientific. The Christian orientates life, he ascends the heights, he attains unto the spiritual. "As I tell my boys in the classroom, Christianity unites the sensory and the scientific, it relates the two, it synthesizes them. In the spiritual realm the perfect individual finally reaches St. Augustine's City of God.

"The intimate relation of reality, Jesus was the first to see. He termed this relation spirit and saw it as the absolute condition of progress. Since this relation is real it will enable one to carry over from the Now to the Hereafter. Progress is knowledge and action. It may be conceived of as on three levels, the sense level, the scientific level, and the spiritual level."

Thus far the speaker had not hinted at Dr. Faison's mysterious note, which he held in his hand. Nor did the audience seem to expect or desire it. But at length there came a hint. "If someone should ask me," said the speaker, "if some day I shall die and pass into oblivion I would answer him and say 'No never.' Whatever essential values of truth, goodness and beauty are in me will never die; they will live forever. The Christian process is the process of infinite growth. The basis of Christianity is love. The finest example of love is that of the Christian mother.

"If we examine the usual criticism of the Bible we find a deep-seated fallacy—an attempt to measure spiritual matters by scientific methods. This may not be done. God is a spirit. He can not be discerned by carnal eyes. Can a quart-cup measure cloth? Can a yardstick measure molasses? Why then should we expect the carnal mind to measure the spiritual?

"And now, my friends, are we not somewhat better prepared to meet the objection of our friend, Dr. Poteat, when he declared that religion must yield to science? If my analysis of the law of progress be correct, the pathway leading from man to God is plain and unobstructed. This highway neither science nor the Powers of Darkness can block. The process of intelligence is truth. Religion is spirit, inerrant, continuous, from everlasting to everlasting. The moral life is a life of principle; it is universal, absolute, infinite. Right is not a matter of place or time. Right is not limited. No man can oppose the right thing. The moral life is a conscious and vital coöperation between God and man. The admission of our good friend, Dr. Poteat, must therefore be rejected. In a conflict between religion and science, religion will always win."

With these solemn words, uttered slowly, deliberately, with deep feeling, but simply and without theatricals, the Old Philosopher closed and quietly resumed his seat. Instinctively the congregation, Dr. Faison included, rose to their feet and stood and did homage to the man who had brought them a great message. But some of the hearers were still unconvinced; they maintained that it was not what the speaker had said but what he had left out that hurt. As for Dr. Faison he shook his head and exclaimed, "He's a slick brother and will bear watching!"

Perhaps the greatest snag Old Horace's venturesome craft ever struck was at a banquet in Charlotte given by his boys for their old Teacher the evening after his address. The time was just thirty days after America had entered the World War, and the war fever was at its height. The *Charlotte Observer* was carrying cartoons of the Kaiser, dubbing him a tyrant and a poltroon hiding behind a screen and with dozens of American bayonets aimed at his heart. On this occasion many reporters gathered, eager for an interview with the stimulating professor. They wished to find out what he thought of the World War into which the United States had just entered. With perfect candor and fearlessness, Old Horace spoke his mind. Yes, he had thought-through the matter and had formed a begriff of foreign affairs. The war in Europe was an economic one, based on the age-old idea of maintaining the balance of power in Europe. He deplored the participation of America in the war. "The United States of Europe is just as necessary as the United States of America," he solemnly affirmed. "And until the United States of Europe are formed, world war will follow world war—forever." Instantly pencils and notebooks made their appearance. What the professor had said was news. Compared with this utterance, his speech of the afternoon was as dust in the balance.

"PROFESSOR HORACE WILLIAMS OPPOSES THE WAR!"

Headlines such as these were flashed to the press of the entire State and were printed in far-away Germany. At Chapel Hill it raised a small-sized pandemonium. Editors castigated the fool-professor. He was an egotist, setting up his immature judgment against the wisdom of the entire world. During the coming months the *Statesville Landmark* and other papers made a target of the unruly professor. He was disloyal, a traitor to America, unworthy to hold his professorship. He must be expelled from the University. At a meeting of the Board of Trustees a motion was proposed to give him an indefinite leave of absence. Whereupon ten, twenty, thirty members of the Board rose to their feet and warmly objected, declaring that Professor Williams was the most popular, and deservedly so, of all the members of the faculty.

So high ran the feeling against Old Horace, on this occasion, that the level-headed Ed Kidder Graham, for once in his life, lost his temper if not his religion. "Why that fellow Williams is a damn fool," he ejaculated, a member of the faculty standing by and listening to the explosion. To counteract the effect of the Charlotte interview and set the matter straight, the University alumni busied themselves.

An elaborate banquet, with Williams as the speaker, was arranged. The function was set for the evening of December 31, 1917. W. D. Carmichael presided. Julian S. Carr, Durham philanthropist, was toastmaster. Chief Justice Clark lent his presence. Distinguished alumni in large numbers partook of the spread. A feast of reason and a flow of soul. But what was Professor Williams going to say? Would he recant? Would he go back on his Charlotte interview?

Slowly the Old Philosopher rose and deliberately began. He traced the advance of civilization from the Hebrew to the Greek and thence to the Roman and on to our own day. He told of clashes, confusion, conflicts, and wars. These, as he said, were in keeping with the dialectic process. Out of wars came treaties and leagues of peace. He cited the Treaty of Utrecht and the Treaty of Westphalia. All this was a part of the world process, he declared. From time to time, philosophers had pointed various and sundry ways for the advancement of civilization: the intellectual way, the mystical way, the sociological way, and, in our day, the natural or mechanical way. But each of these is only a partial truth. They must be combined. Truth is unity. Truth is totality. The German Kaiser has violated his treaty with Belgium. He has overrun that small country. He has violated truth. Germany can never win.

The problem of our day is to find a man, he continued. The process of the particular does not grow a big man. I love, he said, the picture of George Washington in the Philadelphia Convention. The problem was to find a process in which thirteen colonies could function. Hamilton could see nothing but the New York process, his being the largest colony. When the delegates refused to follow him he was angry and returned to New York. Had there been no man present bigger than Hamilton there would have been no United States. But there was a man as big as the problem. Washington arose and said, "Let us erect here a government to which the wise and just for all time may repair."

The result of the Philadelphia Convention was the Constitution of the United States, undoubtedly the greatest document that has emanated from the brain of man. That Constitution guarantees to us our inalienable rights. Under it, religion is free. Thought is free. Speech is free. So that today the free man of America, standing squarely upon the truth can say with Luther, "Here I stand. God help me, I can do no other!"

The Philosopher concluded his remarks and resumed his seat. The audience rose and expressed their gratification. Horace Williams had played the man. He had not recanted, he had not deigned even to refer to the Charlotte incident or its aftermath. "A wonderful speech, a very brave utterance," said President Few of Trinity to Tom Bost, as the two left the hall together. "Twenty years ago such a speech would have been impossible."

"Hold up, Dr. Few," Tom laughed. "We've been talking that sort of stuff at Chapel Hill ever since Old Horace took over the chair of philosophy."

19

IMP OF THE PERVERSE

Poor Doridon, the impe
Whom nature seem'd to have selected forth
To be engrafted on some stock of worth.

THUS SANG William Browne, the seventeenth-century poet who two hundred years later so greatly influenced Shelley and Keats. And what the poet had to say of Doridon applies equally to the paradoxical Williams. As one contemplates the spread between Old Horace's teaching and his conduct, he is not surprised at the misunderstanding of him by some of his associates. The Old Philosopher seemed indeed to have been cut bias. Had his dead body been thrown into the stream it would undoubtedly have floated upward. Not alone the political and the religious groups, but also the social and the regular were ferninst the pig-headed, Irish-minded professor.

Neither Paul Green nor Phillips Russell nor I could move the Old Fellow, when once he had taken a stand. We might urge him to cut loose from Hegel's objective universals and see the other side; we might counsel him to concede something to William James and John Dewey, those workable, bread-and-butter philosophers who were moulding American thought. Our advice would go with the wind. "James and Dewey," he would disdainfully reply, waving them off with his hand, "they are mere experimenters."

Now, from the teacher's point of view, never-to-be-forgotten, was he not correct? Had he taken our advice, had he conceded something to the relative and the exceptional, his philosophy might have degenerated into the commonplace. Never was he willing to lower his flag or admit the slightest deviation from the absolute rule of right. He knew that the world must have an idol. Youth, in particular, demands certitude of its teachers and a candid argument followed by a conclusion, final, certain, and strongly held. These essentials of the good teacher he possessed.

When William Couch sat in the philosophy class he did not approve of Horace Williams, whose mental arrogance and tyranny of opinion irked him. "Why is he not humble, as all really great men are? He offers nothing new. Then why does he speak like an Oracle?"

In this estimate young Couch was not altogether wrong, from his point of view. But in acting Sir Oracle Williams was consciously carrying out a purpose, and, undoubtedly, his very oddities, whimsicalities, and eccentricities have created a more lasting impression on the young than has the erudition of those more learned and profound professors, Greenlaw, Coker, Venable, Cain, Branson, MacNider, Hamilton, Connor, Wilson, Henderson, Pearson, Bell, Royster —or even than the two Grahams.

The mind of youth is not terrestial; it is celestial. Imagination, venturesomeness are its characteristics. Intrepid youth loves to explore far distant shores. "To know is nothing at all, to imagine is everything," says Anatole France. Erudition and profundity may pall upon young people, who demand things fresh and startling. Youth adores the crank! In Horace Williams the student found what he was looking for. "What does Old Horace say to that proposition?" was the campus question when some new idea had been sprung.

So harsh and cutting were his thoughts, though couched in a voice of velvet, that some of his neighbors shunned him, others abused him and only a few understood him. An understanding of Horace required a concession that he was sometimes talking through his hat and taking the other side in order to start something.

Dr. Howard Odum, professor of sociology, imagined that he knew how to handle Old Horace and get away with it. The two would occasionally meet on the street and Horace would set-in for a talk in order to form a begriff of the new and much touted sociological department.

"Dr. Odum," Old Horce would begin, in a crafty, cat-like manner, "they tell me you are doing great things."

"Well, Professor," Odum would laugh, "they are entirely wrong about that."

"Now, Professor Odum, my objective on the class is a conclusion reached through the thought-process and not by experimentation. And—"

"I understand you, Professor Williams. Yes, I fully understand you, Professor," Odum would quickly reply, as he darted off to write another book.

But Old Horace would break even with the impatient Odum. Meeting his friend George Pickard down the street he would dryly remark, "That man Odum's restless. He reminds me of one of my fractious cows, she moves about so fast we can't milk her!"

Old Horace was sometimes social and sometimes unsocial, depending on his mood at the moment. Frequently, in his walk to and from the college, he would run into one of his neighbors, Collier Cobb or Koch or Henry or Lasley or Bell or George Horner, and try out on them the substance of the lecture he was about to deliver; or he would jump some obscure, metaphysical problem of Kant's or Hegel's, taking the wrong side, as Socrates did, to draw out conversation, and discussing the matter with mock seriousness. Reaching the class he would make the conversation he had just had, the theme of an entire hour.

The professor's relations with brother members of the faculty were varied and paradoxical, and his association with them was always with an eye to the main chance. During the noon recess he and Dr. Henderson would often sit perched on a rock pile, regardless of their lunch hour, discussing some problem relating to the absolute and the infinite of Hegel. Henderson, a master of his subject, would perhaps explain in exact terms the significance of two minuses, when multiplied together, producing a plus.

"Nor! You are wrong," Old Horace would, most uncivilly break in.

At one conference when Henderson pointed out the possibilities of the algebraic process, since algebra unfolds itself without postulates, the inquisitive old philosopher was beside himself with joy. The idea was what he had been looking for, for years; the thought was indeed almost a key to the *Ding an sich*. But, so canny and secretive was Old Horace that he never gave credit for the suggestion. The idea that algebra was continuous and self-developing, as suggested by Henderson, really dominated Horace's mind so that he finally made a fetish of it. In old age he concluded that algebra was almost a religion. It bridged the chasm between the finite and the infinite!

Williams' intercourse with other members of the faculty was as practical as with Dr. Henderson. If he encountered Bradshaw of the philosophy department, or Bell, an expert chemist, it would be with the idea of extracting from them something of value to his beloved logic. He was everlastingly in pursuit of the fox, never chasing rabbits!

With only three or four people connected with the University, was he at all intimate. Albert Coates he regarded almost as a son, often discussing matters of the household with him and his wife. Sidney S. Robins, a former student and afterwards a Unitarian minister in New England, was the one man to whom Old Horace uncovered his intellectual soul. For a period of twenty-five years Williams and Robins corresponded and developed their philosophy of life. Francis Bradshaw, afterwards dean of students, was Old Horace's adviser in practical business matters.

But with none of the three did Horace become as personal as with Phillips Russell, teacher of creative writing. Let these two original thinkers get together and speak their minds and nothing was left unsaid. Candor, frankness, and unrestraint, but always with good humor, was the rule, however much they might chaw the rag. One vacation, when Old Horace's autobiography was in the galley-proof stage, he handed a copy to Russell and asked him to criticize it. In a few days Russell returned the file.

"Well, what do you think of it, Mr. Russell?" Williams dryly inquired.

"Why, Professor, I counted two hundred and eighty-seven pages in all and there was a triumph on every page and not a single failure."

"I have never had a failure," Old Horace vouchsafed.

Now this remark, which would have irritated some other person, was amusing to Russell, who was almost as objective and soft-spoken as Horace himself. Indeed, in many respects the two men were not unlike, mystical, enigmatical, and possessing strong personality. But here the analogy stops. If Williams was anti-social Russell was as social as the times demand. Therefore, when these two characters got together and opened up, as I have just said, the fur would begin to fly. If anyone had been sitting in on their conversation and had not known how friendly they were, he would have imagined each had a shillelagh ready for use.

Russell had been a member of the faculty but a short while when he called on his old teacher in the famous den.

"Come in, Mr. Russell," said Horace in his dryest manner. "I have been thinking about you."

"Nothing bad, I hope, Professor," was the reply, fully as desiccated.

"No, not bad. But I've concluded you are a failure."

"Why so, Professor?"

"We expected much of you, Mr. Russell, but are disappointed."

"In what, Professor?"

"Why you seem to have dropped out. What have you accomplished?"

"Well, Professor, what have you accomplished?"

"I hadn't thought of that. And so it goes. But Mr. Russell, I got your new book on Emerson you sent me."

"I hope you approve, Professor?"

"Yes, in a way. But why write about Emerson?"

"What's wrong with Emerson?"

"He's mouthy. What did he add to philosophy?"

"Well, Professor, I might ask, what do you add to philosophy?"

"Why I don't profess to add anything."

"I doubt, Professor, if you read a line of my Emerson."

"No. I didn't, Mr. Russell. Hegel's good enough for me."

"Professor, it seems to me you are not a philosopher at all. You are a mere actor, an artist. You have a streak of perversity in you."

"Do you think so, Mr. Russell? That's interesting, very interesting."

"Yes, Professor, you are merely the introducer of Hegel's idea. Old Sam Johnson might have been speaking of you when he said of a fellow that he was a man of one idea and that mostly wrong."

"Why should I want to know any philosophy but Hegel? Isn't he the master-mind?"

"Well, if Hegel's all you got at Harvard you might as well have stayed here in Chapel Hill. We could teach you that."

"I didn't go to Harvard to learn philosophy. I went there to rid my mind of orthodoxy."

"I get you, Professor, and, as I see it, Hegel twisted your mind out of its orbit."

"How is that, Mr. Russell?"

"Made you anti-social and a worshipper of Things."

"That's an interesting observation, Mr. Russell. Are you a socialist, Mr. Russell?"

"Not a state socialist. But I do hold that the United States should take a hand in the public welfare."

"You get that idea from the Constitution, I suppose. Maybe from the Declaration of Independence?"

"No. I evolved it out of my own consciousness. But we'll let that pass. Professor, I came around to discuss a little business with you. My books have done well, from the sale of my *Emerson* and *Franklin* and *William the Conqueror* I have received money enough to pay my debts, leaving me a thousand dollars. What shall I do with it?"

"Buy cheap Negro houses and get twenty per cent on your investment."

"Twenty per cent! Why, Professor, in five years I'd have my money back and the house besides. That's anti-social."

"Twenty per cent anti-social!"

Once upon a time Phillips Russell had Horace Williams and two or three others out for tea, and as the little party gathered around an open fire and cold December winds began to blow-up thoughts of a southern Christmas, the conversation turned to topics of an emotional kind and to Evelyn Underhill's mysticism. One remark brought on another till the talk reached the stage when each narrated some unusual experience, some deep, mysterious event the memory of which still lingered. During all this time Old Horace sat listless, evidently not interested—undoubtedly provoked that the conversation had not been of his own choosing.

Observing his guest's abstracted manner and wishing to bring him into the conversation, Russell turned and said, "Professor Williams, I am sure there is some event in your life which you look back upon with pleasure and satisfaction. Do tell us about it." The odd old character roused himself and slowly made answer.

"Yes, Mr. Russell," he drawled. "I recall one such incident in my life. At one time I owned a blind horse, though no one could have told it, and I swapped that animal for a good horse and cleaned up one hundred dollars in the trade."

This ridiculous story was probably fabricated, but it exhibits the perversity of the narrator. He was determined to bring the conversation down to earth. No doubt the old philosopher had enough of the David Harum spirit in him to justify the rule of *Caveat emptor*.

Horace's perversity was perennial and proverbial. On one occasion, as the story goes, his niece Leah Smith who was visiting him, and a young friend, were doing some sewing and had no needle. Doubtfully, they ventured into the study.

"Uncle Horace, have you a needle?" Leah timidly asked.
"Yes."
"Will you please lend it to me, Uncle Horace?"
"No."
"Why, Uncle Horace?"
"If I lend you my needle I won't have any needle."

His delight was to put everyone in his place, it made no difference whether the victim was a prince or a peasant. On one occasion when Professor Roland McClamroch was a candidate for the legislature, he crossed the street and shook hands with Old Horace. The perverse man turned to the crowd and dryly remarked that when the professor was not running for office he scarcely bowed, but now he would walk a mile to shake hands!

His near neighbors and friends were the Koches, to whom he showed no more consideration than if they were strangers. Professor Koch was in the habit of cutting through the Williams' backyard to save several hundred steps around the block. Old Horace dropped him a curt note and ordered him to keep off—a demand which the "Proff" considered quite unneighborly but which the Madam thought quite proper.

The philosopher was as rough with social and political organizations as with individuals. In the class one day a student asked him what he thought of the idea of 16 to 1, this being William J. Bryan's pet notion of putting more money into circulation.

"Do you mean stamping fifty cents worth of silver and calling it a dollar?" the professor dryly asked.

"Yes, Professor, the free coinage of silver."

"Well, I call that a lie."

When Dr. Hugh Black delivered a fiery, popular, uncoördinated sermon at Duke University and someone asked Professor Williams what he thought of the performance he answered, "The good man seems to be an ecclesiastical prize fighter!"

Old Horace's pet aversion was the secession of the Confederate States. He was especially critical of Jefferson Davis whom he considered the leader in that unfortunate movement. On one occasion when Otho Ross, Jr., was living with Professor Williams, they went down the main street of Chapel Hill, headed for the postoffice. Alighting from the car, which had been parked by the side of the small Jeff Davis stone marker, designating a highway, the indomitable professor turned to his young companion and drawlingly said, "Some day, Otho, when you have nothing else to do, I want you to kick that thing over."

Nothing more thoroughly delighted old Horace than to get the best of a trade. When the famous hotel, known as the Nancy Hilliard property, went on the market Williams became the purchaser. In a short time he sold a half interest to George Stephens, a Horatian and also a loyal trustee of the University. Stephens let the University have his half at what it had cost him, but shrewd Old Horace sold his half to Alma Mater at a profit of a thousand dollars and never ceased to crow over his dumb-bell associate.

Conduct of this nature—selfishness personified as it appeared—may find an explanation in later chapters, but at this point I deem it proper to suggest several answers to the question, "Why was Williams, the philosopher, also Williams, the horse-trader?" In the first place, as before intimated, there may have been two Horace Williamses. Again Phillips Russell's analysis of the strange old character may be correct. When Horace traded off that blind horse for a good horse and made a hundred dollars to boot, if he actually did, and when he bought-in cheap houses and rented them, making enormous profits, may not this have been the natural result of early poverty? Did it not follow logically in the wake of Civil War destitution? May it not also have been a peasant fling-back—an effort to get even with society which had dealt so cruelly with the underdog?

Not to press the point, a third reason may be suggested. Williams was, above all earthly considerations, an individualist. Beyond all doubt self-determination was the breath of his nostrils. When he proudly declared, "I am an Hegelian," he was speaking by the card. Hegel's doctrine of the One and the many possessed him. Not only in thought but in conduct Williams was an Hegelian, wedded to the idea of the One and the many. Every human being is the One and all else is the non-One.

And by One Hegel meant that which is purely for itself, which is related only to itself and excludes any relation to an other, a single self-sufficient entity. And being-for-itself is precisely the being which excludes any relation to an other. In a word, each one of us is the captain of his soul, autonomous, *sui generis, Ding an sich.*

If this analysis of Horace Williams be correct, he was in all things true to form, even when cashing in on investments at twenty per cent. As a follower of Hegel and a worshipper of the idea of self against non-self, could he have done otherwise? As well expect the pullet not to cackle when she lays her first egg or the duck to cease quacking at sight of a pool of inviting water.

20

HORACE'S PHILOSOPHY EXAMINED AND SIMPLIFIED

THE TASK of simplifying Hegel's abstract philosophy is so utterly impossible that I shall not undertake it, but shall content myself with a mere outline. After completing the synopsis of Hegel I shall take up Old Horace's striking and original method of putting Hegel across to the students.

"I am an Hegelian," Horace Williams often declared. Some knowledge of the Hegelian philosophy is therefore necessary for an understanding of Williams' philosophy. The heart of Hegelianism is the absolute. Absolute truth is Hegel's aim. He had so coördinated and integrated previous philosophies that he concluded his own system embraced them all. The magnitude of his undertaking will appear as we glance at some of the philosophies which he sought to absorb.

The key-word of the strange old philosopher, Socrates, is "Know thyself"; that is, realize that you are not an animated clod but a part of the great intellectual and spiritual process. Plato, whose fame rests somewhat on his portrayal of his master Socrates, conceived of matter as an offspring of mind. "Ideas" is therefore Plato's key-word. Aristotle united the Ideas of Plato and experimentation and is hence said to have given philosophy to science.

The key-word of Descartes is *Cogito ergo sum*, "I think therefore I am." Locke emphasized the importance of matter and conceived of the human mind at birth as but a sheet of blank paper, *tabula rasa*. Berkeley, opposing Locke, carried Plato's "Idea" a step further and put forth the startling notion that matter is nonexistent except for mind. "No matter, never mind," was Berkeley's key-word. Hume took issue with Berkeley and insisted that sensation is the foundation of knowledge.

Kant, with his well-known "categorical imperative," lays emphasis upon the will. The categorical imperative commands us, requires us, to act in accordance with duty, not desire. Morality, based on will, is Kant's thesis. But Kant likewise insisted that the notion that the absolute may be reached by mortal man is a mistake. Discard the fanciful idea that man is a thing-in-itself. The riddle of life cannot be solved. Antinomies confront us. Everywhere paradoxes perplex us. These clashes are beyond human ken.

When Immanuel Kant had reached the age of forty-six, Georg W. F. Hegel was born. In a few years this great German philosopher had entered upon his colossal task of reconciling and absorbing all previous philosophies into his own. Nor was he at all cast down by Kant's candid admission that philosophy could not pierce the veil but must give up all attempts to know reality or to penetrate behind appearances. As Stace dramatically puts it in his delightful treatise called *The Philosophy of Hegel*, no sooner had Kant cried "Halt!" to philosophy than philosophy proceeded, so to speak, with bands playing and flags waving to march victoriously onward to the final assault, confident of its power to attain omniscience at a stroke, to occupy the very citadel of reality itself.

By what methods did the philosophers, with Hegel in the lead, undertake to answer Kant and point the way to the absolute? Whole-heartedly, Hegel went in the pursuit of principle. The absolute, the universal, these were his aims. He wasted no time on the exceptional. Hegel's philosophy visualizes the absolute as idea. The first moment in Hegel's process is called the category of the idea as pure being. The next category is called "becoming." Philosophy is knowledge of the absolute, as idea. And this idea knows itself as object. When the beginning and the end unite and become one, Hegel's task is accomplished and there is a reconciliation of time and eternity, the unity of man with God.

Christianity, according to Hegel, is the one absolutely true religion not because its figurative expressions, such as creation, heaven, the fall, etc., can be taken literally, but because the inner meaning and thought-content of these will be found to be identical with the principles of true philosophy.

But by what system of ratiocination does Hegel refute Kant's major antinomies as set forth in the *Critique of Pure Reason?* Kant had declared that of two contradictions one is false. Hegel came and denied this law of contradiction. He insisted that of two contradictions both may be correct. How did he arrive at this strange conclusion? The ingenious logician employed the dialectic process—a system of reasoning which underlies the philosophy of Hegel, and, in turn, the teaching of Horace Williams. And of all metaphysical abstractions the dialectic process is perhaps the most complicated.

Briefly stated, the dialectic process is the art of arguing. The dialectic is a shrewd method of debating. The dialectician possesses logical dexterity and generally manages to put his unwary opponent into a rhetorical hole. The dialectic makes considerable use of the negative. Thus it discovers in the equation, $-3 \times -3 = +9$, more than a juggling with figures. No one lives except he die: Out of death comes life. The dialectic looks upon the negative as part and parcel of the affirmative. When the chemist informs us that water is hydrogen and oxygen he implies that hydrogen and no-oxygen are not water.

Keeping an eye on the negative, the dialectic process proceeds after this fashion: It assumes being as the starting point. Being therefore is the point of departure. But what is being? Being is essence, mere existence. How, for example, do we know that the clock on our mantel is there at all or has being? Through the senses only. We hear the clock tick, we see it with our eyes, we touch it with our fingers. Our senses and nothing else tell us of the clock. That is, we have no means of knowing matter except through the five senses.

Now a tangible object, such as a clock, is in no sense being as the dialectician conceives of being. In philosophical phrase the only essential of being is "isness." Strip the clock of its attributes—weight, shape, fixtures, and the like—and what is left over will be being, that is "isness." In a word there would remain of the clock the mere idea, a vacuum. The clock is therefore a thing of the senses. Strip it of its properties and conceive of it as being, or ideal, and it is empty, vacant, a pure vacuum. The clock has now become emptiness, not anything, that is, nothing. To quote Stace once more, when we say that a thing is, but that beyond its mere "isness" it has no characteristics of any kind, is equivalent to saying that the thing is nothing at all. In these circumstances being is identical with not-being or nothing. "In consequence of the disappearance of each category into the other we have a third thought, namely, the idea of the passage of being and nothing into each other. This is the category of becoming." The catch in this puzzling method of Hegel is obvious: A negative has been concealed in the affirmative, and therefore the first category both affirms and denies!

It thus becomes as plain as the nose on one's face that Kant was wrong when he admitted that there were certain insolvable antinomies. On the contrary, according to Hegel, everything in life is an antinomy and therefore there is no antinomy. It follows inevitably, that of two contradictions both are right.

It may be asked, Why did Hegel's intellectual process begin with being? The answer is that being is that which first comes into knowledge. Furthermore, everything must have a beginning, or a starting point. As Governor Littlejohn of Oxford used to observe sagely, "How can you have a ziblet unless you have a zib?"

In the month of June, some years ago, I prevailed on Horace Williams to accompany me to Fred Howe's instructive School of Opinion, situated at Sconset, a quaint old sea-going village off the coast of Massachusetts. There we met Phil Wickser of Buffalo, a distinguished lawyer, one of the law examiners of the State of New York, a philosopher as well. Old Horace would often engage Wickser in conversation, when the subject would turn to such abstractions as the One and the many and also the use of assumptions in philosophy.

"Professor Williams," said Wickser, one day, "they tell me you teach knowledge as absolute. How about that?"

"Yes, Mr. Wickser, that's correct."

"Why, Professor, that's an old-fogey notion. Science has destroyed that long ago."

"Mr. Wickser," Old Horace dryly remarked, "I don't know Buffalo and it may be that up there two and two are four on Friday but not on Thursday. In North Carolina, Mr. Wickser, two and two always make four."

This observation put an end to the talk until the next afternoon, when Wickser came up, laughing. "Professor," he said, "have you got any more of those damn mathematical illustrations?"

"Why yes, Mr. Wickser, I had only begun. You ran too quick. And, Mr. Wickser, I have a standing offer of ten dollars to any one who can find a single assumption in my logic."

As I listened to this interesting conversation, I recall that tall waves were dashing against the beautiful bluff at the foot of Sancote Light, sea gulls were darting through a beauteous August sky, hundreds of happy beings were playing in the surf, whose tides always set in and never out. A fairer prospect or one more conducive to reflection and repose could not be asked. "Well," said I to myself as I sat high up on the sands and looked out upon the vasty deep, "Old Horace has met his match at last. Wickser will surely come back at him with a Harvard thrust!"

But Wickser let the matter drop. He doubtless understood Williams' boastful remark better than I did, for, a few days later, Professor Emery, Williams' able assistant down at Chapel Hill, set me straight. "When Professor Williams disclaimed the use of postulates," said Emery, "he was not referring to the first category called being but to his intellectual process. Concede being and the process is flawless all through to the absolute."

In a word, as I got Emery, Williams was as sure of a final victory for his intellectual process as Archimedes had been of his lever and fulcrum process. "Give me a place on which to stand," said Archimedes, "and I will move the earth."

My brief analysis of Hegel's extensive system of logic, I frankly admit, is but a scratching of the surface. The great philosopher tackles everything from earth to sky. Not only does he deal with that branch of philosophy called logic but also with the philosophy of nature and the philosophy of spirit. He divides spirit into subjective, objective, and absolute. He exhausts the abstruse subjects of mechanism with affinity, teleology, chemism, the subjective end, the realized end, and the idea.

Hegel's absolute is indeed still more comprehensive. It embraces universal consciousness. According to Hegel the relation of the absolute and the ego and the non-ego is that of whiteness to milk. Reason and absolute are synonymous. Hegel reaches his greatest height, perhaps, in the dialectic of history, in which domain the whole world is its stage and kingdoms its actors. The thought behind the dialectic of history is that the world-reason must progress through clash and contradictions. It follows that apparent discord and confusion, created by wars and rebellions, are but appearances; the underlying principle is universal reason. "The state is an actualization of freedom. The state is the march of God through the world." Such, in short, is the philosophy of Hegel, and such also is the philosophy of Williams. The thought process of both was, in warp and woof, the same. But the analogy goes no further.

Verily, the moulds must have been broken when Horace Williams first saw the light. Surely never such a human being before or since has been born. The old philosopher had but one thought and that was how to pour himself into his students. Nor was he choice in his methods. If to make a student mad would stimulate thought, he would enrage the youngster, if flattery would work he would flatter, if indifference seemed the best way he would be as cold as an iceberg. And these things he would do regardless of form, ceremony or precedent.

Nothing, in fact, pleased him more than to be talked about and written up and caricatured. From the very beginning of his teaching career his philosophy and psychology had been in the spotlight. The Old Fellow was fond of ducks and, out on his farm, reared quite a flock of these sage, wise-looking birds. Oftentimes he would use the ducks as an illustration in the classroom, to the delight of the boys as well as the cartoonists, who made merry at the professor's expense. The *University Magazine*, in a certain number, caricatured him as an absent-minded, abstracted-looking creature, on his knees feeding a flock of ducks which were quacking and gazing wistfully at the bread-box. Underneath the cartoon were these words, HORACE: "Ducky! Ducky! what is a sensation? How do you know I am feeding you? How do you know that you are my ducks? Have you a continuous personality?"

In another issue of the *Magazine* the write-up of Old Horace showed him in a far different light. In opposition to the bad habit of swiping fruit and wood, which sometimes prevailed, the door of the philosophy room was firmly shut. Horace's honor system was acclaimed, and on the bulletin board were the famous words of Lowell,

*The Ten Commandments will not budge
And stealing will continue stealing.*

Frequently Horace's dialectic method would be hit off in doggerel to the delight of many a social group. In one of these skits called "Hippological Logic," philosophical antinomies were set forth in a syllogistic formula.

*To any ordinary dolt
The horse is father to the colt.
Not so in Horace Williams' mind;
There, most amazing things we find!
Thus, if a horse beget a son
We have our major premise one;
But if the colt beget a horse
The proposition has no force.
The horse, begetting colt, affirms
Himself as colt, not angle worm.*

The skit runs along in this ludicrous vein, depicting the horse as dead and buried and finally transmogrified into hay, which, if the colt does eat he'd be a cannibal, but if he ate it not,

*He then denies his father that
Affirmed the colt and then begat
But who as colt negates, 'tis clear,
Existence as a father here—
Whence, colt, hay, father disappear.*

The most amusing parody of Horace came from the fruitful pen of S. McL. Butt, of which, unfortunately only a distich remains in the memory of man. But that glimpse may serve to illustrate the type process and the difference between appearance and reality,

> *The type-lion never laughs*
> *And apples are not photographs.*

But neither cartoon nor caricature seemed to move the old philosopher. Though he understood that there was a growing hostility towards his critical attitude and biting tongue, why should he worry? He was secure. He had become a myth and a tradition; while in the flesh he had acquired posthumous fame. Not by accident, not by artifice but by concentration and originality he was the idol of the classroom. Simply teaching the dialectic, however, was not enough, he must live the dialectic. Be as full of paradox as the nature of the case required. Concepts, begriffe, antinomies, these he must be.

The teacher, if worth his salt, must be the gadfly. The good teacher must stand out against the thoughtless crowd; he must correct crude and half-baked public opinion. From the housetop the good teacher should, like Jeremiah of old, cry aloud, "'Woe unto you formalists! Woe unto you experimenters, whose chief priests are Ph.D.'s, for ye smatter the Truth. Ye are whited sepulchres, full of dead men's bones.'"

Now the magnitude of his task, as I have said before, Old Horace fully realized. He understood that he would fail unless his boys came to the rescue. His classroom must be the nest in which the thought-process was hatched. He rejoiced to think that from that room there had gone out hundreds of his boys.

"Mr. Gray," he would softly ask, as the philosophy class came together for its first lesson, "What is philosophy?"

"Well, really, Professor, that's what I'm here to learn."

"That's a good answer, Mr. Gray, and I trust I may show you before the term ends, that philosophy is the process of the perfect individual."

At this point the teacher paused and, after a few seconds, turned and said, "Mr. Kenan, do you get that?"

"Yes, Professor, I think so but isn't that definition rather general?"

"Perhaps it is, Mr. Kenan, but as we go along we shall have frequent use for the word process. The phrase is vital. This session we are to study Hegel. I was thrilled one day last year when a brilliant student came to me and said, 'You don't get Hegel in sentences, do you?' 'No,' said I, 'Hegel is a process, a growth, and the goal of that process is truth.'"

What then was precisely the foundation of Old Horace's thought-process? What was his key-word? Beyond all dispute it was *Begriff*. Likewise, the importance of the art of defining. "It took ten years of intensive thought," said he, "to evolve a satisfactory definition of truth." As for begriff, it was the apple of his eye. To exhibit the value of begriff the old philosopher would consume months and months, repeating and repeating and repeating! Turning the thought upside down, illustrating the idea in hundreds of different ways, ding-donging the begriff into the class, unendingly.

The extent to which Horace's teaching was diffused throughout campus life is illustrated by a story which Tom Wolfe narrates in the greatest novel which has come out of the South. Wolfe had a classmate, a red-headed, double-jointed mountaineer from a Fundamentalist family, but very bibulous, who had become inoculated with Horace's new philosophical virus. The boy's name was D. T. Johnson and his nickname, of course, Delirium Tremens Johnson. One morning, very early, Wolfe saw coming out of the woods Delirium Tremens, unkempt, bedraggled, having spent the entire night in the forest. "Hurrah, Tom," he shouted. "I've had a concept!" And Delirium Tremens disappeared to tell the whole brotherhood.

From the September term to the Christmas holidays there was an unending, untiring, unflinching effort to teach his boys how to think. "The begriff unfolds into truth," he would say, "and the work of logic is to furnish a kit of tools to intelligence."

"Professor," said Porter, during one of the lectures, "I have looked everywhere, and I can't find the word begriff anywhere. Does no one treat of it except yourself, Professor?"

"No, Mr. Porter, no one."

"Have you a definition of begriff, Professor," Hudgins asked.

"Yes, Mr. Hudgins, the first fruit of the process of intelligence is begriff."

As the term advanced Old Horace would explain that begriff is not only the beginning of the intellectual process but the ending. In truth he cracked up the begriff to such an extent that the boys concluded that unless they could form concepts and begriffe they were as nothing. Begriff, he would say, is a blueprint of the subject. Analysis, coördination and synthesis, these are the essentials of begriff.

A religious tenet, called Falling from Grace may illustrate the strength of begriff. When the humorous Zeb Vance declared that his brother Bob was a Methodist, believing in falling from grace, but never falling, and he was a Presbyterian who did not believe in falling but was always falling, he illustrated the begriff—in reverse! In Bob's case the individual had God by the hand; in Zeb's case God had the individual by the hand. So with begriff, once formed it has an unbreakable hold.

"In a word, young gentlemen," the old philosopher would declare, "there is nothing wrong with begriff. The wrong is with the one who forms the begriff." Begriff implies thought, unity, integrity, coherency. These result in inerrancy. The begriff of water, as every one admits, is the formula H_2O. The begriff of a building to be erected is the blueprint and the specifications. A begriff of the fundamentals is the bridge which spans the chasm between the finite and the infinite. The begriff of God is Jesus. Around the word begriff cluster all the rules of logic and philosophy.

Hid in the bowels of begriff are the categories and the syllogisms of the logicians.

"Mr. Hancock, how does the intellectual process operate, and how do you connect it with begriff?"

"By means of the categories, I'd say, Professor."

"Yes, and Mr. Battle, what are Hegel's categories?"

"Being, becoming, and relation."

"Quite true, and these, under another name, correspond with my own."

From this point the old philosopher would go on to exhibit his method of tracing the thought-process. Starting with individual, as the unit of human value, he would show how the individual grows into the particular, and from the particular into the universal. Three categories only are necessary. The first category is the individual. The second category is the particular, the third is the universal. The individual grows into the particular, or the group; he joins a church or a political party, he enlarges himself, but always maintains his quality and is true to the type of the perfect man.

When the individual emerges from the group into the universal, he is no longer tagged. He ceases to be a Democrat or a Baptist, he enters wide stretches of thought. He does his own thinking. No more is he group-minded. He has become universal. From the one, and through the particular, he has become the universal. I and my Father are one.

"Young gentlemen," Old Horace solemnly and reflectively spoke, one morning after he had thus traced the course, and was looking with affectionate eyes upon his boys who were hanging on his words, "I have just given you the substance of a paper prepared by one of the best students I ever had, Ed Kidder Graham. It was a perfect paper. I discovered its quality on the very first page. I read no further. It was not necessary. I gave an A."

"Professor," said a belligerent young student, Larry Flynn by name, "I have caught up with you at last. Taine treats of begriff."

"Where, Mr. Flynn?"

"In his *History of English Literature*."

"What does Taine say, Mr. Flynn?"

"Why, Professor, Taine says Goethe passed along the word begriff to Carlisle, who in turn introduced the idea into England."

"No doubt that's correct, Mr. Flynn, but the significance of begriff is not elaborated. The truth is, neither Taine nor Goethe understood begriff. And so it goes."

Such was Old Horace's philosophy, simplified as much as possible. If I have succeeded in presenting a fair picture of the man and the teacher it must be conceded that though he added no new idea to philosophy he was the master thought-provoker of his day. He was a signboard and pointed the way, though he might not be able to travel it. As Cicero and Seneca were Eclectics, he was an Eclectic. Though he made use of all previous philosophies he gave first place to Hegel.

His consuming passion was not the philosophy of life but the philosophy of thought. Above all else he was a logic-chopper, a dialectician. His job was to teach boys to think, to enlarge their intellect, to erase a short view for a long look ahead. He would move his boys from the static to the dynamic and thence into the organic. In this undertaking he employed all of the subtleties and intricacies of the profoundest philosophers.

Nothing did he omit in his search for truth which lies at the bottom of the well of Democritus. One day mystical and metaphysical, next day simple and ordinary. On occasion he would throw the fodder so high in the rack that the animals must stretch their necks to reach it. Another day he would crack up the wisdom of his riding horse or his ducks or he would use Babe Ruth as an illustration, a begriff of baseball.

Quitting the classroom, where he had just expounded the mystical Logos or the logic of the Trinity, he would wander around to the livery stables and swap horses, or associate with his old friends, George Pickard and Tom Lloyd, in whom he found a process of intelligence that fascinated him, strong, clear, full of courage, and rarely wrong. "They were vital; the college man was formal. They were courageous: the college man was foggy, bookish. I came to the view that life is richer than books."

Once only, so far as I can discover, did the good teacher describe himself and at that time he imagined he was describing Socrates. Of Socrates he said he was not a philosopher, he did not claim to understand; he wrote nothing, he did not know enough to teach. He was a man, an ultimate unit of reality. He is known by the children of the world. They do not know what he said or what he did. They know him as Socrates, a man. Socrates was an intelligence. That is, he did not remember what some one had said; he did not imagine a situation. He submitted everything to the intelligence. His appeal was, "Play the man." Socrates was a living begriff. That is, the I is in itself real and yet expresses itself as universal. The I as I is the living universal, the ultimate concrete.

Thus wrote Old Horace of Socrates, and how like it is to Tom Wolfe's estimate of Horace himself.

"We boys didn't know what the Old Man taught," said Tom, "and we didn't give a damn. He taught us to think and that was enough. He was the Hegel of the Cotton Patch."* Nor was Wolfe indulging in hyperbole. On a loving cup presented to the Old Master these words may be seen:

"To Horace Henry Williams, Teacher,
whose wisdom and sympathy discovered to us
the path to a stronger manhood.
From his boys everywhere."

* In one of Thomas Wolfe's novels he disguises the name of Horace Williams as Virgil Weldon.

21

SOLIPSIST

IN THE 1890's, when Horace Williams bought and took possession of the Hildreth Smith property, the place suited his fancy to a T. It was then remote and isolated, lying just beyond Boundary Street and but recently incorporated into the town limits. Only one street and a lane skirted the five-acre tract consisting of hill and dale, brook and meadow, and virgin forest in whose recesses was a cool, bubbling, moss-covered spring, often the theme of Cornelia Phillips Spencer's poet-pen. On the north, east, and south there was not a neighbor, except Og Tenney, who lived near enough for the Williamses to hear his dog bark. They were, therefore, in a sense, pioneers of the bailiwick and had a prior possessory right therein.

And this choice spot of earth was Horace's! His to do with as he pleased, to have and to hold without let or hindrance as long as grass grows or water flows. His the castle from turret to foundation stone. Through its humble roof the winds of heaven might blow, but King George himself dare not violate its threshold. These inalienable rights were Magna Charta buttressed. The deed under which he held, guaranteed them, warranting to defend the title against the lawful claims of any and all persons or corporations whatsoever.

What, then, was Old Horace's surprise—indignation, in fact—when one morning some twenty years after he and his had peacefully occupied the premises, Jug Whitaker, the town constable, appeared on the scene with a warrant for one H. H. Williams charged with violating a town ordinance.

STATE OF NORTH CAROLINA }
COUNTY OF ORANGE } s.s.

State of North Carolina and City of Chapel Hill: To the sheriff or other lawful officer of said County Greeting: You are hereby commanded forthwith to arrest one Horace H. Williams for the violation of an ordinance of the City of Chapel Hill, that is to say for a failure to connect his dwelling with the city water system. The body of the said Williams you will immediately apprehend and deliver it at the office of the Mayor of said City.

Herein fail not at your peril and of this precept make due return. Given unto my hand and seal of office this May 15th 1913.

L. P. McLendon
MAYOR

As the Old Individualist perused this indictment his Irish blood began to boil. True, Will Roberson, a former mayor and a true friend, as his father, the good Dr. Roberson had been, had urged him to connect his premises with the water system, at the same time exhibiting an ordinance requiring property owners so to do. But, as Old Horace maintained, this ordinance was illegal and void. It violated property rights. Property has rights as well as persons. Was a man to be deprived of his lands by such a hocus-pocus? Was the individual to be eliminated—swallowed up in the State? Was he to be run over by a lot of immature boys, many of whom he had taught? No! He proposed to fight. He would spend every dollar to defend his rights.

In this frame of mind the Philosopher and the "law," to wit, Jug Whitaker, put-out, side-by-side, for the temple of justice, where a curious scene was enacted.

"Good morning, Professor," very politely said Mayor

McLendon, a former student and soon to be a gallant Major in the World War and one of the great Carolinians.

No answer.

"We are very sorry about all this, Professor."

No answer.

"You are charged, Professor, with failing to connect your premises with the water system in violation of an ordinance. What do you say?"

"Nothing, sir, except that you and this administration are a lot of whippersnappers. Do you suppose you can tax property out of existence?"

"No, Professor. But law is unity, as you used to teach us and it must be obeyed. [After a pause.] Have you a lawyer, Professor?"

"No and I want one."

"Do you ask a continuance?"

"Yes."

The case was continued for two weeks, and Old Horace again appeared before the Mayor and declared that they had ganged up on him.

Truth to tell, he had consulted Professor McIntosh, a tip-top law teacher, who had informed him that the Supreme Court had just substantially decided a case against him. The Court had held that an ordinance was valid in the interest of public health, which prohibited a livery stable or a cow within a certain town. Perhaps, therefore, the ordinance in question was valid, though the Court, in the case cited, was divided, three judges voting yes and two voting no, on its validity.

"Are you ready for trial, Professor?" asked Mayor McLendon.

"No."

"What is your plea, Professor?"

"Why, I'll have to put water in, I suppose," and out he started.

"Hold up, Professor. That won't do. This thing's been

going on long enough. You must sign up with a plumber and do it at once."

The upshot of the trial was that Old Horace did sign a contract with a plumber to install water in his premises, *but in an out-house*, fully fifty feet distant from the house!

Now this incident the average person might have regretted, but not Horace Williams. It pestered him very little. In fact he rather enjoyed the whole thing. It accentuated his individuality: it gave him a chance to air his views. He had formed a concept of the matter, and that concept he was sure was correct. Civilization of late was artificial and too concentrated and expensive to endure. Bankruptcy would be its end. Extravagance, indebtedness, bond issues, foolish amusements, luxuries, whiskey, dissipation— these evils foretold the coming collapse.

Stocks, bonds, and other intangibles would soon become worthless. Nothing would have any value except real estate. This conclusion was logical and inevitable. For this reason he had bought real estate. And now the government proposed to confiscate that.

But the worst was yet to come; his favorite riding horse and his patient cow must go. No longer could they crop the grass from his meadow or be stalled on his premises, though cows and horses, in ninety-nine out of every hundred home places within the State, were doing this very thing. Indignant neighbors, as I shall now explain, had brought about this result.

Since he had acquired his holdings out on east Franklin Street, that attractive part of Chapel Hill had been greatly developed. New streets had been opened. Tenney Circle, with a clear view of the spires of Durham, on the hinter side of an ancient sea long since evaporated, had been laid out. Many handsome residences had been constructed. Willy-nilly the Williamses had been drawn into the very heart of a fashionable residential section, where homes were screened and equipped with bathtubs, running water, steam heat, and where neither cows nor horses were allowed.

To some of the neighbors the Williams lot had become an eyesore and a nuisance, which they would no longer put up with. At length some of the ladies entered the fight and made complaint to the mayor of the city. The Williams cow and horse must be removed, or else the stables must be cleaned, disinfected, and screened. Ex-Mayor Bill Roberson interviewed his old teacher and advised surrender. Negotiations proceeded until just before the fly-season set in, when a purchase of the cow stall was effected by the neighbors who gave a check for fifty dollars. "Purganum! Fifty pieces of silver!" exclaimed an anonymous writer whose identity has never been discovered. But whosoever he may have been he piled on the agony. In his article, which appeared in the State press, he set out a supposititious contract, with its party of the first part, its party of the second part, its consideration, and all the other legal accessories. Visitors to the commencement, which was then in progress, were informed that they would miss an old landmark on the Hill. H. H. Williams' stables were no more! They had been condemned by public opinion, they had been discussed "morally, socially, ethically, physiologically and profanely!" Though the writer conceded that the professor had not violated any law he charged him with being unsocial-minded.

Strangely enough, even this local eruption did not greatly move the eccentric old philosopher. As he saw it, he was entitled to live his own simple, inexpensive way. He did not stick his nose into other people's business nor did he wish them to interfere with his affairs.

When the bridge club of the Fashionables played for stakes, in other words gambled and violated the criminal law, he did not undertake to regulate their conduct. When certain members of the faculty kept a plentiful supply of ardent spirits in their closets, though the possession of whiskey was a crime, he did not report them. Why should he be jumped on, why should his premises be regulated? The obvious answer, of course, was that he was not only an individual but a member of the community and owed a duty to conform to community regulations. To this, Williams' rejoinder was obvious—"So are you."

At all events Old Horace persisted in being an individualist, a rank individualist, a solipsist—sot in his ways!

Now if the old fellow was himself solipsistic his wife also had her share of peculiarities. Though everyone who knew Bertha Williams loved her, the entire community could but laugh at times because she was so original and so different. Her quaint ways and unexpected sallies made her a great favorite. Her neighbors, the Pratts, the Alexanders, the N. W. Walkers, the Deys, Dr. Kluttz and his wife, the Fred Pattersons, Stacys, Robersons, Kennettes, Cobbs, Bains, Mannings, Mangums, Winstons—all these were delighted when Mrs. Williams was about.

On the occasion, already mentioned, when she had been unable to execute a portrait of Eleanor and had said she had changed the picture into a snow scene, she gave rise to a phrase so original that for years to come it continued a Chapel Hill saying. "Well, let's change that into a snow scene," has brought many a laugh and ended many a controversy.

On a certain occasion Mrs. Williams was to have a reception at her home and was looking around for some pretty girls to assist in serving refreshments. Spying a dark-haired, black-eyed girl and a companion on the street, she darted up to them and said to the dark-eyed damsel, "Oh, my dear, you are just too beautiful and so you must come and serve refreshments at my party. Your dark hair and eyes just match my yellow curtains!" Turning to the other girl, she casually remarked, "I would ask you also, my dear, but I don't know your name!"

At one of the literary gatherings which often met at Mrs. Williams' home, she entertained the guests with a long list of questions relating to music and art. The questions were passed around and after being answered were taken up and a prize given to the one answering the greatest number. Now among the group there were several flapper females having more animation than mentality. As Mrs. Williams approached this group to gather up the answers, they gesticulated wildly and screamed, "Oh, Mrs. Williams, we just couldn't answer a single one of your questions."

"Well, you had better go home then," was the bland reply.

Meeting a friend one day Mrs. Williams gaily burst out, "Oh, you should have been at my party and seen the pheasants, so crisp and brown and delicious and with such variegated feathers all on."

"Why, Mrs. Williams, you didn't serve the birds in their feathers!"

"No," she laughed, "I mean before they were picked."

Some years later when water had been installed in her residence Mrs. Williams was a member of a social party in the village and greatly amused them by one of her quaint remarks. "Oh," she said, "you must excuse me now, I just must hurry home and take a hot bath!"

Mrs. Williams gave a great many small luncheons and teas and occasionally a formal function. But when she undertook anything so elaborate as a set-dinner she ran up against innumerable obstacles. She had but one servant, a green, country Negro girl. Despite this drawback she and her husband insisted upon a certain amount of style and form and ceremony. There must be several courses and the flat silver must be spread out by the side of each plate.

At one of her formal dinners, after the courses had all been dispatched except the dessert, the Negro girl suddenly disappeared. Five minutes elapsed. Ten minutes. The conversation grew thin and thinner, and finally played out altogether. Mrs. Williams rose and went into the cookroom. Instantly a piercing scream rent the air. Not a word was spoken. No one of the guests moved. Old Horace was silent. Mrs. Williams did not again appear. The salted ice-mixture, in the hand-operated freezer, had melted and completely flooded the cream!

These little eccentricities were as nothing, however, when

contrasted with the many excellences of Bertha Williams. It was her solicitude, her tender care, as we have seen, that gave strength of mind, body, and spirit to her husband and enabled him to do the great work in hand. Moreover, unlike her husband, she was thoroughly community-minded. Though not a real artist, as Old Horace imagined, she was such a lover of music that she succeeded in adding a musical department to the Women's Club of the village. She did not sit in the church choir but she coöperated with the organist in developing the best productions of the masters.

In welfare work she also took an active part. In a word, it must be said of this rare, transplanted New England exotic that she was probably the only human being who, for thirty years, could have put up with and loved and honored and made content the strange, peculiar, solipsistic man she had taken to husband. In nothing was he regular; in all things he was exceptional.

When North Carolina voted for prohibition, by a hundred thousand majority, he stood out against the proposition, maintaining that morality was not a question of statutory enactment. At all times William J. Bryan was a North Carolina idol, but at all times a Williams aversion. In later years, President Hoover's "forty key men," he ridiculed. Roosevelt's Brain Trust and their experimentation—trying out this, that, and the other—he considered child's play.

In the name of high heaven, he would ask, why experiment? Why not go about the matter systematically and thoughtfully, assemble the facts and from them draw a wise, definitive, workable conclusion? Little wonder that with such superficiality America was about to go on the rocks.

The modern method of teaching youth was a sore grievance to the old philosopher, whose pole star was the thought-process. "What good is a questionnaire?" he would ask. Did Jesus ever employ such a shoddy device? Why poll the unbaked crowd to get an unbaked opinion? This tabulation, these statistics, this research, it was utterly worthless. Teach the students to think; that, and that alone, was the essential. The Graduate School had become a geometric affair. Their aim is called research. The result is not to master some process in life but to find the type in which some insect lives! If one should ask a Ph.D. a good question, one that was vital and important, the reply would be, "That is not in my field." The economists should not have offered to teach the subject until they had mastered it. They have nothing to teach.

"I ask an economist a simple question, such as 'What is money?' He looks wise and says, 'There are eight theories on that subject.' What can such a man teach? He does not have a begriff of money. No doubt there are statesmen who know what law is, but if so it has not been my fortune to meet them. Economists are creatures of the particular; they seem unable to take a vital view of a question."

Horace's delight was to embarrass his old college mate, his exact antithesis the jovial, much beloved head of the Department of Education, M. C. S. Noble, and to ridicule his modern experimental, educational system. I happened to be present on one occasion and witnessed a characteristic scene, a merciless attack by Old Horace on the head of the School of Education. The incident occurred one evening in May when the then new, commodious Chapel Hill school building had just been completed and commencement was in progress.

Williams was the speaker of the evening. Noble presided and graciously presented the speaker to an enthusiastic, overflow audience. The speaker rose and looked sagely about him. He then made a few prefatory remarks in praise of the mechanical part of the building, its fine structure, comfortable seats, blackboards, a thoroughly efficient plant. But, said he, how about the intellectual equipment of your High School? Are you taught to think? Do you know why you are here? Perhaps you know what education is, but if so you are wiser than your teachers. "I ask them to tell me what is education, but they do not seem to know. Perhaps I am mistaken, and since the Dean of Education is sitting right here by my side I'll suspend a moment and ask him to tell us.

"Professor Noble, what is education?" asked the irrepressible Horace, as he abruptly took his seat and waited for an answer.

The scene that followed was ludicrous. The mass of the audience chuckled and laughed. The pupils opened their eyes in wonder; the scholars were grieved. Noble neither moved nor spoke a word. In a few moments Old Horace resumed. "Since the head of the Educational Department," he said, "cannot tell us what education is I will proceed to do so." And then for an hour or more he delighted the audience, mingling wit and wisdom with nonsense and homely illustrations.

Later, when the speaking was over and the diplomas were being delivered to graduates, Professor Billy Noble had the last word. He turned to the audience and quietly remarked, "These are my education!"

22

HUMILIATION AND TRIUMPH

IN HIS LAST annual report President Ed Kidder Graham made a most agreeable announcement. By the will of Mary Lily Kenan Bingham a gift of seventy-five thousand dollars a year to the University had just been provided paying the salaries of teachers, thereafter to be called Kenan Professors. The gift was intended to honor the donor's father, Captain William Kenan, and her two uncles, Thomas and James, graduates of Chapel Hill, its devoted friends, and gallant Confederate officers in the sixties.

Resolutions were shortly afterward adopted providing that the Kenan Professors should be recommended by a vote of the faculty, whose decision should be reported by the president to the trustees and by them approved, this latter provision being entirely perfunctory as the trustees would not overrule the expert judges under any circumstances. Expectation ran high as to the new appointees, since to be a Kenan Professor meant both distinction and increased salary.

How many would be chosen and who would they be? Undoubtedly Venable, the profound chemist, would be one, and H. van P. Wilson, the zoölogist, affectionately called Froggy Wilson, another. Probably Cain, a great mathematician, would be a third. Would there be other fortunate ones? What about Professor Williams? Surely a teacher so popular with the boys and so much talked about would be chosen. In a few months the balloting took place and Venable, Wilson, Cain, Greenlaw, and MacNider were the honored ones. Horace Williams had been left in the lurch. "The worst blow of my life," the old professor commented. And the decision did indeed wound his pride and cut his comb. He had devoted his life to teaching. He had dropped out of society; he had given his all to his boys; and now the faculty had declared officially that he was not one of the good teachers. "A dreadful blow!"

And yet how could the unorthodox caustic professor have brought himself to imagine that he would be chosen? A hostile faculty were the judges, and they were human beings with human feelings and motivations. What had Professor Williams done to conciliate his associates? Nothing. On the contrary, had he not gone out of his way to declare that science had swamped the University and to belittle his brother professors? Science he was constantly chiding, depicting it as superficial. Its professors were particularists. The Department of English, he believed, had become a yawl-boat of science. The head of the Department of Education could not define the term education. His associates were gatherers of unimportant facts and did not know what it was all about. In his own department he could see no good in any professor unless he was an Hegelian.

No doubt Professor Williams thought his merit as a teacher was so well established that even a hostile jury would overcome prejudices in behalf of the best equipped instructor. But here again an obstacle stood in the way. Some of the professors considered him superficial and not worthy of the honor. Another reason, somewhat philosophical, may be suggested as to why Williams may have expected an unfriendly jury to execute a paradoxical somersault and choose him over so many orthodox professors. He may have been in the same frame of mind as some years earlier, when the brilliant and saucy Tobe Connor was a pupil of his.

"Professor Williams," said Tobe, on the occasion in question, "you have been talking all the term about everything under the sun except music. What do you think of music, Professor?"

"Music! Why, Mr. Connor, I've always wanted to hear a piece of music played backwards."

At all events the piece of music was not played backwards by the faculty when they chose the five coöperative and orthodox professors, in preference to the unorthodox, crooked-rail-in-the-fence, but unsurpassed teacher, Horace Williams!

Soon after the new Kenan Professors were announced, Old Horace wandered, meditatively, into President Graham's office, and had a heart-to-heart talk, an interview full of sympathy and friendliness. For many years the two men had been the closest of friends. "I ranked Ed Kidder Graham as the first student of all my fine boys," Old Horace once declared. In his college days young Graham had majored in philosophy and when he graduated with the highest honors, Williams had urged him to go to Columbia to perfect himself in English. In a few years he left Columbia and became an instructor at Chapel Hill; at that time Williams discovered his ability as an administrative officer and became active in making him president of the University, an office which he filled with marked success.

Only a few months after the first Kenan Professors were chosen Ed Graham died. He had overworked himself in behalf of his country, engaged in a foreign war. He was swept off by the dread epidemic which followed that war—he died a martyr to the cause of democracy.

Harry W. Chase, psychologist, and a thoroughly practical executive, succeeded Graham in the president's office—a change foreboding no good to the theoretical, idealistic Williams.

"I feel rather blue about the University," Horace wrote his friend Robins. "It does not look as if Graham's place had been filled full. We hope. I do not expect to enjoy my work here in the old way any more."

But neither the coming of the new president nor the recent rebuff by the faculty dashed his spirits. He had just begun to fight. He proposed to make the School of Philosophy stronger than ever before. He was sure the scientists and the other departments did not understand him. He was not opposing them, in themselves. So far as they went they might be right. But they stopped short; they should not cut out the logical, the ethical, and the spiritual. The perfect individual is not a product but a spirit, an essence, elusive, ultimate, and eternal. To cut out the spiritual from the teaching-act would be to eliminate the free and the beautiful.

It must not be imagined that Old Horace was a man to run up the white flag and surrender. The greater the obstacles the greater the glory in overcoming them. About this time an unusual student graduated from the University. Paul Green was as original and as promising a youngster as had ever sat under the Davie Poplar, being equally strong in philosophy and in English. On this account he was considered a prize and was eagerly sought after by both as an instructor. The young man had come to Chapel Hill from Professor Campbell's orthodox academy and had selected the University because he wished to be under Old Horace, whose fame as a thought-provoker had penetrated even the wilds of Harnett County, where Paul's people lived.

"No, Professor Campbell," Paul had said to that useful and much beloved teacher, "I shall not go to Wake Forest as you urge me to do. I wish to go to Chapel Hill. I want to study under Horace Williams."

"Going to Chapel Hill! Going to study under Horace Williams! Why, Paul, I'd sooner cast you off and throw your body in a red gully than see you go under that atheist."

It thus came about that Paul Green entered the University and came in contact with Horace Williams, sitting under him for three or four years and at last concluding that he was one of the greatest teachers of all times. "Always he wielded arms for the affirmation of life at its best."

After his graduation, the contest to secure Paul Green as an instructor grew and grew: the Philosophy Department against the English Department, which would win?

PHOTO BY SAM HOOD

PHOTO BY SAM HOO[

PHOTO BY SAM HOOD

PHOTO BY SAM HOOD

Old Horace awarded Paul a sixty-dollar prize in philosophy. The English Department, under Greenlaw, Royster, and Hanford, countered with a salary of five hundred dollars. Horace raised the bid. "Fifteen hundred dollars," said he and won. Undoubtedly Paul Green became a valuable asset to the English Department also, but his joining forces with philosophy put the teeth of the English Department on edge.

In this manner opposition to Old Horace grew and multiplied. Long ago, in political circles, his heresy had made him obnoxious to the dominant party. His criticism of W. J. Bryan was not to be tolerated in a university professor, whose job was to teach, not dabble in politics. An incident in the free silver campaign was remembered. At a time when the village of Chapel Hill was all agog in the Bryan candidacy for president, Williams had mounted the stump and harangued a motley crowd of poor whites and Negroes, Bill McDade, the colored janitor leading the gang. "Rah, Rah, Rah! for Horace," rang throughout the campus.

Nor was a remark which Old Horace had made about the former president, now Dean of the Chemistry Department forgotten. "He is a good scientist," Old Horace had admitted. "A very good chemist. He knows his stew."

Opposition, however, but stirred the old philosopher to renewed effort. His record would stand the test and he proposed to win. From the very beginning of his career as teacher had he not been an acknowledged leader? Were not the *Tar Heel*, the *Yackety Yack*, and the other University journals voicing the sentiment of the boys when they acclaimed him as the most popular and the most useful member of the faculty? Was not the *University Magazine* holding him aloft as the one professor who "drives home things that a student will never forget?"

"Abused as a heretic," the magazine mocked, "a backslider, a hindrance to the coördination of all the parts and yet a man who has the nerve to play the game according to his own rules in opposition to the factory methods of the rest of the faculty." In another issue the same journal nominated him for the Hall of Fame, "Because he has helped set straight in vital matters more students within the University than any other man; because he has helped in building up Carolina's debating record; and because he has always stood for the best things on the Campus."

Moreover, banquets had often been given in his honor, a loving cup had been presented by the debating club. His classroom had always been crowded with students. From that room had gone forth more thoughtful leaders than from any other on the campus. The State, from end to end, was alive with the liberalism of his boys, doing spade-work necessary to bring about freedom of thought and freedom of speech. To thousands of young men and women he had been a provoker of thought, an inspiration and a joy. With this record to back him up his humiliation should be removed. He felt that he should have been chosen a Kenan Professor. He was a teacher, whereas his opponents were mere scientists.

Long ago, Frank Graham, the rising young man of the campus, had pronounced him the athletic progressive of the faculty. So prominent had he been in athletics that he was the faculty member on the all-important athletic committee. In the field of debate who was his peer? In the words of George McKie, Horace Williams was the symbol of the very spirit of debating itself. His debaters had won twenty-nine out of a total of forty-four contests. "If there had not been a path to Horace's study the feet of debaters would have made one."

During the first year of the Chase administration another Kenan Professor was chosen, E. C. Branson, the far-sighted teacher of rural economics and editor of that stimulating weekly, the *News Letter*—a man of strong personality, a publicist, and a choice soul. Nevertheless, on the announcement of this second rebuff of Old Horace, uprisings in his behalf set in. At a banquet held in Chapel Hill Professor Collier Cobb paid a tribute, calling Williams the acknowledged leader in his field. The *University Magazine* proposed a plebescite to the campus on the question, "What professors are closest in touch to the student body?" An election was held. The voting was lively. Three professors were chosen. They were Horace Williams, Francis Bradshaw, and Frank Graham. Williams' name led all the rest.

Another powerful movement began. Graham Kenan, an ardent friend of Horace Williams, an influential trustee, a man of wealth, brother-in-law of Mrs. Bingham, who had just donated several millions to the University, came to Chapel Hill to find out why the Good Teacher had failed to receive a Kenan professorship. Considerable correspondence between Chase and Kenan followed. Chase explained that Williams was not coöperating; he was at outs with some of the faculty and neighbors. Chase indeed went fully into the opposition which had grown up against the eccentric Horace. Kenan pressed the point, and it was understood he intended to air the whole matter before the Board of Trustees, unless Horace was chosen.

In the midst of the contest a significant event occurred. Williams was invited by President H. W. Chase to address the students. The speaker chose as his subject the honor system. Introducing him, Chase said that education was a many-sided affair, but its chief business is to produce men by means of the honor system. "There is no man more competent to present the honor system to you than Professor Horace Williams, whom I now have the honor of introducing."

In his address Old Horace minced no words. He declared that the business of education is the growing of men. There are two methods of doing this. The first is the factory method, the standardization process. If we could thus produce men we might hope for the millennium.

There is another and a better method which is known as the spiritualization process. By this method we produce a man.

Man, in his moral life, is subject to four pulls. The external pull requires one to do right because the State, his party, or the church demands it. Such a man is a mere infant eating only what the nurse gives him. A second group respond to internal restraints; they do right because it makes them feel better. They do not get drunk because they do not wish to have a headache next morning. A third group are good for the sake of a reward. Are you leading a good life because you expect to get to Heaven? If so, what are you going to do when you get to Heaven? Satan is a fine example of this type.

Finally, there are those who live right for right's sake. The greatness of a State depends upon the amount of character of its citizens. Here on this campus we grow the character that determines the greatness of our State. Only one thing this campus will not forgive, and that is hypocrisy. Other things you may do and get away with them but you have to be a man. From this idea comes our honor system. Play the man. Be what you are. That's the honor system. The University Council can't make you an honorable man. That's your job.

I hope to live to see the day, he continued, when the honor system will be so perfect that any man who happens to violate it will ship himself. President Ed Kidder Graham, in speaking of it said: "I love it as I love my wife." The honor system is the sunshine and the fresh air that men feed on. Man can feed on no other diet. "It is yours. Take it, cherish it, love it, work for it."

Thus spoke Horace Williams to his old University. So forceful was he and so impressive that the boys and reporters were deeply moved. When the old philosopher said, "It is yours. Take it, cherish it, love it, work for it," his deep, sonorous voice, his earnest manner, his unforgettable attitude changed the usual morning exercise into a ceremony.

In the month of May following, a seventh Kenan Professor was chosen, the historian, Roulhac Hamilton. Again Horace Williams' name had been passed over. Finally, in June of the same year he was named a Kenan Professor, and with him were two others, W. C. Coker, a botanist unsurpassed in America or elsewhere, and Louis Round Wilson, librarian without a superior.

Naturally there were some who insisted that Horace had inspired the movement to land the professorship. But one day, soon after, this opinion must have changed. Mrs. Graham Kenan handed Professor Williams a check for twenty-six thousand dollars, to be used in enlarging his department. It then became apparent that the interest of the influential Kenan family was not solely in the University but was part at least in the professor of philosophy.

When this gift was made, Old Horace was as near happiness as ever before or since. The next morning, on the convening of his class, he proudly rose and made a statement. "I have a delightful announcement to make," he said. "On Christmas Day I got a letter from Mrs. Graham Kenan, the wife of as good a friend as I ever had or ever hope to have. She sent me a check for twenty-six thousand dollars to found the Graham Kenan Fellowship in Philosophy."

Of this amount, one thousand dollars might be used during the current year. He had divided it into three parts, five hundred dollars to be used to create a new Fellowship or to send a man to Europe. "Ever since I have been here, wonderfully fine boys have come and worked their way through college but have hastened to get into a profession. This is a great mistake; they should have gone further in their studies. I have wanted some chance to give those boys a year of graduate study. That chance has now come and forever hereafter the University is in shape to do this. This is a big thing, it is going to mean much for the University and the State."

And so the victory was won—not a personal victory but a victory for the School of Thought. Increase of salary had not entered into the business, we may be sure. This an incident afterward related by John Umstead may tend to show.

The depression had hit the country, and all salaries except those of University professors had been cut by the legislature. Chapel Hill was incensed at the thought of trimming the meagre salaries of the professors. Legislator Umstead was in doubt as to his course. He consulted Horace Williams. "Why, yes," said the old philosopher, "our salaries should be cut. Are we any better than our fellows?" Umstead acted on this advice and the faculty salaries were trimmed.

After the Kenan professorship fight had been won Old Horace repaired to his study and philosophized, as he often did, in a letter to his former pupil, Sidney Robins, then a professor in a New England college. After describing the heated contest through which he had passed and telling how he had won it he wrote, "When a boy I owned a handsome dog. He was a real dog, quite aristocratic and pleasing to look upon. But when it came to catching a bull by the tongue and throwing him there was a hesitation in his elegance of manner that gave the bull his chance to escape."

Evidently, in the recent fight, Old Horace had not given the bull a chance to escape. He had caught him by the tongue and flung him to the ground!

23

BY THEIR FRUITS

AT THIS TIME Old Horace's exuberance of spirits, because of recent triumphs and the growth of liberalism, found expression in numerous letters to his old boys. All of them he bore in mind. He was fond of Canada, a business man living in Georgia; of the Ross family in Charlotte; of the Rights; of Rev. Henry Clark Smith of California. He often wrote to Frank O. Ray, a brilliant Texas attorney. He and Ralph Harper were brisk correspondents.

Shortly after Williams had staged his unusual comeback and was enjoying his renascence, he wrote to Harper: "To have an intellectual moment is a birthday. When you were in my class at Chapel Hill we were in a stiff fight for the release of mentality, the privilege of investing in thought. We won that fight. Now it is as if the fence were down, and the stock scattered far and wide! The boys come to the fence: the world is open to them. Did you ever watch a herd break over the fence? To talk now-a-days of a fence, or restraint, or principle is crazy stuff. I doubt if they return in my day."

At another time he wrote and expressed a strong desire that good things in abundance might come to the Harpers during the year. Again he wrote: "I have a good class this year. Is it not great to find yourself in a high plane of study? Then one drives the work and begs for time. It changes the attitude toward life. Please give my love to Mrs. Harper and the children." At a later time he wrote Harper that the boys had given him a dinner. "I don't believe a teacher ever had such boys. I declined to attend a banquet in my honor. I could not endure the jazz."

Robins and Harper and Henry Clark Smith were located in other states, whereas Moss, Rozzelle, and Patten, Binkley, and other ministers were nearer home. In fact, it was by means of the pulpit, the schoolhouse, and the courtroom that Horace Williams was handing his clear-cut thinking process to the people. The old philosopher realized that in democratic America the people rule, but public opinion rules the people.

A student of history, he had concluded that there was not an instance in which law or doctrine has won its way against the customs of the people. In the words of Professor Giddings, our legislation amounts to nothing, the statute laws get us nowhere, the decisions of the highest courts get us nowhere, if we do not get the backing of the folkways. Laws without public opinion are vain.

As William Graham Sumner declares, folkways are the function of society and are developed unconsciously; their origin is lost in mystery and they are often the creation of false inferences. But the power of folkways over a people no one disputes. When the customs of a people have been so firmly fixed and set as to be almost unchangeable they are called mores. Since the masses of the people are usually conservative, wholly dependent upon tradition, and accept life as they find it, they are the creatures of their surroundings. If, therefore, Old Horace would change a people he must first change their customs, their mores. The masses lack initiative; they must be led. To penetrate the mores, to change the thoughts and customs of a people, is as difficult as the shaving of Shagpat.

Said Justice Holmes, "The best test of truth is the power of the thought to get itself accepted in the competition of the market." Now how was Horace Williams to meet this test? In what way was he to reach the multitude, to change the thoughts of ultra-conservative people, wedded to the past, thoroughly orthodox and bound by customs, habits and traditions? How was he to get his truth accepted by the masses? As we have seen, his right arm in the fight for freedom of thought was his boys, who had been so impressed by him that they were ready, at all times and in all places, to split a lance in the cause of freedom.

Of Old Horace's impression on students, Higdon, a prominent Atlanta attorney, declares, "I would select him as that one of our faculty whose teaching most deeply impressed a greater number of Carolina men than any other influence." Along the same line Frank Ray asserts, "Of my teachers at the University I consider Williams, Greenlaw, McGehee, and Cobb as great. The Old Master was the greatest of these."

On a certain occasion Charles Maddry, a thinker, and at the time president of the Y, sent two of Horace's boys, Charlie Ross and Gardner Garren, to Trinity College to conduct religious services. Garren, having never before spoken in public, was so badly frightened that he was on the point of resigning. But he reasoned that he would never get anywhere if he backed down. He therefore went to work, outlined his task, rehashing Old Horace's liberal thought-process, omitting nothing. His talk delighted and amazed his listeners.

"Where on earth did that fellow Garren get his speech?" a Trinity boy asked Charlie Maddry.

"Why, Garren was just simply repeating what Old Horace had been teaching him," Maddry laughed.

Nor did Old Horace's teaching cease with college days. It had then but begun. Once a Horatian, always a Horatian. Once a disciple of the concept, of the blueprint, of the begriff, always a disciple. The old philosopher's intellectual route had no detours; his thought-process had no exceptions.

Courts were likewise influenced by Old Horace's clear-cut definitions and logical process. During a term of Harnett Superior Court, Albert Coates happened to wander into the courtroom. At the moment Clawson Williams, a former Horatian, was addressing the jury. This is what Albert heard. "Yes, gentlemen," the speaker was saying. "Up at

Chapel Hill my good teacher Horace Williams used to tell us that truth is unity. Unity in apparent differences, he would say. By this standard I ask you to examine the coherency and the unity of my witnesses in contrast with the disunity of the other side. Thus and thus only will you get at the truth of the case."

And even while Clawson was quoting Old Horace before a piney woods jury down on the majestic Cape Fear, J. H. Winston, class of 1904, our first Rhodes scholar, was quoting him to a United States Judge of the Chicago Circuit.

"Before my clients can be convicted of violating the Sherman Act," Winston was saying, "a conspiracy must be charged and proved. Permit me to quote from Judge John J. Parker, of the Fourth Circuit. 'The basis of conspiracy,' as Judge Parker declares, 'is the unity of design and purpose.'"

Not alone in courts, in pulpits, and in lecture rooms was speech-making undergoing a change for the better but more especially on the stump. In former days there had frequently been a joint canvass between rival candidates. Speaking occasions were great events. Crowds would come together. Barbecue was spread. Whiskey flowed. Personalities were the orator's stock in trade. Epithets, insinuations, and vilification took the place of orderly thought. Fights followed. The spell-binder was indispensable. His side-splitting stories and smutty jokes kept the crowd in a roar and turned the scale. All this was changing. Argument, summing-up, and hard horse-sense, were taking the place of high-flown oratory.

Soon after John J. Parker, of the class of 1907, had been appointed United States Circuit Judge, he ran down to Chapel Hill to attend a meeting of the Board of Trustees and also to visit his good old teacher. Until that visit, as the Judge would laugh and say, he didn't really know what law was. "Old Horace opened my eyes and enabled me to see the relation between fact and the framework of the universe."

When Parker had been a law student he was taught that law is a rule of action, this being the teaching of my Lord Coke and Sir William Blackstone of blessed memory. But since that time much water had gone over the wheel. Coke and Blackstone, Mansfield and Marshall had been succeeded by such far-sighted jurists as Oliver Wendell Holmes, Brandeis, Frankfurter, and W. P. Stacy. Today law is no longer in a strait jacket. Law is flexible, it adapts itself to changing social conditions. Law is unity. Law differs from truth in one important particular, as Old Horace taught. Whereas truth is unity in structure difference, law is unity in action difference.

Often, when speaking of that one hour with Old Horace, Judge Parker loved to relate that he then and there ceased to be provincial and became a citizen of the world.

If a question should be asked, In what manner did Horace Williams coöperate to bring about such radical changes in the body politics? the answer seems near at hand. Always and everywhere the Good Teacher tackled cardinal principles and cut out mere incidentals. As will be remembered, this was the truth which L. R. Wilson carried away from his casual visits to Horace's classroom. It is likewise the impression made upon George Stephens, a public-spirited citizen of the commonwealth.

"George," said I, "did you get anything of permanent value from Horace Williams' classroom?"

"Yes," he answered, "I did, and it was this. If you start wrong don't bull it through. Go back and start all over again." In a word, the old philosopher emphasized a saying of Davy Crockett, "Be sure you're right—then go ahead."

Up to this point I have said but little of the men of wider reputation who came out of the classroom of Horace Williams. I have confined myself in the main to the old teacher's philosophy. Yet the list of noteworthy boys taught by him is an impressive one. Among writers may be mentioned Thomas Wolfe, Archibald Henderson, Ed Kidder Graham,

Paul Green, Lenoir Chambers, Phillips Russell, Frank Graham, Jonathan Daniels, Louis Graves, Julian Miller, Red Buck Bryant, and others.

Among distinguished jurists there were United States Circuit Judge Parker, Chief Justice Stacy, and a majority of the State Supreme Court. In the legislature the list of Horatians is so extensive that it would fill many pages.

The most noteworthy circumstance connected with the liberal teaching of Horace Williams is yet to be mentioned. His thought-process was so comprehensive and universal that from his classroom emerged all shades of thought, advocates of the Right, of the Left, and of the Center—conservatives, radicals, new dealers, standpatters, all stemming from the same root, all products of the dialectic system.

Though I frankly concede that the credit for turning out the writers whom I have named is not due to Horace Williams alone, I do maintain that he was their inspiration. And to whom shall the credit be given for teaching the boys how to think, how to change the thought-process of their fellow-men, and in so doing to create a new commonwealth?

The claim which I am making for philosophy may be illustrated by what is known as the Fundamentalist movement in North Carolina. In 1925 a religious frenzy to legislate the teaching of evolution out of the schools swept the State. What influence was most powerful against the mistaken undertaking? Public opinion, beyond all question. If, twenty-five years earlier, the "Poole monkey bill" had come before the lawmakers, it would have been adopted, *nem. con.* As late as the year 1900 the religious mores of the people would have forced the passage of the measure. But a quarter of a century later public opinion had become so much enlightened that reason prevailed. During the quarter of a century or more, since Horace Williams had taken the chair of philosophy, his boys by the hundreds were living in every county seat of the State. It was their influence which had changed the mores.

When the legislature of 1925 met in Raleigh, Harry Chase, President of the University, and W. L. Poteat, President of Wake Forest College, rendered effective service. But had the contest arisen earlier they would undoubtedly have been powerless in the face of the fanaticism and ignorance of that early day. In that fight, which was waged throughout the State and in the legislature for religious freedom, let us inquire what part Horace Williams' boys played.

First, however, I will acknowledge the debt due by liberalism to the broad-minded W. S. Rankin and Dr. Soper of Trinity College and the effective organization established by them and called Schola Caveat, "Let the Scholar Beware," and to the Baptists guided in part by the virile Livingston Johnson, father of Gerald. Above all, to one of the brightest, wittiest, and most versatile Methodist laymen and lawyers in our midst, Charles Tillett, father of young Charlie, who laughed the State into a good humor. Not forgetting a notable public letter from young Frank Graham in Paris, opposing the Poole bill and advocating free speech under all circumstances.

In the great Fundamentalist fight, Tobe Connor, chairman of the Committee on Education in the legislature, cast the deciding vote which killed the Poole bill in the committee and thus encompassed its final defeat. When the committee met to consider the measure, the excited crowd was so numerous that an adjournment was had to one of the largest halls in the city.

Actively participating in the movement to direct public opinion were many others of Horace's old boys. In and around Charlotte might be mentioned Charlie Tillett, Otho Ross, W. T. Shore, Paul Ranson, Ed Broadhurst, Lenoir Chambers, and many others. These youngsters, mighty in the cause of freedom, banded themselves together to prevent the passage of the reactionary measure. But a powerful host confronted them: Preachers, lawyers, laymen, shifty politicians, judges, besides numerous camp followers, expecting the movement to sweep the State.

Cam Morrison, the popular, public-spirited Governor, had recently outlawed a textbook and banished it from the public schools. The pious Governor had declared that no book with a picture of a man and a monkey on the same page should disgrace the State, a gesture which greatly encouraged the Fundamentalists. Rev. William Black was proclaiming that evolution is the blackest lie ever blasted out of Hell. A Committee of One Hundred, called The Battalion of Death, The Six Hundred at Balaklava, had been formed to see to it that the Poole bill be enacted. Judges Neal and Shaw and the distinguished lawyer and politician, Zeb Turlington, were sponsors of the movement and energetic in its behalf. In the beginning, the conservative and able editor Julian Miller joined the movement. Josephus Daniels and his paper, The Old Reliable, were silent in several languages.

At length the climax of the Fundamental movement was reached. A meeting of the Committee of One Hundred and all other well-wishers was extensively advertised to be held on May 4, 1926, at the hotbed of Fundamentalism, the otherwise progressive and delightful Queen City, Charlotte. Expectation was at tiptoe. Reporters swarmed through the convention hall. It was confidently expected that the meeting would be so harmonious and enthusiastic as to bury evolution out of sight forever.

It was well known that at the meeting plans would be set on foot systematically to organize the State so as to force the legislature the following January to adopt the proposed legislation. But there was a rift within the lute. Horace's boys living in and around Charlotte became increasingly indignant and finally decided that such a thing as that could not happen in their proud city without opposition of the most vigorous sort. Horatians met and formulated their plans—formed their concept. Charlie Tillett got busy and went on the telephone. He called up a number of his friends in different parts of the State who were thought to be deeply interested in the matter. E. D.

Broadhurst of Greensboro was specially urged to attend. He accepted the invitation.

On the appointed day the Fundamentalist meeting was called to order by Judge Neal. Hymns were sung. The general purpose of the meeting was stated. The enthusiasm was great. No one doubted the result. A committee was appointed to draft resolutions. While they were out the meeting was thrown open to general discussion. Robert Lassiter, coöperating with Charlie Tillett, brought up the question as to who would have the privilege of the floor in voting. Some innocent Fundamentalist rose, and in the goodness of his heart made a motion that anyone present could speak and vote. The motion was put and adopted—a decided break for Old Horace's boys. It gave them a legal standing. They felt they were in a position to handle the matter.

While the committee was still out Charlie Tillett took the floor. "Do you propose to gag scientific instruction?" he sternly asked. "Is free speech and free thought to be destroyed?"

"Do you believe a man was descended from a monkey?" was shot at him from all over the house.

As the speaker undertook to explain that it was not a question of man or monkey but of free speech the crowd began to yell, "Answer yes or no!"

Availing himself of the legal privilege of answering yes or no, Tillett then proceeded to explain his position. This made the proponents of the plan more angry than ever. When the lunch hour came the committee on resolutions had not reported. By this time the crowd had swelled to such proportions that it was agreed the afternoon meeting should be held in the Second Presbyterian Church.

During the noon recess several of Old Horace's boys put their heads together and worked out a way to answer what the committee would probably report, that is, they formed a concept of a way that would show up the inherent fallacy of the entire Fundamentalist plan. They figured that the committee would report a resolution to prevent having any teacher at the University who was not an orthodox Christian. This, of course, would eliminate Catholics and Jews, regardless of whether their views were for evolution or against it.

Bill Shaw was selected to pose the question to the committee as to what its attitude would be towards excluding an intelligent Jew from the faculty for the purposes of teaching a nonscientific subject. When the committee reported, it was what had been anticipated. Therefore, Shaw posed the question as to what the committee's attitude would be towards a young Jew who might be employed to teach music. This question put the proponents in a hole. They floundered. Their arguments were hot and heavy. They found themselves in a position from which they could not extricate themselves. Paul Ranson spoke in a manner which carried conviction. Finally Ed Broadhurst rose.

"You are just a bunch of scared creatures," he solemnly declared. These words almost shook the rafters of the Holy Temple. "You had better go home and save the world by preaching the gospel instead of being here trying to pass foolish laws."

At this point the excitement boiled over. The ire of the preachers knew no bounds. A stalwart, broad-shouldered young Fundamentalist jumped to his feet and ran down the aisle. He shucked off his coat, he doubled up his fists as he ran. Approaching the speaker and shouting that he was not afraid of him or of anybody else, he was seized by the spectators. A fisticuff in front of the altar was narrowly prevented.*

The meeting thereupon collapsed. The senselessness of the whole thing was felt on all sides. Soon the Committee of One Hundred ceasd to function. The wise and brilliant Julian Miller resigned from the movement. Dr. Archy McGeachy, a stalwart Presbyterian, likewise pulled out. So

---

* The Rev. Mac Long, a brilliant all-around champion of Fundamentalism, joined in the mix-up, exclaiming, "My God shall not be murdered in his own house!"

also did W. E. Price, the original secretary of the movement.

Several weeks after the fiasco, a friend of Zeb Turlington, up at his home, asked him what was the cause. "Why, our opponents adopted an old political device. They came into the meeting and took it over. When Zeb's comment was reported to young Charlie Tillett, he laughed and said, "Maybe! And so it goes."

There is an interesting sidelight on the Scopes "monkey trial" which had taken place some two years before out at Dayton and which, on account of its novelty and the appearance of William J. Bryan and Clarence Darrow as opposing counsels, drew immense crowds from all over the land. Louis Graves, with his keen sense of humor, and Howard Odum, with his deep interest in sociology, drove all the way from Chapel Hill to Dayton and were interested spectators of the serio-comic affair. Upon his return to Chapel Hill Louis called on Horace and asked him what he thought of the incident.

"It doesn't interest me," he drawled. "Such spectacles settle nothing. Education is the only way."

Old Horace was not only winning the battle; he was winning the campaign. His dreams were coming to pass. Personally he had been honored and his beloved philosophy recognized. But his victory was to be far deeper and more significant than that. It seemed to him that his mission to the South was being fulfilled—everywhere reason was taking the place of prejudice, thoroughness superseding superficiality.

But the practical, immediate work which defeated the unwise Poole bill was that of the broad-minded college presidents, Poteat of Wake Forest and Chase of Carolina. These educators quit their jobs, went down to the legislature, appeared before the committees, defied half-baked public opinion, and hazarded their official lives in the cause of free thought. In the hearts of all far-sighted Carolinians, Poteat and Chase must be enshrined forever.

24

THE PASSING YEARS

SOME YEARS ago, as Judge Stacy and I were talking about Horace Williams, I asked him what lasting impression he had of the Old Teacher. After a few moments' reflection the Chief Justice whispered and said, "Lonesomeness!" He then went on to recall that Horace was wont to say, "The man who thinks profoundly will lead a lonely life." Another pause followed. Stacy then sadly commented, "He did."

When Professor Williams first entered upon his duties at Chapel Hill he imagined that chemistry, botany, zoölogy, and the other sciences would coöperate with philosophy. And undoubtedly this they would have done but for the fact that he demanded too much. He insisted that philosophy was all, the key to everything. No one could be a good chemist or lawyer, or doctor or preacher unless he first had become a philosopher. His notion was that philosophy is the entrance and the only entrance to wisdom. This sweeping claim the sciences could, in no wise, concede.

That the two opposing forces need not have fallen out is beside the point. The fact is they did. That which irked science was the dogmatism of philosophy; that which irked philosophy was the stupidity of science in not recognizing spirit above blow-pipe or crucible. As time wore on the University had expanded; the sciences had waxed and philosophy waned. In these circumstances Old Horace's fighting spirit rose to meet the danger. And they, as we have seen, were formidable.

The old philosopher was fond of the society of the quick-witted women of faculty and village, whose poetic imagination enabled them to catch on to his metaphysical nonsense. In the classroom the puzzle of the female continued a lively topic of discussion.

"Mr. Greenwood," he would solemnly ask, "what should a young man do when he finds himself engaged to one girl and in love with another?"

"That's too deep for me, Professor," Greenwood would laugh, as the boys and girls pricked up their ears.

"What do you say to that, Miss Ross?"

"I guess my answer is about the same as Jimmy Greenwood's."

"Well, I'll tell you what I'd do," broke in the quick-witted Hicks. "I'd smear kerosene all over my hair and you bet she'd kick me."

"Lawyers have a saying," the teacher here suggested, "that hard cases are the quicksands of the law. No doubt that's a hard case. And so it goes.

"But, Mr. Zollicoffer, perhaps you can tell us this. Why does your girl's canary sing sweeter than other canaries?"

"It doesn't, Professor. It's imagination."

"Imagination!" retorts Porter. "Why everything's imagination."

"Not the biscuits you ate for breakfast I hope," Kerr corrects.

"I agree with Porter, Professor," Colton interposes. "Doesn't Plato say matter came out of idea?"

"I'll tell you why," Humphrey pipes up. "That fellow was in love and a plumb-fool."

"No it's not, either," the imaginative Hawkins suggests. "It's a transference of values."

"What values?" asks Patterson.

"Why, reason for sentiment."

"I don't agree," says Nina Cooper. "It's because the canary actually sings sweeter. That fellow had spent his last dime for the best bird."

"What is your answer, Professor?" Smith inquires.

"Now, Mr. Smith, you must think it over. I may ask that question on the next exam. And so it goes."

At a certain mid-term examination, it is said, Old Horace put but one question to the boys: "If one of you were invited to address a girls' school on philosophy, how would you treat the subject?"

Lockhart, witty and original, wrote this as his "paper": "I wouldn't go." Lockhart passed.

It has been wisely said that men possess thoughts but ideas possess men—a statement which describes Horace Williams. In the colossal task which he had undertaken he was absorbed. Ideas possessed the man. The thought that ideas are weapons engrossed him. So closely did he stick to his task that his health suffered. As age crept on, its usual infirmities beset him. He went under the surgeon's knife, Dr. Foy Roberson, a son of his old friend, operating in a most skillful manner.

Illustrating Old Horace's total absorption in philosophy strange stories continued to circulate in the village. It was said that he and his wife had entered into a compact, whereby they divided the day into six periods of time. One hour was set apart for Mrs. Williams' painting, another for her music, a third for marketing, and still another for visiting. The period from seven to eight in the evening was *sui generis*—it was called the affectionate hour!

On a certain day, and during the music hour, as the story goes, Mrs. Williams' servant came into the studio and announced that the potato man was at the door with a bushel of potatoes which she had ordered. "Tell him it's not my hour for receiving potatoes," was the naïve message sent back! So original and delightful was Mrs. Williams that she had become a curiosity, socially, as her husband had philosophically. As we have seen, however, she differed from him in that she was coöperative and beloved, whereas he was sometimes suspected and feared.

One morning Mrs. Williams met her friend Mrs. Whitehead in the drug store, a kind of gathering place to discuss a limeade. Without warning or preface the artless Bertha burst out, "Oh, Mrs. Whitehead, I would so love to paint a portrait of you."

"Why that's a great compliment, Mrs. Williams, but why do you select me?"

"It's this way, Mrs. Whitehead. I can see beauty in even a gnarled old oak."

But however quaint and original Bertha Williams might seem to others she was the one dear object on earth to her equally queer and original husband. Though they were but babes in the woods, they thoroughly understood each other. The public must have been mistaken in their opinion that they were right-down stingy. This, assuredly they were not. During their fruitful days, they were saving up for old age, an agreement, as we have seen, long before entered into and firmly observed. She being his junior, would, in the course of nature, survive. The motive behind her husband's sacrifice and economy was not selfish; it was devotion and loyalty to her.

Horace Williams considered his home an ideal one, based as it was, on thrift, frugality, moderation, common-sense and mutual respect. So much was he enamored of his wife that he wished every one of his boys to get married. In a letter to Sidney Robins he wrote, "I am heartily glad to hear from you things relating to your inner and fuller life. By all means go ahead and get a wife. I should love to come up and give my blessing to you both on the great day. I am strongly interested and hope you will keep me posted. It is the thing I wanted for you since you left Harvard. Loving companionship of a fine woman will put a new note into your work."

A few months later, upon hearing from Sidney that the marriage day had been agreed upon, he wrote, "I have wanted to write you for a long time, but somehow could not get to it. Today I have your letter stating that June 4 is to be the glad day. I am heartily glad. You must use your tact and good judgment on Mr. Ford [the father]. He will come around gradually. Be a good Hegelian and hold him as Aufgeboten. I want to send Miss Frances a little wedding present. Shall I send it to Cambridge or Plymouth? I wish I were free to get away. It would be a joy to be present and see the beginning of the new chapter in your life.

"To build a fine home-life is not easy. Many fail in it. It can mean the inhibition of all development to the woman, it often does. This to me is an unpardonable sin. When true woman commits her life to a man, it should mean deeper, richer, fuller life and steady maturity into perfection. I covet this result for both you and Miss Frances. And I hope you will hold it steadily before you.

"Man has the advantage, and it is so easy to forget it and take for granted. And I suspect Miss Frances is that exalted kind that accepts without complaint. So you must not forget but always give her a square deal. Steady sympathy and thoughtfulness on your part will bring the richest returns. Am I preaching too much: if so you must forgive me. I desire greatly your success in this step, and I know the failures are many and the successes never come save by the highest efforts."

As the years passed, his attentive wife became, more and more, his solace and comfort. In the home, in the studio, and in social gatherings she was his ideal. He also found relaxation as I have indicated in the society of women. Writing to his friend Robins and telling him of the interesting Miss Lord, he said, "For about two weeks I promised myself to clear up things so that I could command an hour of quiet and peace and write to Miss Lord. Do you suppose she will let me write now? I want to get acquainted and to know that we share our friendship with her."

In the same letter Williams laments the death of Mrs. Ed Kidder Graham. "We have had a sad time here," he writes. "Mrs. Graham died last week. She was sick, desperately ill, for six weeks. It is a loss to every good interest in Chapel Hill." At an earlier date he had lamented the loss of Dr. Eben Alexander, "a very great teacher." He wrote of the death of his friend, Collier Cobb, with deep emotion. Likewise, he expressed his sorrow when Parson Moss passed away. "Mr. Moss has been failing for two years," he wrote. "He was away all last year. This fall he returned but attempted no work. Thursday evening he was at supper and was lively and bright. After retiring he became ill, summoned the doctor, seemed to improve. Then after sleeping a bit the doctor was recalled and before he could do anything the end came. He was buried Sunday afternoon. It was a community event, each one feeling that he had lost. The church was packed and many were outside. It was impressive to see the state of the village. No one can express his feeling yet each one wishes to do so. It is as if one would tell about his loss as the sunshine fading."

After Horace Williams had been teaching about a quarter of a century he began to think of resigning and calling his young friend Robins to be his successor. He broached this idea to the president and though it was well received it did not materialize. In a letter to Robins he thanked him for sending a paper setting forth a philosophical doctrine with which he agreed. "Let me tell you about myself," he also wrote. "I am planning to leave Chapel Hill. I want to get off in July and go to Jena and study with Eucken or to Harvard. Which do you advise? I want to write a logic. I am also divided on this point: I prefer you to all men to come here and do my work. And if I go to Harvard I should need your criticism and inspiration. I shall be fifty-six next summer and shall have completed twenty-four years here. This is enough. I may come back and teach a little. But my desire is to take some time for meditation and writing. Tell me how you feel about coming here and what you think of my plan?"

So far did he proceed with the scheme of resigning that he sold his home and was all packed up and ready to move away when the prospective purchaser backed down and the trade fell through. At this time the idea of becoming an author took possession of him. He wrote to Robins and suggested that they collaborate and write a book to be called "The Principles of Christianity." They would use Hegel and Harnack and Everett as the basis, and the result would be a publication of world service.

At this time, in his extensive correspondence, he continued to lambast the bread-and-butter philosophy of William James and the pretensions of the Ph.D.'s. James he called a joke. In a letter to Robins he said, "I am going to Asheville tomorrow and make a talk at the Teachers Assembly. I call it, 'After Education, What?' I trace the parallel between our present movement and scholasticism, I end about this way: 'No salvation outside the church,' thundered the Priest; 'No truth outside the scientific method,' echoes the scientist. 'Join the church and you are a Christian; get a Ph.D. and you are a great teacher.' When St. Peter gathers his choice ones about him, on one side will be a priest and on the other a scientist. And should they lose their labels St. Peter will be unable to distinguish between them."

In another letter he thanks Robins for a dissertation which interested him. "I wish I could ring your door-bell this morning. I have a distinct and vivid picture, not of the eye but of the imagination, of Mrs. Robins, and my plan is to compare it with the original next summer. I had hoped to do it this year but it seems impracticable. My plan is to sell all such things this fall and get a few years of freedom. So please expect me next summer."

In the conclusion of his letter the old philosopher was as rough-tongued with his former pupil as if he were a stranger. "I do not like your paper," he writes. "It does not sound like you. Pragmatism is not a philosophy. It can't be. A good kitchen, busy with the food for the feast, can never be the feast. Making a wheelbarrow can never be a science of physics and mechanics. You say, 'I am seeking a word for that in which knowledge and being and value are not to be discriminated from one another.' How confusing such a word would be. Please, if you find it, burn it promptly. It is our business to bring light, not confusion, to men. To me the value of knowledge is this: It expands the individual. Action produces individuals; knowledge overcomes the limits in action. You say pragmatism will save us from war. As I see it, pragmatism is the cause of war.

"Suppose you and Mrs. Robins go to breakfast. There is one biscuit on the table; both of you are hungry; one grabs the biscuit and eats it. This makes war. A fight is action, not knowledge. Of course truth will work. It is the only thing that will work. But this is not to merge the truth in the action. Pragmatism is not as interesting as Russell's attempt to merge philosophy into mathematics. Spinoza tried this. A quart pot is not a yardstick. With all good wishes and apologies, I am your friend, H. H. Williams."

What with teaching philosophy, writing stacks of letters, toying with authorship, laying plans for a School of Thought, delivering lectures, reviewing the *Education of Henry Adams* and elucidating in the *Monist* the One and the many, addressing the Y.M.C.A., at the invitation of its secretary, Harry Comer, distinguishing between physical and spiritual miracles, supervising debates, answering his critics, and not neglecting the business of trading horses, mules, and cows, purchasing cheap houses and collecting rents, the old philosopher was kept busy.

Some of the troubles incident to his farming operations he outlined in a letter to his friend Robins. "At times it looks as if I could get away for a few days. Then a horse gets sick, the steers break out and invade the cornfield of some neighbor. And a dozen other things. I am afraid to promise."

A curious incident arose out of the purchase of a Percheron stallion. It seems that about the year 1914 Old Horace and his neighborhood friends, George Pickard, Jim Ray and others purchased the stallion and gave their notes for $600 to the vendors. The horse, a beautiful, shapely animal, arrived but there were no results from his activities. Old Horace and his associates thereupon undertook to repudiate the trade. Suit on the notes was brought and Old Horace got a big kick out of the litigation. Indeed, he formed a begriff and laid a trap for his opponents.

He admitted the notes but pleaded a counterclaim of double the amount because of defects in the animal purchased. The jury found for the defendants. They validated the notes but gave judgment for double the amount by way of counterclaim. It resulted that Old Horace not only got the horse but was in-to-the-good by $600! The case was appealed to the high court. After argument an opinion was handed down affirming the judgment as to the notes but setting aside the counterclaim. The defendants had failed to notify the owners of the horse of its defects, as the bill of sale required. In a word, though Horace and his lawyers had formed a concept, Bob Sykes, the lawyer on the other side, had formed a deeper one, and blown his old teacher out of the water. And so it goes!

The amusing part of the case was that in remitting his check in payment of the judgment, Horace wrote a letter to Sykes and asked, "I wish you would let me know what sort of power or influence or legerdemain you used on the Judges of the Court to get them to set aside the finding of the jury and give your client judgment against us?"

Judge Sykes made this reply: "When I was a student in your psychology class, I recall you said many times that in every complicated question, particularly in every lawsuit, there is a scarlet thread of truth running entirely through it from beginning to end, and if a lawyer could get hold of one end of that scarlet thread of truth in the beginning of the case, and follow it to the end, he would usually be successful. I followed your advice in this case and if any error has been committed you can charge most of it up against what you taught me."

As session followed session, so busy did the philosopher become that he forgot to remember the Sabbath Day to keep it holy. Sunday morning would come, and the church bells would ring, but not for him. Seated in his study he would be poring over Socrates and Plato, Hegel and Eucken, totally oblivious to all things around.

"My dear," said the churchly-minded Bertha to her philosophical spouse, one Sunday as the bells were urgently calling to church, "why do you insist on working Sundays?"

"Do I?" he languidly replied, looking up from his book.

"Why of course you do. You are becoming a slave to teaching."

"It's this way, my dear," the logician answered. "I don't have to go to church. My whole life is sacred, not just Sundays."

Occasionally, however, he and his wife would get away from the Hill for a visit with sister Lucy Wells, or they would run up to New England and spend a summer in the exhilarating White Mountain section. During the Christmas season, and on New Year's Day, he would take his pen in hand and write to his old boys extending greetings and choicest blessings, sending little presents to the children of the household.

"The best way to begin the new year," he writes Sidney Robins on January 1, 1912, "is to have a word with you and to thank you heartily for sending me the photograph. I have enjoyed it very much and immediately placed it upon my mantel by the side of Phillips Brooks. I have spent the holiday here at work. I am trying to show that the Parsees laid the foundation for the Egyptian theory of God." After much elaboration of this thought he concludes with these words, "I hope you have acted more wisely than I this gala season, and given yourself over to fun and happiness."

He was constantly complaining of the failure of institutional Christianity. "As I see it," he wrote, "the time has come for a man to do work kindred to that done by Philo—a supreme synthesis of the contending elements in consciousness. This synthesis must work itself out first in the individual experience. Hence the storm and stress of the deeper life today. All truth is painful in process. Great ideas tear their way into individual experience. It is the truth of the

Man of Sorrows. All great things come into the world by way of the Cross. I see this fact. I do not know a single exception to it. And I cannot understand it."

Despite numerous activities Old Horace gave time and thought to the growth and development of the University, specially along ethical and liberal lines. The choice of new presidents, as vacancies occurred, had given him concern. When it was discovered that Venable would likely resign he had set about to assist in choosing his successor. With absolute confidence he had hit upon his old pupil, Ed Kidder Graham, as the learned Venable's successor. Upon the election of Graham, he was so well pleased that he wrote Robins and declared that Graham was making a good president, "The best the University has had in my day. He combines the good points of Battle, Winston, and Alderman. I think he will be the greatest College President in the South."

A few years later the Good Teacher expressed his opinion of Graham in an address before the Summer School. "Who is the man in North Carolina in this century who has won his way into the heart of all North Carolina? What name is it that thrills the soul of every youth in the State today? It is a schoolteacher who in four brief years has written a chapter of service to the State that will forever make it a place where men big and free shall rejoice to dwell. He did this because he was the living spirit, simple, sincere, passionately devoted to the truth. Let us then as teachers have done with the apologetic attitude for our existence. Let us put behind us forever the forms of slavery. Let us become conscious of our worth as the high service to truth."

Ed Kidder Graham was perhaps the ablest and most universal-minded scholar who ever sat under Horace Williams. He died on October 26, 1918. In a later chapter I shall endeavor to point out his excellences. Coördination, unification, integration, these were his characteristics. And a whole-hearted devotion to truth. Undoubtedly, as his Good Teacher declared, he combined in himself the best qualities of his able predecessors.

The task of finding a successor to Graham had seemed almost impossible. But after several months of searching and sifting and investigating, Victor Bryant giving of his time and labors to the task, the problem had been solved. At the commencement of 1919 Harry Woodburn Chase was chosen. It is a significant fact that several months previous to his selection Horace Williams had picked him out as Graham's successor. In a letter to Robins, written early in the year he said, "We are still drifting as to Mr. Graham's successor. Chase is doing well and may be made President."

The most paradoxical aspect of Old Horace's paradoxical teaching was his fixedness, his obstinacy. Once "sot in his ways," he never changed. His orders were law. If he selected the teacher's job for one student or the pulpit for another or the law for a third, they dared not disobey; they must knuckle down and do as told or take a tongue lashing. The case of Sidney Robins, and also of Ralph Harper, is in point. Harper became an Episcopal minister and still wears the cloth. Robins became a Universalist preacher, but soon shifted to a chair of philosophy in a northern college, giving up the ministry no doubt because of criticisms of his views on philosophy by his old teacher.

In the main, however, the tone of letters from Williams to Robins was cordial and helpful. "Your new theory of sermonizing is just the thing," he writes. "A sermon is not the unfolding of private syllogisms—it should be an interpretation of the audience to themselves. 'I am come that ye might have life,' should be the motive in every sermon. I enjoyed reading the sermons you sent me and intended writing you of them. I liked all of them except the one concerning the church. I think there is a deeper view of the institution."

At the urgent insistence of Professor Williams his brightest boys generally finished off at Harvard. The best or nothing was his objective. One of these boys was Harold Rights, who wrote his old teacher, acclaiming the loyalty of thought at Harvard. In a terse reply Horace signified his approval of the Harvard spirit of freedom and individuality. He added, in his cryptic way, "I do not want a priest to eat my food and save me the trouble of digesting it."

No doubt the high-water mark of Horace Williams' career was reached about the year 1920, when he was chosen a Kenan Professor. Such were then the manifestations of affection, approval, and confidence that he felt rewarded for all the sacrifices he had made. Trustees were backing him. Students enthusiastic, college journals selecting him as one of the leaders on the Hill. The failure to name him as Kenan Professor had aroused his old boys. Judge Parker wrote the *Magazine*, naming Williams as the greatest teacher in the State's annals. Newspaper reporters doted on him. If Bob Madry or Tom Bost or Le Gette Blythe or Lenoir Chambers ran short of news they sought him out. Parson Moss in the *Magazine* added a word of high praise. His man Horne stood by him.

So much in the limelight and so toasted and feted was the vain, egotistical man, though protesting the opposite, that on such occasions he would mount his horse, leave town, and take to the woods. No doubt a dialectic gesture!

At this time Horace Williams was perhaps less lonesome than at any period of his career. There was not the sensitiveness and flinching from criticism which afterwards developed. He could take a joke on himself, as an incident related by Scrubby Rives, the University cheer leader, may show. One afternoon during a baseball game, the seventh inning had come around, and the people in the stadium were standing up and wildly cheering for a Carolina victory. "I looked in front of me," says Scrubby, "and saw an elderly man sitting very calmly in his seat. Without thinking very much about it I caught a hold of the old fellow's shoulders and jerked him to his feet, saying, 'Get up, old man, get up and shout.' The old man happened to be Professor Williams and all through the years when I was in college he laughingly told of the incident and said he could never again remain seated when the crowd around was standing and cheering."

But it was neither the admiration of students, the backing of trustees, nor the successes he had attained that brought a measure of satisfaction to the lonesome old character. This accomplishment was the work of his home and his wife, from whom had come the depth of inner experience and enlarged usefulness.

Alas for the husband's peace of mind, a loss beyond repair was near. Bertha Williams died October 18, 1922. She had just reached home from a happy visit to her sister Lucy when the fatal heart-attack came.

25

THE HUMAN TOUCH

WHEN Bertha Colton Williams died in the fall of 1922, numerous were the expressions of sympathy and affection which came to her husband from all parts of the country. In response to a letter from Sidney Robins, the old philosopher wrote as follows:

CHAPEL HILL, N. C.
January 15, 1923.

My dear Mr. Robins,

I want to thank you for your letter. It was a fine and gracious expression of sympathy. I shall keep it. I should have answered at once, but it has not been easy to write. For the first time my philosophy has failed me. I am not yet adjusted. My home life was so congenial, so satisfying that I am unable to give it up. What a big thing it is to secure and hold the love of a noble woman for thirty years. Not once was I ever conscious that anyone came between us. I was always first with her. I am deeply grateful. So now I do not know what to do. So far it has not been possible to work. All my life the path ahead has had such a tremendous appeal, now it is silent.

Last year was the wonder year for me. I explored, roamed, gazed upon the Eternal City of God, the inner mechanism of intelligence. And I had planned a preliminary volume to be called, "The Evolution of Logic." This would deal with all those phases of the content of knowledge, such as hypotheses, a priori, assumption, etc. I have seen enough to say that every position in superstition, theology, and philosophy can be explained. Today we uncovered the basis of Platonism and the transcendent character of the Ought, showing how the nature of quality has been moved to the opposite of itself. You would revel in this. We have visitors every day, about as many as members of the class. It still appears queer to me that any should voluntarily attend a class on logic. But the old swing is not present now. Like the hibernating bear, I am consuming my own fat.

This summer I want to get away, clear away, up into Canada, or somewhere, and see if I can get back into my stride. What are you planning to do? How would it do to go and see Harper? Years ago he would have suggested it.

The University is going ahead materially. I am afraid we are not doing better work. Prosperity is as difficult to digest in the case of an institution as in an individual. I wish I could have a good talk with you. It seems such a long time since the summer in Cambridge.

I am planning to get two Cornell men to assist me next year. One of them is Paul Green, an old student of mine, now at Cornell on the Graham Kenan Fellowship. With all good wishes, I am,

        Sincerely yours,
        Horace Williams

Emotional letters of this kind the old philosopher did not often indulge in. He was less communicative. The proud, intellectual man indeed rarely reveals himself. His innermost thoughts he keeps locked up in his own breast. If he suffers, he suffers alone; if he is misunderstood, he makes no explanation. He has no entangling alliances. I once heard Walter Clark, the intrepid, ambitious, Chief Justice of our highest court say of friendship that it is both useless and costly. For a different reason Old Horace avoided friendships. He considered them a sign of weakness. The individual should stand the strain; he should be the captain of his soul. No difficulties should daunt him.

The individual is the I, all else is the Non-I. Were the individual to indulge in the restraining influences of friendship he would weaken himself. Friendship, as Horace Williams seemed to conclude, is a call for help, an admission that life is too great a burden to be borne alone. Friendship is a capitulation with fate, and this the masterful are by no means willing to make. An artist should stand to his work. The hero would rather die than run up the white flag. Such at least was the case with Horace Williams.

In all the world the old philosopher had no intimate friends, except his mother, his wife, and his sisters, Lizzie and Hallette. Nor was his love for these dear ones based on ties of blood. According to his austere philosophy, to love your brother or your sister because you have the same parents is to be group-minded. He was fond of those relatives only who had a similarity of taste. His mother had been a friend and a supporter in the needy days of his youth. His wife had been a helpmeet, coöperating in laying up a competency, catering to his wants, and in all respects meeting his every expectation. Sisters Lizzie and Hallette, who had entered into his life at a later period, were dear to him because of their quiet, old-fashioned ways and their fund of common-sense.

The winter after Bertha Williams died, sister Lucy Wells and her daughter Polly came down to Chapel Hill, at Horace's invitation, and spent several months at the Williams home. The University and the village gave them a hearty welcome. Polly became a social favorite. At the Christmas frolics she was a leader, being one of the best dancers on the floor. In truth Mrs. Wells was kept busy chaperoning the popular Polly. In a letter giving an account of this visit, sister Lucy writes me as follows:

"Horace was a most brilliant man—his generosities were very large, and his idea of saving money had behind it a future hope of a deep expression of love and loyalty to Bertha and the University. The four months I spent with

Polly at Horace's were so full of Polly's dancing work—and her beaux—I seem to recall few conversations with Horace himself. He talked but little.

"My sister visited me many times. Yet we were so engrossed with old friends and my children, and spending the money Horace *so* generously always sent her, that we had little time for Chapel Hill or her home gossip. I can see her face shine as she opened a special delivery letter enclosing an unexpected extra $100 to spend on her beloved New York.

Faithfully yours,
Lucy Colton Wells

137 High Street
MIDDLETOWN, CONNECTICUT

As the summer of 1923 approached, bringing the usual vacation, the Good Teacher was overwhelmed with invitations to visit his students then living in various sections of the country. In a letter to Robins he informed him that he had written Harper that "I expect to ring your doorbell about the middle of July. Could we meet in Boston and go up together?" To these words he added, "I look upon the year closed with little satisfaction. Too many compliments were given me and too few stimulating theses from the students. The Trustees gave me two assistant professors and I hope for more results next year. I am going to Greensboro tomorrow to speak in the Quaker Church. I shall endeavor to explain Philo's effort to solve the problem of the First Century. Then I go to Charlotte to speak to the Bible Class of the Presbyterian Church. My subject is, The Wise Life."

During the following summer Horace paid a visit to sister Lucy at her cottage in Maine. He enjoyed the sea breezes. The summer following he and I spent at the Tavern on the Moors, where Fred Howe's famous, hedonistic School of Opinion was in full swing. The quaint little village of Sconset never knew what would come next, as, day by day and night by night, Sinclair Lewis, Bruce Bliven, Floyd

Dell, George Middleton, Kallen and Mayo, and their likes took the floor and discoursed upon Freudianism, Karl Marxism, complexes and various neuroses. Philosophy was taboo, of course, the prevailing idea being that there is no such thing as spirit or soul. The School of Opinion was not interesting to Old Horace; he never ventured inside the classroom.

During the summer vacations, for the next ten or twelve years, Horace would visit his friends the Harpers or the Robinses, or he would run up into the mountains of New England or enjoy its seacoast. He grew to be very fond of the numerous Harper children and also of the Robins family. In letters to their parents he often referred to them and the merry times they had had together. From the hamlet of Islesford, Maine, he wrote Robins and thanked him for his cordial letter of invitation.

"You and Mrs. Robins are certainly good to me. I can't imagine anything more interesting than another day in Plymouth with you and Mrs. Robins. Hence I shall plan for it and thank you very much. I suppose it will be the last of the month before I start South. It seems to agree with me here. I love the sea and am enjoying it daily. Saturday we went to North East and I called on President Eliot. I admire him and we had a good talk of an hour. I have also had a talk with Newman Smyth of New Haven, he was the big preacher in New Haven when I was there. It is very interesting to compare the mountains and the sea, two ultimate forms of life and yet quite different. I shall want to ask you a lot of questions when I get to Plymouth."

Upon receiving a letter from Robins which announced the expectation of a new arrival in the family he replied, "I do not think there can be too many children, such as Ann and John. I should like immensely to frolic with John. I hope Mrs. Robins will do splendidly. I wish you were coming East. It would be a keen pleasure to see each of you again. I am planning to go to Sconset about July first. I am fond of the place. There is good food, the utmost freedom, golf, tennis, swimming, walking over the moors. Nobody bothers you. I hope to work all summer on the Logic and finish it next year. If you and Mr. Harper will come over to Sconset I promise to listen to your sermon and not go to sleep. Give my love to the children. I am sure they are a constant delight to you."

Again he wrote, "It was real pleasure to get one more letter from you and to hear that you have had a good year. Mr. Harper seemed to have had a fine year. I wish it were practicable to see the Robins family. I picture Ann and John as fine to look upon. Tell John, 'He is no good,' and beat him to the laugh. Please give all greetings to Mrs. Robins and the children for me, and believe me, Cordially yours, Horace Williams."

The correspondence between the old philosopher and Ralph Harper extended over many years and covered almost every phase of human experience. The Harper children interested Horace—both those in esse and those in posse. When he was visiting their parents they were his companions and very close to him. After receiving a letter from Harper that an increase in the family was expected he wrote and expressed his pleasure. "Let's hope it will be a girl and exactly as the mother is. I can think of no better fortune. Please give her my love." At a later date, and when a boy was born to the Harpers, he wrote and said, "That Mrs. Harper is given a beautiful son is fine. Why? I do not know."

At other times he wrote and said, with Socrates, that virtue is knowledge and vice ignorance. "When you get off the trail stop barking. . . . The essential thing in a big crop of fruit is the sound tree." Again he wrote, "The ten tribes perished because they had no Isaiah. The big thing after Moses is to see Isaiah. Isaiah saw the actual vision. Religion is the organizing principle in a people's life. The unity from Abraham to Jesus is vital and progressive. Abraham was great and so were Moses, David, Elijah, Elisha, Isaiah, St. Paul, but the greatest of them all was Jesus."

The relationship of Horace Williams and the Rosses of Charlotte was refreshing and beautiful. It smacked of the good old days before hospitality had become a lost art. Visits were often exchanged. When Otho, Jr., entered the University he lived in the Williams' home. When the daughter Jane majored in philosophy under Horace she wrote a valuable thesis which won a Fellowship. Occasionally Dr. Ross checked over his Old Teacher and prescribed for him.

At the doctor's suggestion several teeth were extracted and plates were sent down. "I took them to Durham and watched the dentist enjoy them. The teeth are gone. They had done me much service. It was hard to see them go unsung and unwept. Such friends deserve better at our hands. But what is one to do? I thought of several ways to exhibit my appreciation. What do you think of a tight box with this inscription: In this box are two teeth long the servitors of H. H. W., may they rest where there are no abscesses."

Letters to Dr. Ross bordered on intimacy. "You are a great friend, and each time I see you my sense of obligation is deepened." In another letter he declared that the doctor was "good beyond words to me. This morning I enjoyed again the girls and Otho getting off to Sunday School. It was that way in my home."

On commencement occasions the Parkers and Shaws and Tilletts and Battles and Winslows and Umsteads and other old boys would enjoy a luncheon in the home of their Old Teacher. Once Dr. Ross was absent, whereupon Horace wrote and expressed his disappointment. "I wanted you and Mrs. Ross to join Judge Parker and Mr. Shaw for breakfast with me. They came, we missed you. I should like to date you now for the next time you are here. You are a great friend."

Though the home at Chapel Hill was lonely now without its mistress, and without the cats and the horse and the cow, Horace made a brave effort to bring good cheer and to overcome the solitude that almost always surrounds the martyrs of thought. In the village there were a number of sprightly, philosophically-minded young women whom he would have around at frequent afternoon teas, or for a horseback ride through the woodsy bridle paths, and at whom, as Madame Grundy was whispering, he occasionally cast sheeps' eyes. But his mind ran to philosophy and not to women. Gus Long, his old college mate, attests this. "That he was ever stirred by the flash of an ankle," said Gus, "or the flutter of a skirt is unthinkable."

However these things may be, Old Horace laid in a supply of handsome linens, doilies, napkins, table-cloths and the like. He likewise ordered from abroad the choicest brands of coffee and tea. In this struggle for rejuvenation he had good support from his friends the Bradshaws, the Koches, the Kennettes, the Umsteads, the Cobbs, and others. One summer up at Sconscet he had Mrs. Bradshaw as his guest. The young women students of the University he took much interest in, specially those who were self-supporting. His admiration for the splendid work of Mrs. Marvin Stacy, Dean of Women, and widow of one of the greatest young Carolinians of the early 1900's, found expression in many ways.

He would call at Mrs. Stacy's office and ask if he could not help some of the poor worthy girls through their college course. Time and again he endorsed the notes of these fine young people. The queer old man considered himself the very best possible judge of the human countenance. In fact he toyed with mind-reading and considered himself an expert in phrenology. Nor was he unwilling to back up his judgment. Since he knew an honest person by merely looking him in the face, he knew whom to aid and whom not to aid!

At the beginning of one session of the University he signed a young woman's note for tuition. Presently the installments fell due and the conscientious girl made prompt payment. Whereupon Old Horace wrote and said she was paying off the note entirely too fast. She must go more slowly and be sure not to stint herself. Numerous acts of kindness, unknown to the public, he performed. He contributed $500 towards the endowment of an excellent Methodist College at Louisburg.

It was a pleasure for Old Horace to continue his wife's subscription to the Circle of the Episcopal Church which bore her name. With the first remittance after her death he wrote the Circle and said, "I believe it would give her the keenest joy to know that you had named this Circle for her. Therefore I beg the privilege of doing something that I know would please her. As I wrote Mrs. Hudson there is nothing during the year that gives me quite the pleasure that I have when paying her dues. I know it would make her happy." In this letter he likewise wrote that his wife loved her art and her violin and in her studio spent many hours alone with her chosen joys. "She read French and subscribed to several French art journals. I do not believe she ever destroyed one. She lived in Chapel Hill thirty-one years. She looked upon it as home and lies buried here."

When Horace made a contribution to any worthy cause he did so cheerfully and ungrudgingly. If Francis Bradshaw came around for a contribution to the Y.M.C.A. he would ask how much was his part. He would then draw his check without quibbling or complaint. Whenever he was invited to address the Y.M.C.A. he complied, and never skipped an appointment. Though many people were afraid of the erratic old philosopher, this was not the case with Mrs. Cotten, the accomplished assistant in the Archives Department. She unhesitatingly called on Old Horace, the big property owner, and informed him that one of his tenants was sick and unable to pay rent. "All right," said Horace. "Let him stay and I'll also put in water." The house was occupied rent-free during the six following months.

One day when Old Horace was quite lenient with a delinquent renter, Francis Bradshaw said to him, "Professor Williams, why are you easy on some renters and hard on others?"

"It's this way, Francis," said the original old character.

"If a renter is trying-to-come and is in bad luck I let up on him. But the sorry ones I turn out."

"Why, Professor," said Bradshaw, "You are letting that drunken fellow Smith occupy rent-free. He's been there a whole year now."

"Yes, that's so. But Smith has a good wife, and she's industrious."

When a niece of his wrote and asked him to relinquish to her his interest in a piece of land which the Williamses had inherited, he cheerfully assented. Nor was his generosity to those humble ones who served him as domestics less marked. Celia Johnson, a colored girl from South Carolina, faithfully presided over his kitchen for the space of seven years. He was grateful to Celia and made her an out-and-out deed to a comfortable cottage in the fashionable colored section of the village.

When one of Horace's plantations was vacant he advertised for a renter. Mr. Bennett applied and asked for the terms. After talking the matter over Old Horace said, "Mr. Bennett, I'll rent my farm but you must first get married and after that stick to your job." The bargain was closed. Bennett moved in and in a few years had laid up sufficient money to buy a farm of his own, from which he later sold timber for the sum of $8000.

His little acts of kindness were as numerous as they were unheralded. It pleased him to present a cedar chest to the Bradshaws and also to the Umsteads. The number of rugs, made from tanned calf-skins, which he gave away, was not a few. When his new assistant, Professor Kattsoff, arrived on the Hill, his salary was small and his earthly possessions as meagre as his salary. Old Horace called on him in his humble cottage. On the inexpensive little center table he descried a vase of natural wild flowers, on the walls were simple reprints of the masters. Nowhere was there any foolish display. Old Horace was delighted. The very next day he sent around to the Kattsoffs a leg of choice mutton and a calf-skin rug. Soon afterwards he presented the new professor with Everett's *Science of Thought*.

The affection of Horace for sisters Lizzie and Hallie was not only brotherly but beautiful. For a year or more Lizzie was the honored guest in his home. Afterwards she married George B. Smith, moved to Virginia, and reared an interesting family. Her son, Spotswood, became a student in the University and lived with his uncle, coming under his special care and training. Spots was one of the shining lights of the Hill, graduating president of the Phi Beta Kappa.

So congenial were Horace and sister Lizzie and so greatly did she admire him from childhood up that she called him her hero. "I loved him with a passion," she would declare.

Hallie was younger than Lizzie. She, too, lived with Brother Horace for a year or more. Her affection for him was no less deep and genuine than Lizzie's. Her account of her brother's manifestations of affection is indeed touching. "He imagined I looked like our mamma," she said. "When I first went to live with him, and he saw me after a separation of several years, he was overcome with emotion. He placed both of his hands on my cheeks and kissed me tenderly and lovingly. Over and over again he kept on saying, you are the exact imagine of our dear old mother."

While Hallie was a guest at his home brother Horace supplied her with handsome dresses and other apparel. The family car was at her disposal and everything was done to make her feel at home. Hallie's husband was Bruce Hooker. When Horace was attacked with pneumonia, "the old man's friend," she came to Chapel Hill and nursed him back to health.

But the philosopher's interest in his sisters and neighbors was as nothing when compared with his solicitude for his boys. The botany professor, John Couch, tells of a characteristic incident, which occurred at a meeting of the faculty. A hot discussion was going on because of a case of drunkenness. A motion had been made to expel the offender and it was about to be adopted. Whereupon Old Horace rose and took the boy's part. "Is it our purpose," he solemnly asked, "to expel this young boy, and put the institution above the man? Not with my vote. Let's save this boy. Let the institution go."

The plea had the desired effect; the boy was not expelled. Today he is a worthy citizen of the State.

There is an old saying, "There is no fool like an old fool." Horace did not fall in this category. He was not a fool. His feet were on the ground. On occasion he could be as rough as nails. His biting, rasping tongue had lost none of its sting. His fighting spirit was still at the crest. He could trade horses with the best judges of "hoss" flesh. He could spot a faker no matter how disguised he might be, with oily tongue and smiling countenance selling bogus securities. The craze of speculation, sweeping the land like a cyclone in the late 1920's did not move him, except to pity and sorrow. He avoided stocks. The collapse must come. From every street corner he proclaimed that a great disaster impended. In letters to friends he ridiculed the idea that real prosperity would follow spending and borrowing, or that something could come out of nothing.

When he heard that the government proposed to lease a lot of cotton land and then not work it, he wrote and asked Robins, "Why not hire a lot of professors to do nothing and let them draw their pay as they smoke cigarettes about the drugstore." When he ascertained that his young friend was leaning towards John Dewey and his socialistic, trial-and-error theory, he was disturbed. "Analogy and assumption belong to poetry and literature," he wrote. "They do not appear to have any place in logic or life. Imagine a rose some fine May morning bestirring itself with an analogy. Imagine yourself with your family taking ship for Europe. You ask the pilot, Is this ship sea-worthy? He answers, I do not know. If it is not, we have another ship in the dock. We will try that."

In a word Williams continued to be a stern, relentless prophet, denouncing shallowness of thought and warning the credulous, uninformed, poorly-led people of the wrath to come. A curious story is told of a faculty meeting at which the course of study for the following year was being formulated. The scientists were in a clear majority and were about to win. Among other changes in the curriculum it was proposed to put science in the Liberal Arts course and take Greek out. Silent and enraged Old Horace sat by, intent and boiling within, asking himself if the faculty really knew what education is. At length he rose and in his quavering voice said, "Mr. President, I move the appointment of a committee of five to retire and report what is education."

At another time, and when the law officers of the State were meeting at Chapel Hill Professor Lee Brooks, professor of sociology, and Horace Williams were chosen to address the convention. Brooks spoke first and employed the modern approach to the subject. Crime is an economic problem. Increase wages, improve living conditions, give the underdog a chance and crime will disappear. Professor Brooks finished and resumed his seat, and it was plain that he had made a hit. But not with Old Horace.

Slowly walking up to the speaker's desk, and with neither notebook nor memoranda in hand, he opened up with the bold, flat-footed assertion that his learned colleague was wrong, wrong in his premises, wrong in his conclusions. "Pragmatism is the curse of the day," he solemnly proclaimed. "Trial-and-error is heresy. Principle only can cure our troubles. Our honored speaker is photographic, he deals with the surface. He should penetrate to the heart. The Kingdom of Heaven is within you."

Having broken these few remarks, Old Horace quietly resumed his seat. Brooks was amazed. He turned to Dean House and said, "What have I done?"

"Oh, don't mind him. That's Old Horace."

Next morning at the village postoffice, where faculty and students assembled to get their mail and gossip, Old Horace sidled up to Brooks, as though nothing out of the way had happened and said, "Professor Brooks, what is social pathology?"

Brooks fled.

Once only did any person get the laugh on Horace and that was on an occasion after he had addressed the Phi Society in his usual manner decrying shallow thinking and predicting a total collapse of civilization unless there was a radical change. His old college mate, Frank Winston, jovial, popular, and optimistic replied. Frank cautioned the boys not to be alarmed at Horace's grouches since he was born that way and nothing ever pleased him. "He reminds me of old Uncle Tom Bazemore down in Bertie. Uncle Tom is just like Old Horace, never satisfied. He looks on the dark side of things. Why, when we were building the railroad from Windsor to Ahoskie Uncle Tom came in my office one day and I said, 'Uncle Tom, see Windsor is going to have a railroad.'

"'Never!' Uncle Tom growled and stalked away.

"Next month Uncle Tom came in again.

"'Didn't I tell you, Uncle Tom, Windsor was going to have a railroad? See out there, the ties are already down.'

"'Don't you fool yourself, Frank. Windsor ain't never had no railroad and hit ain't gwine to git one now.'

"Well, in about four months the road was completed and the old man came to town and walked into my office looking kind of sheepish like.

"'Come in, Uncle Tom,' I gaily called out, taking the old man by the hand. 'Let's join the gang and go on the excursion.'

"Well, we lit out, old man Tom and I, and we got on the train, and the bell rang, the whistle blew, the conductor called out 'All aboard,' and then the engine, she began to choo, choo, going faster and faster. Presently I looked around and there sat Uncle Tom crouched up in his seat and holding on for dear life.

"'Didn't I tell you, Uncle Tom, we were going to get a railroad?'

"'Yes, Frank, you sure did, and here she goes and all Hell can't stop her.'"

It was many a day before Old Horace recovered from this unphilosophical larruping.

26

WHAT THE GOOD TEACHER TAUGHT ME

UNTIL I HAD reached the age of sixty-odd and was sitting in Horace's class I had never looked inside a philosophy book. My early training had been classical with a sprinkling of science and astronomy. Furthermore I had started to school so young and my mind was so immature that I grew up over-night, much as a Jonah's gourd vine.

I entered college at fourteen and at the age of eighteen had graduated. A few years later, and while disqualified by reason of non-age, I was elected to the State Senate. Before I was thirty, I became a judge and entered upon the delicate task of adjusting the differences of nearly three million souls. Such precocity was something to brag about, but did not make for depth or breadth of thought. On the contrary, it had the effect of precipitating mental indigestion. I was long on memory and short on ratiocination. I was what Old Horace would call group-minded. I galloped with the gang. Unlike Emerson, I considered consistency a jewel and by no means the hobgoblin of little minds.

"Ed Pou," I said to my able Solicitor at my first Court, "Let's be orthodox."

It thus becomes plain that when I entered Horace's philosophy class, orthodoxy and non-orthodoxy met face to face and the professor had a tough job on his hands. I was subjective and introspective, he objective and detached. I was wedded to the past, he often an iconoclast, smashing images to left and right. My mental apparatus was telescopic, it spanned sea and sky; his was microscopic—but also telescopic. My method of argument was personal and direct; it abounded in ridicule, satire, the grotesque, the *ad personam*. Horace's manner was thoughtful, abstracted, logical. In debate, if I was a Harry Hotspur he was a patient, oracular Socrates.

Always, I began firing at the first tap of the drum. Horace waited till he could see the whites of the enemies' eyes. I shot a short-range, sawed-off gun; Horace shot a long-range rifle. I would fly the eagle-bird or make the welkin ring and bring forth shouts of applause from the emotional multitude. I could wring big verdicts from sympathetic juries. Horace, on the contrary, synthesized unrelated facts and drew the most surprising conclusions.

Naturally, my entrance into Old Horace's classroom delighted him, though he was too proud and uncommunicative to admit the fact. But one evening in his study he unbosomed himself to his young friend Garland Porter, who was then living with him.

"Mr. Porter," said the old philosopher, "did you see Judge Winston on our class today?"

"Yes, Professor, I did."

"Isn't it remarkable that such a successful, business lawyer can find something in our classes?"

The Good Teacher then went on to say that it was not only a phenomenon but a source of satisfaction, since his teaching was evidently spreading and taking root. And yet his appreciation of my presence did not soften his manner towards me.

"Mr. Winston," he asked, shortly after I had taken my seat in his class, "what is law?"

"Generally speaking, Professor, I would say, with Blackstone, that law is a rule of action."

"What do you say to that, Miss Liddell?"

The young Portia glibly repeated Old Horace's well-worn definition of law, unity in action difference.

"Yes," Old Horace added, "law is not a rule, law is unity."

"Why, Professor," I hotly broke in, "you are in a sad minority!"

"Yes, Judge, and so was Noah on a celebrated occasion."

As the class snickered and enjoyed my discomfiture, I returned to the attack.

"Why, Professor," said I, "under that definition where does punishment or sanction come in?"

The old philosopher smiled a sardonic smile. His chance had come. My question gave him an opportunity. After a significant pause he carelessly and dryly remarked that the old idea that law is a rule is error, harmful error. There is a great difference between a rule and unity. Rule is rigid, unity plastic. A rule operates from the outside, unity operates on the inside. Rule implies force, unity implies love. The one is external and photographic, the other internal and organic. One is death, the other life.

"Young people, rigidity of thought has brought civilization to its present pass. In our time the institution is supreme. The spiritual is ignored. Not until mankind realizes that life is a spiritual process and has truth for its goal, will real progress come about. When truth becomes our goal there will be no further use for rules or courts or sheriffs. The absolutely orderly is the absolutely necessary. The truth of order and necessity is freedom. And this is the begriff. Four is in itself four. It is not possible to influence a four. It is what it is absolutely in itself and this is ultimate freedom, the ultimate negation of all outside influence, the capacity to be itself within itself."

Though this excursion into the metaphysical floored me for a moment I soon came back, and in my old didactic hip-and-thigh manner.

"Professor," said I, "it seems to me you are chasing myths and shadows. Did you bring that transcendentalism with you from Harvard?"

"No," said the old philosopher very sadly and after a pause and a longing gaze out of the window. "Not from Harvard. Socrates taught me—Jesus taught me. 'The Father and I are one,' is my guide."

The Good Teacher then went on to explain that he was a student at Harvard in the late 1880's. At that time Everett was transplanting the *Verstand* from England to New England. "The idea thrilled me—the substitution of thought for emotion. My duty was plain. I must transpose the *Verstand* from New England to the South. Not an easy task. On all sides there were obstacles: Preachers who condemned free speech and the pursuit of truth, scientists who denied that there is such a thing as truth."

"Mr. Kerr, what do you say, is law a rule?"

"Well, Professor, that's what I was taught in the law school."

"Mr. Fuller, you come of a legal family. What's your idea?"

"Really, Professor, your views are so revolutionary and different I'll have to think it over."

"Professor," I said one day, "When we have formed a concept how do we know it's a true one?"

Pausing for a few seconds, and quietly looking the class over, Horace softly replied, "Judge, when you had read all the books about Andrew Johnson, talked with dozens who knew him, visited his birthplace, gathered the facts, analyzed them, synthesized them and drawn a conclusion and put it in your book, did you have any doubt that you had a concept?" Of course the class snickered and I subsided; how could I go back on my own concept?

Hours such as these greatly pleased Old Horace. His delight was in questions and answers, and the rougher the better. In his walk home, in company with young Porter, he would remark that it had not been a bad morning. "I seem to have kindled a thought in the minds of the students."

"Yes, Professor," Porter replied, "and you certainly left that old Judge out on a limb."

"No, Mr. Porter, not according to the law books. Why, until I taught Judge Parker and Judge Stacy otherwise, they had an idea that law is a rule. Now they know better."

A few days after this interesting experience I wrote Justice Stacy and gave him a humorous account of what had happened. In a short while the Judge replied. He said that Henry Horace Williams was an enigma to some, a great teacher to others, and his definition of law might furnish a cue to this division of opinion. "Law is unity in action difference," Old Horace would say, "and to those who are not willing to dig for the meaning of this definition it is meaningless. To others, it represents a workman in the thought-world striving for the real, reaching for the thoughts of the Infinite. It is close akin to Tennyson's 'Flower in the Crannied Wall.'"

This letter of Stacy's greatly influenced me, since I was one of those striving for the real and reaching for the thoughts of the Infinite. And Old Horace was beginning to let in the light. Of the brilliant Madame de Staël it was said that she had more heat than light. Such, I confess, had been my case. But now, under Old Horace, my mental attitude was undergoing a change. He was affecting me in the same way that Voltaire was affected by Spinoza. I was finding that which stilled the emotions. A wider and freer prospect over the physical and moral world disclosed itself before me. So new and entrancing was my experience that I looked eagerly forward to the next philosophy hour. I was beginning to see the unity of life: its totality, and myself a necessary part of the whole. My own place in the truth-process was beginning to appear.

"The individual," as the Good Teacher would say, "sees himself in the process of reality. At one end of this process is the individual and at the other end the Eternal One. Each is the complement of the other. The individual is the process that finds itself in the begriff." The individual is the infinite embodied in the finite to be developed and returned again to the source of energy. There is no individual apart from God.

Types go down in the struggle. The mastodon is gone. Ancient Greece is gone. The sixteen-to-one type went into the hands of a receiver. The H_2O type dissipates into a formula of motion which yields to the biologist's formula of life. In other words, there is an organizing principle, a force in the type that commands the organization. The H and O could not do anything if the force were not there to bring and keep them together in the H_2O compact. Man is not the product of environment; this the objects in nature tell us. The environment of rain and sunshine comes in on a grain of wheat, but that grain acts on its own environment, assimilating it to itself. There is something in the wheat more than grain and environment. Reciprocity takes the place of environment.

The real individual is a power in his community. He lifts his fellows up to his own level. Once only in history has the perfect man arrived. He was the Eternal Logos. He did not write a logic; he did not unfold the life of the mind in conscious thought-forms. He did more than this. He lived logic. He was the Logos, the spirit of truth, goodness, and beauty.

The effect upon me of such a novel discourse was far-reaching. I was exalted from earth to sky. I was delocalized, though intensely local. I had become dialectic. In the words of Paul Green, Old Horace had implanted a great idea, the glory and dignity of being an individual. I was becoming part of a continuous process whose end and goal is truth. I began to understand what St. Chrysostom meant when he declared that the true Shekinah is Man. My mental befogginess was giving place to orderly thought. I was learning to arrange my mental process. I was catching a glimpse of Old Horace's begriff. I was striving to generalize and to draw conclusions.

Never again would I go off at half-cock. I would follow through to the very bottom of things. Unity, totality, these should be my goal. The whole, not a part, the circle, not a segment of the circle. The dialectic process my method of approach. As lecture followed lecture the idea of unity deepened and broadened. From the concept of law the Good Teacher advanced into the domain of truth. If law is unity in action difference, truth is more profound. It is unity in structure difference.

"The unity of life no one has ever seen as clearly as did Paul. 'God is before all things,' says Paul, 'and in and through Him the universe is one harmonious whole.'"

Since truth is fundamental it is absolute. It transcends the particular. The mystery of life is the ability of the finite to transcend itself. The scholar invites the individual into life, which is the synthesis in the individual, as individual, of all the values in the process of reality. The scholar challenges the individual to an infinite existence in the process of absolute values.

Thoughts and ideas of this exalted and stimulating character were daily put forth by the Good Teacher, in a manner and a voice impressive beyond words. And not one important utterance escaped me and my appreciative notebook. In a short time it came about that I caught on to the meaning of *Sein* and *Wesen* and *Begriff*, and synthesis, integration, coöperation, coördination.

At the conclusion of such a lecture I would wander through the lonely woods and commune with myself, and as I reflected upon the past so self-centered, so earth-bound, so ignorant of real values, I could scarcely realize the change which the Good Teacher's words had wrought. It pleased me to quote a line which I had recently read, "Why so hot, little man, why so hot?"

I sat down and wrote out my thoughts and published them in the leading magazines of the country. I was determined to tell the world. To my notebook I likewise confided my reflections. I wrote that I had been a ship without a rudder, floating aimlessly upon an uncharted sea of thought.

What then precisely did the Good Teacher teach me? The answer is this: He taught me how to think, to think in terms of the infinite and the universal. He gave me a kit of tools. He glorified the concept. He extended my reach. He would have me hitch my wagon to a star. Unity was his battle cry. Truth, goodness, beauty his shibboleth. Perfection his goal.

He did not endeavor to put me into moulds, or into a strait jacket. In matters of politics or religion his boys might do as they pleased. Just as he formed his own concepts so the boys must form their concepts. It concerned him not a whit whether his boys became teachers, or preachers or lawyers or whether in politics they turned to the left or the right or the center. His job was to furnish a kit of tools, his pupils must do the rest.

In this cosmopolitan atmosphere, and under this intensive thought-process, I came to think upon Old Horace somewhat as Kittredge did upon Shakespeare. I considered him universal in thought and full of antinomies. I realized that he absorbed types and formulas. His was not accuracy but principle, not the particular but the universal—the absolute with no exceptions. I concluded that his vision was by no means narrow. He was striving to create universal individuals, leaders, such as Moses and Socrates and, through these leaders, to develop an educated citizenry and a broadly religious people.

Undoubtedly his aim was to restore the spiritual to its old place in the hearts of men. To this end, as it seemed to me, he had in mind not only his classroom but the misguided multitudes, not today but tomorrow. Not time but eternity. Had the old philosopher been able to put across to the nations his consuming idea of the thought-process who shall say that he might not have revolutionized the world?

It is to be regretted that Williams, in old age, undertook to become an author. His effort was a failure. He had not trained himself to write. He had ignored Aristotle's Rules of Rhetoric. His pen was clumsy. His three books, which he called *The Evolution of Logic, Modern Logic*, and

The Education of Horace Williams, were wretchedly "massed." There were no chapter headings, no table of contents or index, and few paragraphs. As a writer the old philosopher seemed to be under a constant strain and ill at ease. There was lacking that free and fearless expression of his own idioms which had delighted his classes. These defects Paul Green and I pointed out when he handed us the manuscripts to correct. We urged him to permit us to lick them into shape. "No!" the Old Fellow proudly growled. "They must stand as written."

This must be said, however. Nowhere does the writer recant or apologize; he is as bold, original, and unorthodox as in the classroom. Whether as author or teacher he continued to blame the evils of our day on half-baked thinking.

The Peace Conference of 1919 he contrasted with the Peace of Westphalia which brought new life into Europe. "These delegates at Paris were assembled to take counsel and report a remedy. Yet the only concern of the American delegates seemed to be that nothing must be done to affect the price of cotton. As to the French economist he could see nothing but the interest of France. The same was true of the English representative. Our own Congress had been as dumb as oysters before this biggest of modern problems. They had not been grounded in the principles of social process. As to Clemenceau he is a high grade crook."

Though Professor Williams' autobiography was widely read and brought about a correspondence with McDonald, Ray of Texas, Canada, the Harpers, Parkers, Robinses, Rosses, and many others, it must be conceded that Williams, the author, was not in a class with Williams, the teacher. In the preparation of his books he had neither analysed nor synthesized. Nor had he formed a begriff!

There is another view of Old Horace's obscure, puzzling books. As Curtis Bynum conjectured, they may have been intended as a huge joke! Old Horace was kidding the public as he did the boys in the classroom.

27

A LOVE LETTER

ONE EVENING, at about the hour of nine, a student called on Professor Williams. He found his old teacher alone, engaged in a game of solitaire. Not another human being was in sight. The rambling, ghost-like house was empty, neither man nor woman, cat nor dog, was to be seen. The spectacle was significant. At a glance it was obvious that the sole occupant was lonely, desperately lonely. Yet this predicament was not to be wondered at. For the better part of life he had held the world at arm's length. Philosophy, not friendship, he had wooed. The mind, and not the emotions, he had cultivated. He had given everything to his profession.

And now his life was almost spent. He was approaching the ripe age of seventy. Was he so far gone in years that he could not retrace his steps, repair the damage, renew his youth, and have another fling with a more human approach? He thought not. There were difficulties, of course. He recalled the unsuccessful attempt of Monckton Milnes to rejuvenate himself, and his failure—how this international statesman, having spent his mature years in diplomacy, to the neglect of the humanities, had striven in old age to humanize himself, and how, after failing, he had uttered a dismal note:

> *Oh the bitter thought to scan*
> *All the loneliness of man!*

Nature by magnetic laws
Circle unto circle draws,
But they only touch when met,
Never mingle—strangers yet!

Did subconscious thoughts of this kind arise to perplex the old philosopher? As he sat alone in his dwelling, did his mind revert to those neglected hours with Bertha, his dead wife—moments which he might have spent by her side but which he had given to his classroom and his boys? Occasionally he would wander across the street and call on his friends, the Coateses. One afternoon he found Gladys Coates with garden hoe in hand, busy with her flowers.

"Mrs. Coates," he said, "you mustn't do that. Don't over-exert yourself. I regret so much that I didn't look after my Bertha's health more closely."

On another occasion he spoke to Phillips Russell and told of the hard bargain which he and Bertha, in their young days, had made with Fate. "A great mistake," he said. "We should not have taken life so hard."

"Well, why did you do it, Professor?" Russell asked.

"The dread of poverty. My early days were spent amidst warring armies and shooting-gunboats. Down East, on the waters, we often went hungry. A nickel was a lot of money. A nickel meant bread and meat. Every penny had to be saved. The dread of poverty I cannot shake off."

"Professor, they say you drive hard bargains. Is it true?"

"That's life, Mr. Russell. Life is not a smooth business. I fight, but I fight square."

"Why, Professor, isn't fighting contrary to your philosophy?"

"No, it's in line with it. Struggle and conflict is the dialectic."

The loneliness which now engrossed Old Horace he determined not to endure. Neither teaching nor writing filled the gap of time. The loss of Bertha left a void which he was resolved to fill. A companion he must have. And Fate seemed most kindly disposed.

One day in his classroom, his eyes fell upon the strong, beautiful face of a young woman sitting by the side of his friend and pupil, Madge Kennette. In a moment his heart was touched. He sought an interview. The fair creature was visiting at the home of the Kennettes, just across the street from him. He gave her a luncheon and she sat at the head of the table. He and she strolled through the Tenney Circle section. They drank water from the Roaring Fountain not far away at the foot of the hill. They rode horseback together; they discussed art and English and philosophy. In tastes and dispositions they found themselves at one. In a short time he laid himself at the feet of the cultured and modest Miriam Young Bonner.

This young woman, born in Beaufort County, was descended from Colonel James Bonner, founder of the City of Washington. Her father's dearest friend, whom she called Uncle George, was Justice George H. Brown of our highest court. At the moment she was teaching English at the Woman's College in Greensboro. She had already attained many honors. At the University of California she had won her A. M. and had received the Phi Beta Kappa key. At Columbia she had been a Fellow. She had likewise taught in the schools of California.

In this choice young spirit Old Horace soon found an understanding which he needed, and in him she seemed to find a stimulation for her mental life. In a word it was love at first sight. The following epistle tells the tale.

CHAPEL HILL, N. C.
June 6th, 1923

My dear, dear Friend,

I have read your letter several times. It is just like you, splendid. You desire to do the wise thing. Your point of view is more comprehensive than mine and equally sound. I think you are very, very lovely. It is true as you say that we have seen little of each other. This applies to you and I am prepared to be patient. My mind works swiftly in the matter of the individual. You know I taught psychology several years. And all the emphasis was placed upon the human rather than the animal side of us. I became almost uncanny in seeing the kind of edition a boy was.

You attracted me the moment you took your seat in my lecture room. Then I sought a short interview with you in the auto in front of Mrs. Henry's. Then do you recall being placed at the head of the table? I am satisfied. The only doubt is grounded in the fact that I am so much older than you. I do not feel the limitations of age, but the almanac says the age is there. I have taken good care of myself, the only excess ever permitted is that of study. At Yale I broke and had to loaf a year. I ride a horse half a day without fatigue or walk half a day.

I should like to win your complete devotion. And then I should want to hold it. One cannot control age and each stage of life has its own forms of expression. An old horse simply cannot go with a young horse and when forced to do it generally balks or kicks. In either case failing to be as fine a horse as it should be. This is your question. It would destroy me in hope and ambition if I found it beyond me to make you happy—and that through no fault of either of us. My hope is that your real interest is intellectual, and the intellectual is not a matter of age. It is the social and physical that are dominated by age. The social has always criticized me.

I have not been spared since a boy. They do not approve of me. Several years ago I sat at dinner in the Greensboro Hotel and heard myself annihilated by two strangers. It was very interesting. I waited until my dinner was ended and they had made an end of me. Then I simply introduced myself as the corpse. Then it was my heresy. Now it is my social irregularities. I have done nothing in secret and do not intend to do anything below my standard. I had a lovely home and a companion that inspired all that was fine in me and never failed me. We were lovers to the end. The last year was the best year. The loneliness this Winter has been terrible.

I do not like old people. All my friends are young people. I have sought relief among them and they have been very kind. A few days ago a little girl about four, one of my many friends, saw me and with a squeal left her mother and ran to me throwing her arms about my neck. It was beautiful to me. I look to the young people for companionship.

The work must go on. The book must be completed. I must have one companion else my home is gone. Among them all you stand out. I will love you utterly if you will say that I can satisfy you, can make you happy. I am asked to go to Charlotte for an address Monday after our Commencement. This will be the 18th. I should like to stop in Greensboro and see you. Would Saturday night and Sunday be too much? I made the address at the High School Monday evening. It went fairly well. Then two finals yesterday and another Friday. My sister comes Saturday to see her son graduate. He is president of the Phi Beta Kappa. She is a lovely sister, a graduate of N. C. C. W. and very wonderful. I wish you and she knew each other. I think I met Judge Brown when we gave him LL.D. I know Mrs. Shepherd quite well. Her son Brown was a prize student of mine. His wife and I exchange letters occasionally.

I am glad you are to be in Asheville this summer. It is interesting. My plans are about completed to go to North Conway, N. H., for the summer with two of my old boys. I must work all summer on the Logic. But as soon as I read of your plans, I lost my interest in the White Mountains. Asheville seemed to be far the better place. How fine it would be to tell you in the evening all I had worked out during the morning. This is a long letter. The only excuse I can offer is that I love you and it is such pleasure to talk with you even under these limits. May I not sign myself,

Lovingly yours,
Horace Williams

P. S. Miss Madge has won a $60.00 prize in Philosophy and Mr. Greenwood a fellowship of $700.00 next year.

H. H. W.

When Horace Williams and Miriam Bonner met for the first time he was sixty-five and she barely twenty-seven. A rare friendship was in the making. In a short time she began to feel a deep affection—that of a daughter for a congenial, sympathetic father. When marriage was proposed, however, the disparity in age, which Old Horace in homely phrase had likened to an old horse and a young horse hitched up together, proved a hurdle at which the young horse balked.

But the friendship continued. Scores of letters passed; interviews took place. Thus did matters remain for the three years while she taught at a Greensboro college. Finally in the early part of 1927 she went to London to perfect herself in philosophy, history, literature, and economics.

The following summer Professor Williams joined her in London, where he made the discovery that his suit was hopeless. Nor could it have been otherwise. Though the two were devotees of philosophy they were as opposite as the poles: she a practical worker in the ranks of the poor, he a theorist immersed in concepts and begriffe. But the old philosopher could not bear the thought of losing the agreeable young woman. He therefore proposed to adopt her as his daughter and sole heir. She consented, subject to the approval of her mother, then living in California. To Horace's delight, Mrs. Bonner approved. Thereupon Old Horace expressed appreciation in noble words.

GRASMERE
England
Aug. 28–27

My dear Mrs. Bonner,

I wish to thank you for letting me have Miriam as my daughter. She brings light and joy into my life. She will not love you the less. I was very lonely, she makes me fully happy. Her companionship leaves nothing to be desired. I count myself most fortunate. She will contribute in many ways to my work.

I think the conditions at Chapel Hill will be friendly to her tastes. She will have leisure, her own study, a stimulating atmosphere, an adequate library, a saddle horse to take her out into the woods as often as she wishes, and a kindred spirit who rejoices in her happiness.

With all good wishes, I am,

Cordially yours,
Horace Williams

Williams proceeded with adoption papers. He wrote a letter of adoption, signed by President Chase and Dr. Bell of the University, both of them then in London. After a few weeks there Horace and Miriam travelled through England and Scotland, and then took ship for America. In New York proper papers were issued under the direction of Gordon Battle, a Chapel Hill alumnus, a lawyer of international fame and a friend and former pupil of Old Horace. In a few days Williams and his adopted daughter arrived in Chapel Hill and took possession of the old dwelling which had been his home for a third of a century.

The arrangement was not a success. It was a failure. Some people arched their eyebrows, others scoffed. A few were sympathetic. The Cobbs, Kennettes, Henrys, Lawsons, Adam Kluttzes and a few others called or invited the new daughter to their homes. The Williamses gave a formal dinner. Dr. Katherine Gilbert, the Henrys, Parson Moss, Madge Kennette, Robert Williams were present. I was also of the party. There were several vacant chairs. The atmosphere around the table was far from cordial. It was manifest that we were pulling up-stream. Lovely little Chapel Hill had taken on a spasm of righteousness—most unusual in a community usually so liberal and free of unjust suspicions. Whether it was real or a cover for long-cherished dislikes for the lonely, eccentric, desiccated old professor, will never be known until the Judgment Books are unrolled.

Merciful heavens! As well suspect Peter the Hermit!

Shortly afterwards Williams was stricken with pneumonia. His faithful adopted daughter and a trained nurse aided him to recover. Thereupon I called. The daughter and I sat side by side on the antiquated sofa. Just as I was about to take my leave she turned and said to me in a low, sad voice, "I am going back to California."

"Not for good?" I protested.

"Yes, for good."

In a few days she was gone, never to return. She spent the next ten or twelve years teaching in New Jersey, New York, California, and North Carolina. Her work was among the poor and the Women Workers in Industry, to which she devoted herself to the exclusion of society or other matters.

The departure of his daughter shook Professor Williams from center to circumference. He was broken-hearted. Out of the depths he wrote and begged her to come back and brighten his lonely home.

Dearest Miriam,

Thank you for the letter of the twenty-third. It is one of your fine letters. You have a strange power to make me happy. There are elements in it that are new. I have had two ultimate relations in life. One was with my Mother. One was with my wife. Now this one with you. I suppose if I had children the relation would not be new. There is in this relation something that is both real and fine. Hence I am unable to give it indifference. The prospect of your struggling for five or ten years, then—the picture frightens me. Clearly I did not do my duty by my daughter! Then Miriam Dear I love you, not your body. I love your spirit, your individuality, that which is you. My admiration for you does not suffer.

In all these hard, cruel days I know you are groping for the way forward along lines that are true and beautiful.

From the beginning we have sought that line. For me there is a large list of beautiful experiences. We lived steadily weeks and weeks. There was not the jar of a word. I do not know of two people who had a more intelligent or a more beautiful summer in Europe. That summer does not lose with time. Then came a new step. It was new for us; it was new for society. For six months we were under fire; fire from each other; fire from society. So far no one has cited a single error. You and I know that we kept the faith. We thought we could. At times it was hard. To climb a high mountain is always difficult and dangerous. We did it. The rough places are mastered and behind us. Today you are dearer to me than you have ever been. The physical is mastered; it is your beautiful self, your nobility of mind, your steadfast passion for things that are right that I love.

How our future shall shape itself I do not know. So far I have given no heed to the evil-minded. I owe them no good thing. They have said all manner of harsh things. Last week I heard of a student at Duke who wanted to come here; his father refused on the ground that at Chapel Hill there was that atheist, Horace Williams. In our case it seems that the criticism is directed at you. I do not believe it has in mind any good to you, to me, or to society. Hence I am not interested in it. When we have finished our plan they will be equally loud in praise. So lets forget that. Lets do the thing that is best for you. There is a place for sacrifice. If it is best for you that we sacrifice all our companionship I must submit. It was something of this kind that made Jesus exclaim, My God, Why hast thou forsaken me? What good will it do you to deny yourself the happiness of a beautiful companionship? I do not know. I thrilled at the sentence in your letter, "I am not afraid." Fear springs out of unsound conditions. I have been waiting for that sentence.

Fear is back-wash that clogs any machine. Intelligence does not move serenely in muddy fears. Twice you said, "I am not afraid." I rejoice in both sentences. We have had so much; it was so beautiful. I can see no good in retreat. I can see many disadvantages. Was it for nothing that we loved, planned, hesitated, tested every way? For six years we did our best. Is the outcome of that conscientiousness to be only harm to you? God forbid. Now there is no answer to the critic. He can say, Yes, you knew you would be exposed. I do not believe any woman has been more high minded than you in this experience. You have my entire admiration. It tore my heart to see you suffer in London and in the pain my admiration blazed. You have gone steadily as you could see the path of right. It is not just that you should suffer for such action.

I went to Duke Thursday evening and talked on Logic to the Math Club. Mr. Rankin said it went over one hundred per cent. I enjoyed it keenly. Now Dr. Emery and I are going for tea with the Gilberts. Her Mother, Father, and Sister are with her. They all came to hear me in Duke. I thought it was nice. If you were here what a fine visit we should have.

Monday Morning

The visit was agreeable. The Father is strong and simple. We had cocoa, crackers, salad, cake, peanuts. We returned at nine. I wondered what you would think of Dr. Emery. The heater is working well. It makes the hall, dining room, and your room comfortable. The stove in the study seems necessary. The radio is entertaining. I think you will enjoy it. But Miriam Dear there are no substitutes for you. I miss you dreadfully. Please love me. I need it.

Faithfully yours,
Father Horace

What did Horace mean by the expression, "We have been under fire from each other?" The answer has been given by Miriam Bonner herself. "If we had been following the same interests," she wrote me, after she had returned to California, "if we had been studying the same subjects, if we had been trying to understand the same problems there would have been no conflict, but my year in Europe had made it imperative for me to study and learn new and different things, things of no concern to him. In Chapel Hill I led his life, but if I were not to be miserable I had to live my own—and so I went away. This was a blow to him, far more painful than my not marrying him. He begged me to accept help from him, he wished to send me to any university or to Europe. At times I felt I could accept his offer and go off and write something which would give him a feeling of pride. But then I reflected that I would not be free. I would be under the necessity of pleasing him."

Actuated by these unselfish motives Miriam Bonner left the home of her adopted father and returned to California. The correspondence between them continued unabated. It was of the most affectionate character. He wished to bestow gifts upon her; she refused. She proposed to make her own way in life. After a few strenuous years at the Bryn Mawr Summer School for Women Workers in Industry, she had a nervous breakdown. Her adopted father furnished her with funds and wrote, "The feature of this holiday is that you are almost yourself, ready to challenge life once more."

During a period of ten years he sent her monthly checks. After about ten years she married. When she wrote her adopted father of the intended marriage he replied, "Tell your husband if he will be appreciative, gentle, and affectionate, then no man in all California will have a more companionable helpmate."

In the course of nature a child was born. "I hope it will be a boy and very much like its mother," Old Horace wrote. When she informed him of the little fellow's satisfactory development, he replied, "With such a mother he has the right to be unusual. It is a theory of mine that every great man begins with a great mother."

Despite this philosophical episode the old philosopher went steadily ahead with his task, but there was a lack of the dash and spirit of former days. Shortly after Hoover had been elected President, John M. Mecklin, a learned professor of sociology at Dartmouth, came to Chapel Hill and asked me to aid him in sitting in on Professor Williams' classes. He humorously declared that he was anxious to learn why his orthodox mother and sister, Alabama Democrats true and tried, had voted the Republican ticket. He had been told that no one but the logical, dialectical Williams could explain the phenomenon.

In the class that day the subject under discussion happened to be how to connect the Finite and the Infinite. To my surprise and sorrow Old Horace boldly asserted that the answer was to be found in algebra. The transition from time to eternity is algebraic, identical with the transition from arithmetic to algebra. I was amazed and anxious to extricate the aged man, now more than seventy, from his false position.

"Professor," said I, "that illustration is but a rough analogy, of course?"

"No," he gravely rejoined. "Not an analogy. Algebra is self-generating, continuous, a thing-in-itself." Nor would the old man modify this statement in any respect.

Otherwise there was no change in his life and habits. Though there were premonitions of heart trouble, and a severe attack of hernia, he uttered no complaint. When he wandered down the streets of Chapel Hill or through the campus he held his head as high as in his best days. Correspondence with his old boys increased. Summer vacations were spent at Nantucket or elsewhere in New England. The loneliness of his home was somewhat overcome by the presence of Hood, a young, congenial philosophy student with whom he would discuss the recitation work, current events, and village gossip. When a philosophy club, embracing Duke University, Wake Forest, State College, and other institutions, was organized, he was chosen president. He continued to be a stout advocate of the honor system and the inspiration of the distinguished order of the Golden Fleece.

A life-size portrait of him, executed by Mary Graves,

daughter of his old math teacher, was presented to the University by grateful Horatians. His birthdays were still State news. Banquets were as frequent as of old. At one banquet a ludicrous mistake occurred. The event was celebrated in April, though his birthday was in August. In a newspaper report by Bob Madry the mistaken date was cracked up and the reporter wondered if it would be corrected in August. At this banquet Parson Moss presided. Judge Parker and Chief Justice Stacy spoke. President Chase, Dr. Connor, and Carter Dalton added their presence. I, too, was in attendance. Dr. Ross raised a laugh when he lauded Old Horace's *Evolution of Logic*—"Too deep for me, but a good sedative."

The old philosopher was frequently interviewed and his original views sought after. He addressed schools and colleges and spoke before Alumni Associations. Preachers and ambitious men and women continued to attend his classes. So greatly did he impress one brilliant young minister that he often attended seminars in the old philosopher's home.

One Sunday morning this preacher, indoctrinated with Horace's profound thought-process, entered the pulpit and proclaimed that there had been only three great teachers, Jesus Christ, Socrates, and Horace Williams. Whereupon the good women of the church rose in their ecclesiastical wrath, and rebuked the rash speaker, but did not change his mind.

Rev. C. Excelle Rozelle, an earnest seeker after truth, was swept along by Horace's philosophy though he did not accept his Universalist views. The impress of Horace Williams upon the mind and conscience of Rozelle was not only marked but characteristic of others who came under his influence.

Speaking of the old philosopher, Rozelle proclaimed him a teacher superb—molder of more and greater men than any other southern college professor—builder of brains, a dynamo who supercharged thousands of students with new life and with finest ideas—encourager of individual thinking

—hater of modern social and psychological claims—opponent of materialistic philosophies, wrecker of superficial thinking—bitter foe of Atheism yet called by many an Atheist, a mighty stimulus, but a poor guide in details, apparently cold and unfeeling yet sympathetic with all earnest seekers after truth—possessing a soft sarcasm that always cut like a razor's edge—critic of every one, both friend and foe yet meaning only the best—seldom leaving an ache or a scar—on the surface seemingly flippant and cynical but always as unmoving in position as the Pole Star, an exponent of the old verities in faith and experience, yet keeping up with and abreast with all the new-fangled knowledge, and despising it with all his soul—caring little for outward appearances—quiet, modest, cold, unfeeling, yet on fire with white heat for truth—always truth.

Though this tribute is a trifle overwrought it is not greatly out of line with the estimate which his boys, on and off the Hill, entertained. Commenting on an address which Horace delivered before a graduating class and called "Citizens in the Kingdom of Truth," the *Carolina Magazine* sounded a similar note. "A molder of thought. A maker of men. An interpreter of Carolina," declared the *Magazine*. "These are the attributes of Henry Horace Williams, Professor of Philosophy. No man has done more for the spirit of the University than he. No man who leaves Carolina can get the full breadth and spirit of what this institution means if he fails to hear Professor Williams interpret the meaning of the University and its relation to the individual."

28

THE UNIVERSITY UNDER THREE PRESIDENTS

IT IS SIGNIFICANT that during the fruitful period of the past thirty years two of the University's presidents, Ed Graham and Frank Graham, were Horace Williams' pupils, and Harry Chase, the third, an associate with him in the faculty. Beginning about the year 1913 and not yet ending, the growth of the University has been phenomenal.

During these momentous years the faculty has been more than doubled in numbers, the enrollment has increased from one thousand to more than four thousand, the maintenance fund from two million to nearly four million. More than six million dollars has been invested in permanent improvements —a percentage of growth not excelled, perhaps not equalled, by any other institution in America, save by our neighbor and friend, Duke University. But it is not of this physical development I would speak; it is rather of the spiritual, that subtle, all-pervading influence without which no physical growth could have come about.

The love of Horace Williams for his Alma Mater was deep and enduring. In the dedication of his autobiography to its Trustees he acknowledged his debt of gratitude. Though they were often tempted to fire him, he said, they stood firm. "For twenty-five years I was the center of a storm. . . . But we all loved the University. The battle was won and not a heresy trial."

When Horace Williams made this confident claim he was

seventy-eight years of age. What battle had he won, what victory had he in mind? Was it a triumph of industry or the sciences or the classics? By no means. It was a deeper triumph, a victory in the wider field of thought. It was the spade-work necessary to progress and development. And though it was iconoclastic it was also constructive. As Horace imagined, he had succeeded in shaving Old Shaggypate! He and his boys, now three or four thousand strong, were eradicating harmful orthodoxy. They had changed the mores of the people. They had broadened and liberalized the concept of religion and of politics. They were also overcoming sectional and racial prejudices. They had done for the people at large what the old philosopher had done for me in his classroom, taught them to think, to take nothing for granted. He had given them a kit of tools, opened up a broader vision, made them citizens of world-thought, lifted them out of themselves, and brought the periphery to the center.

And this great work, as Old Horace concluded, was not only coincident with the administration of three University presidents, indoctrinated with his thought-process, but it was largely due to their influence. In this conclusion was the old philosopher correct? Do the last thirty years register the high water mark of intellectual freedom and progress in the University and in the State? If so, did he and his boys play an important part in bringing about the change?

In the early 1890's when Horace Williams arrived in Chapel Hill and began his task of liberating human thought he had no complaint to make of the sciences or the classics, in themselves. And as for his associates then and later, who conducted those classes, he criticized but held them in high esteem. He realized that they were unexcelled in any southern college. He was proud of the labors of Odum and Vance in sociology, Carroll in commerce, Branson and Hobbs in rural economics, Coker in botany, Henderson in mathematics, MacNider in medicine. He appreciated the fact that many of the University departments had gained national recognition: the Graduate School under Greenlaw, Royster, and Pearson; the Playmakers under Koch; the Extension Department under Grumman; the University Press under Couch; the Department of Chemistry under Venable; Historical Research by Hamilton, Connor, and Newsome; Library Science under L. R. Wilson and his associates; the writings of Paul Green and Phillips Russell; the School of Journalism under Louis Graves, Gerald Johnson, and Oscar Coffin. Likewise the thoroughness of the departments of law, medicine, arts and sciences, modern and ancient languages, geology, zoology, psychology, English, the School of Pharmacy, and the admirable administration set-up.

These important facts he realized and appreciated. No one of the departments would he have changed. They were as good as the best and this he knew. But his task was different from theirs. And vaster. They could reach a handful of students only; they could not go out to the people and change their thought-processes. Their subjects were limited, his were not; theirs technical, his liberal. They dealt with the particular, he with the universal. He was concerned with principle, they with incidentals. They were not trying to shave Old Shaggypate. He was—a gargantuan task, I grant.

His was the job of uprooting the fixed, well-set habits, customs and manners of an old, well-established civilization. A home-loving, self-satisfied people must be shocked out of complacency and beguiled into dealing wisely with the complexities of modern life. Religious over-zeal, race hatreds, caste distinctions, narrowness of thought, group-mindedness, these attributes of the descendants of a proud, slave-holding people must be changed, must give place to their opposites. That this great change in the life of the University and of the people occurred at about the turn of the century needs no citation of authority to prove. The census tables speak.

The necessity for an enlightened public opinion as a prerequisite to genuine progress seems likewise too plain to need discussion. In a Republic public opinion rules. In a Republic the people are supreme; they make and unmake. The President, Congress, and the Courts bow before the popular will. Without public opinion laws and statutes, decisions of courts and presidential ukases are as sounding brass and tinkling cymbals.

Solon being asked if the laws he had given to the people were the best replied, "I have given them the best they were able to bear."

Since a change in public opinion was necessary before the liberation of thought was possible, it may be asked what connection was there between Horace Williams' teaching and this transformation. What was it that so suddenly altered the thought-process of the people, exalting them from rigidity and fixedness of mind to placidity and the universal. Why were conservative, debt-despising North Carolinians willing, yes eager, to burden themselves with taxes, to issue millions of dollars of bonds and other obligations to provide schools and free textbooks, highways and hospitals? Why did the State cease to be provincial and become cosmopolitan? What caused Old Rip to wake up from his slumbers?

Undoubtedly time was a factor, an important element. So were frequent communications and business relations between North and South and the going of southern boys to Harvard and Princeton and the coming of northern boys to southern colleges. Northern capital invested in southern industries might be mentioned, and also the unifying influence of the World War. Yet these agencies existed in other southern states where they seemed to be less potent for good than in North Carolina. Why was this? I must conclude that there were other causes than those set out which account for the progress and development of the University and the Old North State.

Is it claiming too much for Horace Williams and his three or four thousand boys, active, rejuvenated, logical and patriotic, to say that they played an important part, almost controlling, in changing the mores of North Carolina and in advancing her progress? That Old Horace was the immediate cause of this transformation no one would claim. That he was the mediate cause no one should deny: The liberator of the thought of a people is a Columbus, the discoverer of a new world.

Admittedly there are other southern colleges which equal Carolina in the Arts and Sciences, in scholarship and in research. But which one of them is Carolina's peer in a breadth of freedom, in liberality of thought, and in genuine progress? Since the turn of the century which southern State, indeed, excels our ancient Commonwealth, but lately so backward, so unassuming and so modest that my brilliant college mate, Edwin Alderman, has characterized her as that Valley of Humility between two Mountains of Conceit—a State now wide-awake, educational-minded, humming with industry, traversed by good roads which make it possible for artist and nature-lover and traveller to gaze upon verdant, cloud-piercing Mitchell or listen to the roar of ocean-waves dashing against the strands of treacherous Hatteras, or wander through the inspiring campus of our ancient University, with its homelike, domestic atmosphere, or enjoy the beauty and artistry of Duke, or feel the practical, uplifting influence of Wake Forest and Davidson, or admire the commodious, well-equipped free public school buildings dotting a thousand hills of the Piedmont?

In a recent volume of the *Dictionary of American Biography* there is a thoughtful sketch of Edward Kidder Graham. Its author, Louis Wilson, makes an interesting statement: "In Graham's stimulating chapel talks," Wilson writes, "he developed his conceptions of student conduct on what has been characterized as the most democratic, self-governing campus in America." High praise from a high source! But broad and sweeping as the statement is, no North Carolinian questions its accuracy. Nor will anyone who is acquainted with the part Horace Williams played in molding the mind of young Graham be in doubt as to the source of his inspiration. The very term, self-governing campus, is in truth but Old Horace's dream, his labors, and his very words.

Unquestionably there will be those who will deny the influence of Old Horace upon Ed Graham. Some will shake their heads in protest, and likewise others who are classicists or materialists or innocent, uninformed religionists, or scholars and scientists, who resent Old Horace's sweeping claim that his logical process is the gateway, and the only gateway, to wisdom. These good people will dissent from the claim that the Philosophy Department of Chapel Hill changed the thought-process of the people and will say that philosophy is but the dead bones in the valley before breathed upon by the Prophet. But even those who deny Old Horace's potent influence must admit his transcendence as a Teacher.*

"Bob," said I to Robert Connor, first United States Archivist, and the son of a very dear friend of mine, "what do you think of Old Horace?"

"He was a bad citizen."

"That's interesting. Give me a bill of particulars."

"Why he never coöperated. He was a kicker."

"So you are against him, eh?"

"Oh no! You may put me down as saying this, Horace was a damn good teacher."

My eldest son, now a Chicago lawyer, and at one time a student under Horace but a classicist and, therefore, rather impervious to dialecticism, once said to me,

"Why, father, Old Horace did nothing unusual. He simply brought down in advance the thoughts of Emerson and Channing. In thirty or forty years they would have come anyhow."

"Did Old Horace do all that?" I teasingly replied. "Wonderful!"

"Yes," came back the answer, "we had been beating up one egg in a dish with a kitchen fork. Horace brought down a little gadget to beat up a dozen eggs at a time, that's all."

* The influence of Horace Williams upon his boys may be illustrated by a remark made to Charlie Tillett by Ed Graham, who said that "if it had not been for the stimulating presence of Professor Williams at Chapel Hill he would never have been willing to have stayed at the University."—Letter to author.

"More wonderful still," I rejoined. "What other individual has moved North Carolina that far forward?"

An estimate of Old Horace by Curtis Bynum, a former pupil, seems to me to be nearer the mark. According to Bynum, in those pioneer days North Carolinians were Fundamentalists, soaked in scholasticism. Then came Old Horace with his psychology, philosophy, metaphysics and the rest and was the embodiment of new thought. His philosophy was revolutionary, bold heresy. "It thrilled us, he was the heresiarch. In those days we southern boys had no notion which way to turn for life's work. We were desperately lonesome and hungry for advice and sympathetic consideration of our personal problems. Many of us thought the professor of psychology should have peculiar insight into matters mental. We went to him to be analyzed. I do not know whether Old Horace's methods were original, it makes little difference. His methods were new and interesting; he became the protagonist of our epic of philosophy and vocational guidance. One of his favorite utterances I shall never forget: 'Greatness consists in identification of one's concrete life with an ideal, with a principle.'"

The first one of Horace's boys to become president of the University was Ed Graham. While a student this remarkable lad had sat under Horace and taken all of his courses. The first term he tackled Philosophy 1, the next term Philosophy 2, and finally Philosophy 4. During these fruitful years the young student became saturated with Horace's thought-processes. The dialectic approach, analysis, synthesis, unification, the Hegelian system of reasoning, absorbed him. Early in life he began to think-things-through and to form concepts. He played with begriffe and became a fighting conciliator, a valiant unifier, a superb synthesizer. He saw both sides of a question. Passion he discarded. A thinker, he was thoroughly objective. He was immersed in Old Horace's methods of thought, though he often differed from his good teacher in his conclusions. Young Graham could not go along the entire way with Horace. He discovered faults; Achilles had a vulnerable heel. Horace was lacking in the human touch.

He should not only have taught but should have coöperated and taken a part in public affairs. Plato's idea of a Geometric God might be all right to theorize about but not to live by. God must be nearer and more personal. Nor should public opinion be flouted. Conciliation was better than ridicule or ever so much ratiocination. This fact I repeat and emphasize: Ed Graham and Horace Williams were one in their thought-processes but often differed in their conclusions. Though their methods of thought were identical, the concepts drawn from a given state of facts were often opposite—a situation which the Good Teacher would not have changed in the least. His job ended when he furnished Ed Graham with a kit of tools; thereafter the young man, as well as all other students, must do his own building, draw his own conclusions, form his own concepts, work out his own begriffe.

An important question may now arise. In what manner did Ed Graham make use of Old Horaces thought-process? An answer to this inquiry may be found in President Graham's inaugural address and in his official papers, some of which have been collected and published under the title of *Education and Citizenship*. In these writings one may find hundreds of words and phrases and ideas and illustrations which so often had enlivened and fructified Old Horace's classroom.

The idea of the unity or oneness of all things is illustrated by the vine and its branches, and by the insistence that the University and the State are one and should be a coöperative organism in the equal distribution of the good things of life. A controlling thought is that the whole value of University Extension depends upon the validity of the purity and power of the spirit of truth from whence it is derived. There is an insistence upon the coöperation of all the forces of State and University to liberate the faculties and aspirations of the people; a vision of teachers and students given wholly to the pursuit of truth. Such examples as these, by the dozens, illustrating the identity of the thought-process of Old Horace and his pupil, might be cited.

Other phrases likewise occur: Teacher and pupil must have the same unifying point of view. The source of a student's spiritual insight is a scent for reality; and such words as growth, progress, evolution, the intuitional process, constructive coöperation, truth, goodness, beauty, unification, and the like.

In the preparation of his inaugural President Graham ransacked the entire field of education. He assembled the facts, digested the facts, and then put the facts together again. In a word, he followed the advice of his good teacher. He formed a concept. He insisted upon a creative period overcoming ancient obsessions; he pinned his faith to ultimate thought and to higher levels and the supremacy of human values, to the abolition of ignorance, to life as a whole, a vital organism. At one point in the address he all but quoted Old Horace. "The line of memory and repetition," he said, "is the line of least resistance to student and teacher, as it is in the dead routine of every field of effort." Again he said that teachers and students must have a unifying point of view. Of the University he declared, "It recognizes no antagonist in this general business but ignorance. Ignorance it conceives as the unpardonable sin of democracy."

Truly did the artistic Alderman say of Ed Graham that he used his mind to think with, and, as a sort of intellectual conscience, kept it ready for instant test.

The distinctive service, therefore, which Ed Graham rendered State and University is apparent. He coördinated and unified the hostile educational forces which had so long retarded intellectual advancement. He integrated and made one the public schools, the University, and the denominational colleges. He coördinated and utilized the distinguishing traits of his four admirable predecessors in office. He possessed the kindliness of Battle, the force of Winston, the culture of Alderman, and the research of Venable. Under President Ed Kidder Graham the ancient, hurtful denominational fight waned and almost went out. The University campus became coterminous with the State's boundaries.

Ed Graham had been president but a short time when the Rev. Columbus Durham, a man of great force and a deep religious conviction which moved him to look upon the University as an agency of Hell, launched a sweeping newspaper attack. In a few days Graham replied and exhibited his method of thought. He neither ridiculed nor manifested contempt nor anger. He struck a higher note. His reply was masterful, soft, dialectic, and without passion. He thanked Dr. Durham for his publication. He was confident it was an honest inquiry, made in good faith. If the University was such as Dr. Durham thought, it should be abolished. He was satisfied that the good Doctor had been misinformed, that the University was not so bad as he had painted it. Let the facts speak: the active, voluntary, religious life of the University, the very large number of self-help students, the absence of disorder, the kindly relations of rich boys and poor boys, the democratic spirit, without caste or snobbishness, the earnest effort to create a new and a better world with equal opportunity for all.

President Graham had struck a new note in controversy. He had solved old Dr. Holmes's hydrostatic paradox of controversy! Unity, brotherly love, the Sermon on the Mount had won. Dr. Durham was convinced, he dropped the subject.

Ed Graham was succeeded by Harry W. Chase, a distinguished graduate of Dartmouth. The Chase administration proved a success. The new president, both as executive and as presiding officer, was without a superior. He could get the best work out of every department and without a particle of friction. In a word, he carried forward the policy of Ed Graham, that of conciliation, reconciliation and unification. And he had a decided advantage over his predecessors. The Alumni had been organized and were thoroughly coöperative. Fiscal aid from the State had been greatly increased.

North Carolina was now blessed with one of her bravest and most progressive governors. Cameron Morrison was not only unafraid but willing to take long chances. The Governor anticipated the coming of an early era when North Carolina would soar aloft as a young eagle. Valiantly he waged a fight for enormous bond issues, the proceeds to be used for public improvements, for public schools, and for higher education.

The momentum of Ed Graham's administration was accelerated by Chase, who was not only wedded to experimentation but to idealism as well. A man of patience, tolerance, and liberality of thought, his task was relatively an easy one. He had but to sit steady in the boat. He had but to follow Ed Graham's trail. The people needed no leader. They asked nothing except a clear path. At last the old North State was alive with energy. She was feeling her oats! Before the legislature, which was expected to vote bonds, convened to consider the matter, the University Alumni had put on a far-reaching, preliminary drive. This movement covered the State from east to west. Alumni associations were especially active.

Young Frank Graham was appointed to the job of carrying the message of the University to the body of the people. He gladly accepted the appointment. Traveling from sea to mountains, and speaking as he went, he aroused the greatest enthusiasm. When the legislature met, the public had been thoroughly awakened to the cause of education. In the Capital City the scene was set with dramatic effect. Hundreds of teachers and preachers and industrialists, together with progressive farmers and others from all parts of the State, assembled. The committee room was not large enough to hold the crowd. Over to the commodious hall of the House of Representatives they rushed. The movement went over with a bang. The bonds were authorized and issued. Millions of dollars came to Chapel Hill, doubling, trebling, quadrupling its capacity for service to the people.

Next into the presidency came young Frank Graham, late a lieutenant of marines, a rare, social-minded interpreter of history, unassuming and modest and yet valiant in the cause of the poor and needy, and conscious, to his very marrow bones, that a man's most precious property is his labor. Frank Graham had been a student of Williams and in later years an associate with him in the faculty. He was, therefore, speaking of his own knowledge when he declared that "Professor Horace Williams has been for half a century a University institution and would always be a University tradition. He stood for the integrity and freedom of the individual and always championed the freedom of the mind. Through his influence on the thought of many college generations, he was as much responsible as any other person or factor that North Carolina did not have an anti-evolution law."

"Professor Williams made more University students intellectually conscious than any other professor in the history of the University," Frank Graham once again declared. "His prize students and devoted followers, such as William D. Carmichael, Herman H. Horne, Edward K. Graham, Sidney S. Robins, Ralph Harper, William D. Moss, Otho B. Ross, John J. Parker, Ed McDonald, A. L. Ray, Walter P. Stacy, Charles W. Tillett, Kemp D. Battle, Francis E. Winslow, Gladys Avery Tillett, Henry C. Smith, Robert B. House, Adeline McCall, Francis F. Bradshaw, Paul Green, Anna F. Liddell, Thomas Wolfe, George Denny, Jane Ross Hammer and countless others caught up his communicative flame and lighted the lamps which will never go out on this campus."

Neither Frank Graham nor his cousin Ed Graham belonged to the ancient, slave-holding South. Hence they were well fitted for their liberalizing task. Unfettered by family traditions they were free to blaze a new way. They were not suspicious of new ideas. They had no disposition to act from emotion rather than thought. In their conception of duty, sentimentality and false values played little part. Their father's grandfather Graham had come over from Scotland and was a worthy representative of that land of Calvin, oatcakes, and sulphur, in truth, another Douce Davie Deans, God-fearing, honest, respected of all men, standing stoutly in his shoes, a man whose offspring have gone forth and blessed every clime.

After arriving in Fayetteville and going into business, the founder of the Graham family in North Carolina married and reared a family from which sprang several sons: one, Archibald, who lived to see his son, Ed Kidder, president of the University; another, Alex, the father of Frank.

Young Graham did not wish to become president of the University. He was content to teach history and the social aspects of history. His classroom was his delight. Students by the scores sat under him and were captivated by his friendliness, his accurate knowledge of history and his simple ways and personality. In truth, the matter of the presidency, as it was thought, had already been settled. It was generally conceded that Professor Robert D. W. Connor, a man of scholarly qualities, would be chosen. But to the gods it seemed otherwise. Old Horace's boys had broken the slate. Some months before, without his consent or knowledge, they had quietly organized, such men as Tillett, Ross, Shaw, Battle, Parker, Winslow and others and had determined to spring the name of Frank Graham upon the Trustees. And yet, according to the *Atlantic Monthly*, Graham was "to unfriendly critics a synonym of Communism or something equally horrendous, such as the New Deal!"

Presently the Trustees met. One of their number rose and stated, authoritatively, that Frank Graham would not accept the presidency if offered him. This act of renunciation sealed the young man's fate. That was the kind of president the Trustees wished. Dr. Otho Ross removed the only objection, the health of the unwilling candidate. "It is good," he declared. The Trustees would take no refusal, and so Frank Graham became the eleventh president of the University.

Dr. Ross and other Horatians were jubilant. In letters to his old teacher the doctor disclosed how he and his associates had brought about the election of their young friend, an ardent Horatian. He likewise predicted for the new administration the greatest measure of success. Old Horace replied in a like tone of rejoicing. "I agree with you," he said, "that Frank Graham has the qualities of the good teacher. He knows the process of civilization. He realizes that a beautiful life is not a dream and the perfect life can be lived. But is he physically strong? We must look after that, we must see that he rides horseback at least one hour every day." *

The people and the press were equally well pleased. The election of such a liberal evoked favorable comment. The *New York Times, The Nation, The Baltimore Sun, The Southern Review* and the press generally approved. Trustee Josephus Daniels, and other notables, ascribed the election of Graham to his winsome personality and to the flaming enthusiasm of youth. In so doing did they not overlook an important factor? Were not Frank Graham's liberality of thought and keen sense of social justice the immediate cause of his election?

But a few years previous, bloody strikes had taken place at the factories of Marion and Gastonia. In these unfortunate affairs young Graham, at that 'time president of the Conference for Social Security, had played a notable part. Conceiving the idea that the laborers had not received justice in the courts and were being railroaded to prison, he not only raised considerable sums of money to employ counsel for the friendless strikers but he wrote appealing letters to the press demanding justice for them. He likewise prepared and spread abroad a platform of principles, a chart

---

* In consequence of this letter, an alumnus came to Chapel Hill and offered to present the new president with a well-broken saddle-horse and to build stables. Frank Graham declined this gift, as he has done all others.

of human freedom, which shone like the Pole Star midst the conflicts and antagonisms of the hour.

The substance of the document was as follows,

1. All persons, regardless of race, religion or occupation have the legal right of freedom of speech and of assembling together to discuss their grievances.

2. Labor has the right, as fully as capital, to organize and bargain collectively.

3. Because of unrest and disorder in many southern mills, a nation-wide survey of the whole field of textile industry should be provided forthwith.

4. Since social adjustments lag behind industrial advance there should be a reduction in the sixty hour week, a gradual elimination of night work for women and young people and a strict enforcement of the social code as between capital and labor.

The explosion, on the part of industry, which followed, is inconceivable. "Turn out the young Radical! He is a disgrace to the University," was the cry. Letters by the dozen flooded the mail of Governor Gardner, Chairman of the Board of Trustees, all of them denunciatory. The young man's answer to these attacks, and to others because he favored free thought and free speech as taught by Old Horace, was simple and bold. "North Carolina will never shut the windows to outside light," he declared. "It will never close the book of knowledge." *

Now as to this simple charter of human rights, it must be remembered that it was promulgated several years before the birth of the New Deal and was therefore considered red, revolutionary, and horrendous. This also may be added: so much did it resemble Old Horace's teaching that it might have come from his pen. As we have seen, to Horace's mind the right of free thought, free speech, free conduct, and of labor to organize and assert itself was as clear as the noon-

---

* In the efforts of Frank Graham to aid the Gastonia and Marion strikers, Horace Williams actively coöperated. He not only agreed to the principles involved but contributed of his means to see that justice was done.

day sun. The election of Frank Graham to the presidency, in these difficult circumstances, is one of the worthiest and most notable chapters in southern history.

On November 11, 1931, Frank Graham was inaugurated. Soon after the ceremonies the new president called at the home of his good old teacher to pay his respects. The old philosopher was away on his horse. Seated at the historic table where he and associates had so often gathered, President Graham wrote these words:

CHAPEL HILL,
November 11

Dear Professor Williams,

I am sorry to find you away from home. I called to thank you and to say that when I finished my speech this morning I realized it was just your organic method.

Faithfully your old student,

Frank Graham

Beyond all doubt President Graham's liberal administration has proven the most fruitful, as well as the most popular, since the Founding Fathers sat under the Davie Poplar to lay the foundation stone of the first State university in America. The basis of this success, it must be conceded, was the idea of unity, totality, and brotherly love, as taught by Old Horace.

There are some, as I have said, who may question the statement that Horace's thought-process so permeated North Carolina as to change the people's mores. And these doubters may be correct. When one enters the philosophical field of causation he is likely to lose himself. Was not the philosopher Hume right when he denounced the search for causes, and affirmed that no one thing causes anything else? The idea of necessary causation between one thing and another is pure conjecture and is derived from impressions.

Now it would lie in the mouth of Old Horace to claim

that his teaching was the cause of a change in popular thought. He seemed to agree with Hume that causation is unknown and unknowable, a statement which may find confirmation in a little Chapel Hill story. It seems that one day Collier Cobb, the geologist, and Horace Williams, the philosopher, were strolling through Piney Prospect when the geologist stubbed his toe on a paleozoic boulder.

"Ouch!" exclaimed the geologist. "That rock has certainly caused a lot of pain."

"How do you know the rock caused the pain?" queried the philosopher.

"Why," retorted the geologist, "don't I feel the pain?"

"Haven't you felt pain in that toe on other occasions, from rheumatism or neuralgia?"

"Yes, but I saw this thing."

"No, you saw the rock and you saw the toe, but did you see the cause?"

Frank Graham had been president but a few years before his broad, humanitarian ideas and practices were recognized throughout America. He served as Chairman of the Association on Interracial Relations. The President of the United States appointed him on the National Mediation Board to adjust the disputes between labor and capital. He became Chairman of the War Emergency Board, and a member of the powerful War Labor Board.

In the management of the University he concurred with his old teacher, Horace Williams, that student government and the honor system were necessary. He espoused the principle of clean athletics, and became the author of the Graham plan to bar from sports all students except those bona-fide enrolled and without subsidization. Under his leadership the Woman's College at Greensboro and the State College at Raleigh were successfully consolidated with the University and thereby created the Greater University of North Carolina. He saved the Medical School to the University and was so well recognized abroad that the Secretary of Labor heralded him as one of the greatest Americans of all time.

President Graham was not content to advocate the idea of unity and coöperation. He must put these principles into practice. At one time when the legislature was predominantly liberal they dropped one of the University trustees, David Clark, a fighting reactionary, always out gunning for Graham, demanding his scalp, and charging him with destructive and revolutionary ideas, such as "membership on the Board of Moscow University." At a meeting of the subsequent legislature a petition was presented to replace Clark upon the Board. "What would Frank Graham do?" everyone was asking. He had Clark restored to his old position.

A few years later a New Dealer, Ralph McDonald, exponent of everything that was hateful to old-line conservatives, and a really alarming fellow, made bold to enter the race for governor against Clyde Hoey, a regular of the regulars. When McDonald took the stump and laid down principles which smacked of Tom Watson and the La Follettes he stirred the plain people to the center and caused cold shivers to run down the spinal column of the Old Guard. On election day he all but defeated the Regulars.

Frank Graham made a study of McDonald's record and concluded that he would be a useful member of the University. He could go to the people and extend its liberal principles. Sometime after McDonald's defeat the University Trustees met. Graham rose and urged his incorporation into the University. The motion prevailed. McDonald became a member of the faculty.

Surely it were a sight for gods and men to behold David Clark, standpatter, and Ralph McDonald, radical, marching arm in arm to the Chapel, as the voices of George Coffin Taylor, South Carolina aristocrat, and Eston Ericson, stimulating Montana wild-cat, singing out of the same hymn book to the tune of "We are not Divided," lined out by the unifying, well-beloved Frank Graham! But that's the University way!

May we not venture to predict that here at Chapel Hill the vision of Isaiah is in the making: "And the suckling child shall play on the hole of the asp and the weaned child shall put his hand on the cockatrice's den."

29

CONCLUSION OF THE WHOLE MATTER

WHETHER or not Emerson made the observation that if a man builds a better mousetrap than any one else the world will make a beaten path to his door though it be in the woods, Horace Williams illustrated the saying. He became the greatest of our teachers. For nearly fifty years boys by the hundreds beat a path to his door.

"Horace Williams was the great teacher of Chapel Hill," declares Julian Miller of the class of 1906, Charlotte editor. "As an intellectual he was a Colossus. His teaching of truth and justice and spirit opened up contents of new thought and made of them the clearest, cleanest, deepest scholars in North Carolina."

On a certain occasion I was interviewing two of the indefatigable, well-furnished professors, Edgar Knight and Kent Brown, and asking them to give me an estimate of Old Horace, their associate and neighbor. They did not admire the man. He was anti-social and given to flattery. "Quite true," added Brown. "He was so ignorant that, as Dr. Stuhlman declares, he didn't know an atom from an electron. But this I will say, he could certainly hold the folks. I recall an incident. When Coach Cartmel came down here the campus was so full of Old Horace—his strange sayings and doings—that the newcomer was amazed. 'Why,' said Cartmel, 'I never saw such a place! Everybody in Chapel Hill is talking philosophy and freedom!'"

The attacks on Horace Williams' general knowledge may be well-founded since he had confined his labors to only one subject. Yet this must be said—the wisest men, all down the ages, have been similarly criticized and charged with ignorance, oftentimes with gross ignorance. As will be recalled, Aristophanes in his ridiculous play *The Clouds*, holds Socrates up to derision, picturing him as an ignoramus, with merely a semblance of wisdom, uncouth in speech, coarse, arrogant, impious, and so unconventional that he made innumerable enemies.

The service which Horace rendered to his generation may be likened to that of the signboard. The old philosopher was a signboard—this, and nothing else. He pointed the way. Should he have done more? Should the signboard be expected to leave its post of duty and accompany the traveler on his journey? What service is greater than that of the accoucheur to undelivered thoughts, the teacher making his fellows thought-conscious? How poor the world would be had no Socrates ever lived. Yet Socrates founded no school and organized no religious group. He was but a gadfly. So with Horace Williams. Though he taught the value and necessity of organization he never organized.

When Horace was at Yale and Harvard he was considered one of their best scholars. The letters of Dwight and Eliot and Everett, commending the young man to the Carolina authorities were not perfunctory. They described young Williams as a profound thinker, devoted to his work and giving promise of the greatest usefulness. But after arriving at Chapel Hill and setting out on his task Williams narrowed. He became a student of Hegel and of no one else. Nor did he keep up his association with Yale and Harvard or with the outside world. He was satisfied with the kind of knowledge he had acquired. Why should he make further search?

In 1923 Dr. Harold Smart, now of the Cornell faculty, but at that time a much beloved assistant to Williams, coming down to the University of North Carolina, was profoundly impressed by Old Horace's knowledge of Hegel, but not with his general scholarship. As Smart sized up Williams, he had an unfortunate way of dismissing the views of other thinkers. "Apparently many of his younger colleagues, as well as I, were puzzled by the apparent paradox of his great reputation and influence as over against the simplicity and dogmatism of his actual intellectual make-up. Thus I have to confess, like many another, that I was never able fully to understand the *man* and to discern the sources of his power. I was even more puzzled as to what to make of the *thinker*. But that he was a great personality there can be no doubt at all, in view of his profound and widespread influence, his ability to evoke loyalty and affection on the part of those who knew him well and shared his ideals of human life and conduct."

A somewhat similar view is expressed by Sidney Robins, professor of philosophy in St. Lawrence University. Robins concludes that his greatness was ultimately as a teacher, in the Socratic sense of that word, rather than as a constructive, systematic thinker. "Like a multitude of others, I was indebted to him for an immense amount of personal criticism and prodding. And it has been one of the wonders of my life to see how his interest in students persisted. He placed his faith in men, not always with perfect judgment perhaps, but uncovering many able men of the future. Into every personal relationship, with men or women he brought a certain delicacy and respect, thoughtfulness, and fineness of soul that was uplifting. Nobody was a match for him in conversation, and his views were masterful in their impression. There at the Hill he was the Piney Prospect of the mind. His influence upon me has been pervasive and deep and will be lifelong."

Along the same line speaks Lenoir Chambers, of the class of 1914, now a constructive Virginia editor. Chambers remembers Old Horace "as a great tradition, a fearsome yet challenging kind of teacher whose classes one must have entered for the sheer experience of them and for the test they enforced. That Horace was a great teacher is not open to question or that he introduced hundreds of students, perhaps thousands, who had been concerned primarily with the business of learning to the business of thinking—a process in which they quickly found that no parrot mind could succeed. No longer could the boys get anything by memorizing.

"Textbooks in Horace's classes were of little importance. Students had to use their own minds. Once started, some of them have been using their minds ever since. If they remembered nothing else about Old Horace they were certain to hold on to the difference between superficial thinking and what he laid down as the real essence of thinking.

"After all these years I am no judge, but if I were pinned down I should hold that one who had tried to understand Horace and had made any appreciable progress in that direction would not be likely, at any time thereafter, to accept any doctrine, belief, tradition, or flat statement without a close look at the basis on which it rested."

After reading and considering tributes of this kind, I greatly regretted that those thoughtful and virile men Jonathan Daniels, William Couch, and others, could not have been under him in his best days. They berated him. They declared that he did not impress his equals, but stirred the young and ignorant. Granted. But was not that his job?

While I was trying to get a line on Old Horace I called on his successors in the Department of Philosophy, now ably conducting the work. I inquired of Bradshaw, Emery, Kattsoff, Kuhn, and Browning, asking them to tell me if Old Horace had really added anything new to philosophy. "No cardinal principle," they replied. "But he did one unusual thing; he gave philosophy such popularity that it became a campus revelation and is now a tradition."

One phase of Old Horace's character, to which I have made reference, continues to puzzle me. How could a man of such lofty ideals, insisting that nothing less than the perfection of life would save religion, come down out of the clouds and trade spavined horses in some dirty back lot?

This psychological nut I handed to English Bagby, the freely-giving-himself-out professor of psychology. I asked him to crack the nut. "Why that's easy," said the psychologist, "Old Horace was not like other folks. He was a law unto himself. He had a vision. He was a mystic. Why, at one of our Phi Kappa Sigma banquets he spoke and looked exactly like an Easterner. He asserted that Hegel had made only thirteen steps or judgments on the road of perfection but Jesus had taken eighteen. With a far-away look on his face he alluded to a tree in his yard, a beautiful magnolia, and called it his Bo tree. The idea being that he was a second Buddha, instructing the youth and piercing the veil.

Bagby had shed a new light on the many-sided Horace, confirmation of which I discovered on further investigation. In vacation time Horace would attend the exercises of the Clarkton Colony, a little way out from New York, Dr. Bernard being in charge and the instruction of an occult and mystical character. Old Horace likewise claimed to be able to judge a man's character by an inspection of his face and on more than one social occasion exhibited his skill as a phrenologist.

A few years ago the learned and popular philosopher, Ernest Hocking, came to Chapel Hill and made several talks. As he was giving an account of a personal experience, in far away India, describing the self-abnegation of the Yogi and their followers, I could but think of Old Horace and his manner of life. Hocking had gone out to India, with the hope that the Vedanta philosophy would quiet his nerves and cause him to slow up a bit. In India he became acquainted with a Yogi and informed him that he wished to be inducted into the mystery and the serenity of Eastern philosophy.

"Follow me," said the Yogi in his abstracted way. Side by side the two wandered with never a word spoken. At length they came to a secluded spot.

"Be seated," the Yogi quietly said. On the ground they sat.

"Take the shoes from off your feet." Hocking removed his shoes.

"What is your name?" Hocking gave his name.

"Do you drink wine or other stimulants?" Hocking said he rarely drank.

"Do you eat meat?" Hocking replied that he seldom ate meat.

"You are not qualified to become a Yogi," was the sad reply, as the Priest slowly departed leaving Hocking to his meditations.

Now in Yogi land, I am sure, Old Horace would have been able to qualify. In abstemiousness, in simple living and in isolation Horace was a Yogi of the Yogis.

In truth his religious leanings were not altogether away from Sankhya philosophy. He seemed to lean somewhat upon the Vedantists, and to admire their individualism, though it might become so intensely individual as to cease to be individual. "The Parsee is the moral man of the world," Horace would declare. "He exhibits the philosophy of the Amesha-Spentas, those special messengers of God, sent from above." The necessity of any such messengers, however, Old Horace repudiated, and relied on the intellectual and the spiritual. According to his thought-process, Christianity was superior to Buddhism. He defined Christianity as a synthetic life. The individual loses himself in reality and finds himself in reality. The individual must go in pursuit of truth and become part of the man-god, god-man process.

If Horace Williams had continued to live in New England, undoubtedly he would have been an independent Congregationalist—the faith of his mentor Everett of Harvard, and of Emerson, Taft, and other liberal-minded people.

Now in Old Horace's religious conclusions I did not concur. To my mind religion is too deep for concepts or begriffe. Religion is a matter of faith. Religion is all or nothing. If Jesus be not the Christ how is Christianity superior to any other benevolent organization? I cannot understand the mysteries of the Christian religion nor do I wish to do so. If I comprehended mysteries religion would cease to be religion. Life is a mystery, entirely beyond us. A religion which would explain this mystery must therefore itself be mysterious. I often talked over these matters with Horace Williams. I insisted upon both mystery and divinity; he was content with mystery and the thought-process.

That Old Horace's religious views had nothing whatever to do with his greatness as a teacher must be conceded. Nevertheless when thoughtless or uninformed people charge the old philosopher with atheism a word in his behalf seems in order: Such accusations are without foundation. No one held Jesus in deeper reverence than did Horace Williams. His offense was not infidelity but lack of orthodoxy. He simply would not accept a literal Bible, a vagary which offended the Fundamentalists, who cast him out and classed him with atheists, infidels and "Romanists." Lack of Protestant orthodoxy was almost a crime. In my youth I have heard many a sermon from a Fundamentalist pulpit in which the Scarlet Woman of the Bible and Anti-christ were assimilated to the Catholic Church and the Pope, by a gesticulating pulpit-orator who proved his point to the satisfaction of the faithful!

In Old Horace's crown there is no jewel more precious than the change which he wrought in the minds and hearts of our people, softening them towards Jews and Catholics.

It is not Horace's religious conclusions, however, or his other erroneous concepts that matter, but his ability to teach, or, as the thoughtful Kemp D. Battle puts it, "To lead the youth to a realization that the world of the mind can be as thrillingly interesting as the laboratory or workshop or even the athletic field."

Horace Williams' influence over all who were willing to put themselves in the way of introspection and self-revelation was almost hypnotic. Not unlike Socrates he was inspired with the thought of a mission on earth. "Know thyself," was his motto. Know thyself as in and of the stream of tendency. On a certain occasion when the old philosopher presented his autobiography to his young friend, Ross, then living with him, he mysteriously remarked, "This book may explain yourself to yourself."

The hypnotic effect of this dramatic personage was in no wise meretricious. There was no table rapping. No holding of hands. No sex appeal. No shutting of the eyes, nor closing of the mind. No darkened rooms. No sensuous music. No Nirvaña. But precisely the opposite. In the old philosopher's classroom when Ralph Harper was so overcome that he did not wish to go to Heaven since he was already there, when leonine, Whitmanesque Tom Wolfe rose and fairly shouted, "Professor, where do we go from here?" and when young Fred Koch was so impressed that, in after years, he declared, "I can honestly say that of all my college courses Horace's remains the most damnably provoking, enjoyable and profitable I had," these virile youngsters had not been moved by adventitious surroundings. There had been no legerdemain. They had seen themselves as part of the cosmic plan and as necessary to God as God was to them.

Horace's influence over the tender, sympathetic mind of women was overpowering. Said a young woman to me as she came out of his classroom, "On the lecture today when Professor Williams unfolded his idea of standard and said of spirit it is that which is the source of its own impulse and the strength of its own activity and has the end within itself, I am sure I felt as Emily Dickinson did when she lost herself in a poem. My body was so cold no fire could ever warm me." Young women students indeed could scarcely talk of Old Horace without a moisture of the eye. They seemed to feel as Coleridge sometimes did: The mist which stood betwixt them and God had defecated into a thin transparency.

Perhaps the old philosopher would have emerged from the static into the dynamic and reached the highest level, that of the spirit, and would be exemplifying the spiritual as manifested in the life of Nicholas, or St. Francis. "God must be lived," he would say. Here he would pause and wander slowly away to his favorite window, his hands folded behind his back, and gazing abstractedly out into space. In a few moments he would resume.

"The individual must exhibit the universal attitude of life," he would go on. "It is this profound essential that makes St. Francis a permanent ideal in the process of civilization. St. Francis loved. He loved widely; he loved deeply; he loved continuously. Love is the absolute synthesis, the consciousness of the individual that he is in and of the cosmic process. Every particle of matter in the universe is attracted by every other particle. This is the master vision of Newton. There is in any particle of matter the quality of response to the cosmic process. This absolute unity is the law of science, and the truth of philosophy. It is the God of religion."

Almost exhausted, the teacher would conclude, standing speechless and abstracted. Not a student would move. The spell was too profound for interruption.

The mystery and elusiveness of the old philosopher greatly impressed Dr. Katherine Gilbert, of Duke, once a valuable assistant in the Philosophy Department of Chapel Hill. She visualizes Old Horace not only as a mystic but as a poet. To her he always seemed to be *un poète*. The first appearance of Old Horace on her horizon was as of some magical patron. With the slightest of introductions he offered her on trust a Kenan Fellowship; and so began six happy years of writing, studying, and reporting on progress made at the Tuesday night seminar in his study, where discussions seemed to be in a special language and based on some unusual rules.

"If I were to work usefully," she declared, "I must learn to play a new game; to check and counter-check, exchange pieces, and count up loss and gain on some pattern that was apart from the common logic of philosophical discussion, and that threw off entertainingly and remarkably into a hyper-logical atmosphere. When I became assimilated to the game I always felt a certain exhilaration in the novel intellectual motions, propositions, and relations that passed current in this philosophical *faerie*. Certain words seemed to be used as arresting 'spells' or 'incantations.' They were signals for intellectual gestures or postures: *Wesen; Begriff*.

"Skill in a novel art almost a power of enchantment," concludes Dr. Gilbert, "seemed to be Horace's great gift. He interpreted himself as a logician and thought it foolish to claim the faculty of a creative artist. And yet it was under this latter rubric that I came more and more to place him. He was a natural story-teller. Facts metamorphosed themselves instantly for him into the colors and images of a legend or dramatic fancy. There was difficulty sometimes at the border-line where Horace's poesy and most men's prose meet. The border-line was not clearly marked. But once this philosopher was grasped as a unique, solitary, creative spirit, there was singular joy in knowing, listening to, and playing games of the mind with him."

It would be unfair to the memory of Horace Williams, and to numerous friends, not to set down an opposite view. Those who intimately knew the clear-headed old man will deny that the occult influenced him, the least particle. Albert Coates indeed is of the opinion that Horace was far from mystical, that when speaking of the occult he was merely toying with the subject, talking through his hat, starting something and gypping the listener.

And much may be said on this side of the subject. Old Horace was intensely practical. The conclusions which he drew from the affairs of life were well-nigh perfect. He foresaw the fearful panic of 1929 and guarded his estate against it. He anticipated the complete failure of national prohibition. After the first World War and the Peace Treaty he was depressed in spirit; he concluded that this affair would be the breeder of a second World War, more terrible than the first. He insisted also that there should have been a comprehensive convention to organize the United States of Europe. He said that so long as Europe was broken up into small nations discord and confusion would be the portion of the human race. He held that all peoples were equally good. Original sin, he repudiated; the doctrine was an insult to mothers.

His concept was that force, violence and selfishness had brought the world to the brink of ruin. These evils should be supplanted by coöperation and love. He thought the idea of a hell of fire and brimstone a hurtful myth and that a life based upon truth, goodness, and beauty would lead to the pearly gates, and nothing else would. He demanded absolute freedom for the human mind. Labor should be free to organize. Capital should be free to grow and expand. He was not afraid of big business. He concluded that the Government was able to manage it. In a word, though the old philosopher was individualistic to the core, he was also universal.

That Horace Williams lived up to his high standards no one should insist. His teaching and his conduct often parted company. He omitted the human and therefore the copula that unites mind and matter was wanting. And yet must it not be said of him as Voltaire said of Newton, "It will not be making him too great a compliment if we affirm that he was valuable even in his mistakes?"

My views of Horace Williams, that he was the liberator of human thought and rendered a distinct service to nation and State, I expressed to Josephus Daniels who had known Old Horace half a century. I asked Mr. Daniels to give me an estimate of Williams and of the effect of his teaching upon the mores of the people. In a humorous reply the former capable and beloved Secretary of the Navy dissented. He recalled an animated conversation between himself and Locke Craig and President Winston and myself.

It seems that we had been talking about a book which had recently appeared, *The Education of Henry Adams.* Governor Craig spoke of it as the greatest book which had appeared in a decade. Thereupon Winston asked, "What did Henry Adams do?" The answer was that he was a scholar, a traveler, one of the foremost men of his day.

Again Winston broke in, "What did he do?" Without heeding the interruption the Governor proceeded to recount the greatness of Adams as a learned man, a great scholar. "What did he do?" again Winston insisted. "At the end of the conversation," as Josephus concluded, "when the persistent, 'What did he do?' had put the Governor at his wit's end, I was bound to think that President Winston had spoken a parable in bringing out that Adams was a dilettante."

To this letter I made a courteous reply. I set forth Williams' value as a teacher, a provoker of thought, a liberator of the human mind. In due course Joe Daniels came back at me and quoted Josh Billings: "I never argy agin a success." He then went on to say he had gathered from serious-minded students that Horace Williams had awakened their minds, stimulated their logical thinking, enabled them to weigh evidence, and to put devotion to truth as the highest virtue. They regarded him as the personification of inquiry and diligent search after truth and never closing his mind to new evidence, and as setting an example of uprightness of mind and living.

"But over and above all the conflicting accounts," Daniels concludes, "one thing stands out in my view: Men like Ed Graham and scores of other students, who became leaders of righteousness, found inspiration and direction from his teachings and close association. The lasting test of his place in the University and State will be found in the fact that Horace Williams *never sold the truth to serve the hour*."

In a lengthy rejoinder to this thoughtful epistle, which indicated that my old friend and client was beginning to see the light, I gave numerous illustrations of Horace's fruitful labors. I stressed the fact that out of his thought-process there had stemmed many divergent schools of opinion: Left-wingers, Right-wingers and Members of the Center. I asked if there were more useful or liberal-minded leaders than Frank Graham and Charlie Tillett, or wiser statesmen than

John J. Parker, W. J. Brogden and W. P. Stacy. I called attention to the remarkable changes in our people's habits and methods of thought: almost a revolution in religious tolerance, in racial relations, in the absence of political animosity, in freedom of thought and speech, and in the exorcism of social ostracism for opinion's sake.

I cited the progress of his own paper—ten times stronger in circulation and influence under his liberal, enterprising sons than in his day, when the personal and the vituperative found expression in the columns of an apocryphal, nonexistent, terrifying side-partner, the "Rhamkatte Roaster." I asked, "Why this change?" "Why had North Carolina—the only one of the Southern states—broken the fetters of a beautiful, caste-ridden past?"

In a few days a reply came,

MEXICO, D. F.
March 25, 1941

Dear Bob:—

You are eternally right. One who opens and stimulates the mind of youth is greater than he that buildeth a city.

Sincerely,

Josephus Daniels

After Old Horace passed the seventieth milestone he began to slow up. No longer was he "the livest thing on the campus," to quote rough-tongued Oscar Coffin. "No longer was he able to cut the feet out from under the boys and make them swim their way to one bank or t'other, through the whirlpools of doubt and the eddies of convention."

About the year 1935 he gave up regular class work and taught irregular groups Tuesday evenings in his study. In a letter to Robins, he laughed and said, "Babe Ruth to the benches!" Nevertheless he continued to be the campus puzzle and wonder. Even the critical young Jonathan Daniels looked upon him "as dynamite, dangerous to complacency, to mental lethargy, to the rut of conventional thinking of colloquial minds. A man who helped set the mind free in North Carolina. On such freedom rests in large measure now the strength of the state." Louis Graves, editor of the delightful college exponent and rambler, the *Chapel Hill Weekly*, though not a Horatian by any means, quoted the great men of the State who called him "a superb teacher who had accomplished the task of training young people to think."

From Currituck to Cherokee the press was acclaiming him, "The plainest man and the greatest teacher in the State."

30

HAIL AND FAREWELL

As the shadows lengthened the Fates were kind to the Old Master. His last days were his best days. Though his body was wearing away and he must lie in bed under the watchful eye of sister Hallie or attentive Mrs. Vickers, the village nurse, he never complained. Old age and decay was a part of the nature process, to be enjoyed as freely as air or water. The immortal part of him was intact, and that was enough: His spirit was growing younger and, with Cato of old, he could boast that his soul was secure in its existence,

Unhurt midst the war of elements,
The wrecks of matter and the crush of worlds.

Neighbors were kind and attentive, often calling and bringing flowers and dainties. Old students, visiting the Hill, made their usual pilgrimage to the shrine of early intellectual stimulation. Reporters continued to interview, going away with stories of no uncertain sound and with predictions of coming events, some accurate, others far otherwise. The Old Philosopher was experiencing posthumous fame and enjoying it. Not only did no sick-bed atmosphere prevail but there was an air of satisfaction and contentment.

In the City of New York Tom Wolfe, a devoted Horatian, had recently passed away, dying ere his prime. Before taking his leave Tom had paid a tribute to the Old Master which expressed the sentiment of many. "To me," said Wolfe in *Look Homeward, Angel,* "you were above good, above truth, above righteousness. To me you were the sufficient negation to all your teaching. Whatever you did was, by its doing, right. And now I leave you throned in memory. You will see my dark face burning on your bench no more; the memory of me will grow mixed and broken; new boys will come to win your favor and your praise. But you? Forever fixed, unfading bright, my lord."

One afternoon when the old philosopher was convalescing from a heart attack Francis Bradshaw and I called and found him as keen-witted as ever.

"Francis," said I, "what is it Professor Williams told you a miracle was?"

"A law operating on a level it had never before operated on."

"I didn't say that," the Old Man growled.

"What did you say, Professor?"

"I've forgotten."

We did not press the point but changed the subject.

"Professor Williams," Bradshaw ventured, after a short pause. "You are looking stronger today."

"Nor. My work is done. It's time for me to go." Then, after another pause, he said, with an innocent smile on his face, "I guess I'll try being an angel a while."

His chief ailment was a bad heart, which caused sleeplessness. His physician, Dr. Fields, therefore cautioned against exercise or exertion. But Old Horace disobeyed. One evening, after Celia, the faithful cook, had gone home, he observed that the car had not been put up. Out of doors he went, crawled into the vehicle and stepped on the gas. Down the steep incline rolled car and philosopher. Into the garage it plunged, crashing through the back of the little shack, headed for Roaring Fountain, some three hundred awesome yards away. A friendly tree intervened and stopped the runaways. Picking himself up, he managed to reach the house with no bones broken and no fatal injury. Again his doctor warned that he must be more careful and take less exercise.

As soon as I heard that my old college mate was well

enough to receive company I called to find him in his study and quite himself again. He was glad to see me, in fact he had been thinking about me since he was on the eve of making a will. He had talked the matter over with Attorney General Seawell and wished my opinion. He proposed to give his entire estate to the University. "I came to Chapel Hill more than half a century ago," he said. "I love the place. The ambition of my life has been to establish here a School of Thought. The income from my gift will be enough to engage several additional instructors in philosophy and start the school going. The scheme I shall soon execute."

As the old philosopher unfolded his extensive plans, I was greatly moved. Was this the same Horace Williams, who some people said was so stingy that he would squeeze the Eagle till it screamed? And then a wicked thought popped into my head. Which one of his critics had moiled and toiled, scrimped and saved for Alma Mater's sake, and finally given her the hard-earned savings of a lifetime?

In a few days the will was prepared, signed, sealed, witnessed and delivered to Dean Bradshaw, executor and trustee. By this instrument, *"All my property of every description and all of it is given to the University to be held in trust forever, the income to be used for Fellowships in Philosophy."* Hereunder the University acquired an estate of great value, fifteen hundred acres situate on the outskirts of the village, twenty or thirty rentable houses in Chapel Hill and Durham, and the Home Place of six or eight acres, in the center of the residential portion of Chapel Hill.

A solace of the Old Philosopher's declining years seemed to be the consciousness that he was winning his fight to change the people's mores. He had overcome narrowness, provincialism, and hurtful orthodoxy. No longer were Baptists and Methodists jowering as to which was right, sprinkling or immersion, free will or predestination, close communion or open communion.

As for politics it had become so liberalized that he and fully a fourth of the faculty had recently voted for a Republican president, and no head had been chopped off! Bill Couch, Head of the University Press, was spreading abroad such revolutionary and unorthodox racial and socialistic literature as twenty years earlier would have sent him packing—and, strange to relate, the people were approving.

These changes were comforting to the aged philosopher but they were not enough. There still was too much of the mechanical and too little of the spiritual. As of old he was a dreamer of dreams. He insisted that every one should have an intellectual moment (that is, get religion!)—an experience such as that of Saul on the road from Jerusalem to Damascus. "Moses too had this experience when he stood upon the Mount in the presence of Jehovah and the Hebrew civilization got under way. Gautama sat under the Bo tree and the great moment came to him. Gautama became Buddha."

No doubt inspiring thoughts of this character moved Dean House to pronounce Horace Williams not only "the greatest teacher of a generation but the greatest religious and moral force. The work he has done in upholding religion, morality, and a standard of a wise but tolerant and open mind has helped directly to build the University of North Carolina and the Commonwealth which it serves."

A short time after the will was executed the Government began negotiations to acquire land for an airport at Chapel Hill. When Old Horace heard of the scheme he was greatly pleased. The thought of an airport was directly down his alley. Time and again he had said to friends that some day flying would take the place of other methods of travel. A town without an airport would be left in the lurch.

In the effort of the National Government to establish a port the University authorities coöperated. It resulted that four hundred acres of the Horace Williams' lands, devised by his will to the University, were chosen as a site. But the devisor was not yet dead, and before the Government was willing to expend vast sums on the project it required immediate occupancy and a good, fee simple deed—not a will.

Would Professor Williams anticipate his death, give immediate possession and execute a deed for the four hundred acres the Government required? Many people doubted, but Billy Carmichael, the efficient and affable University Controller, was sure he would. At all events he would undertake to sound out the old philosopher.

"Yes," he cheerfully assented. "I'll execute the deed and give immediate possession."

In a few days the deed of gift was prepared, conveying to the University the four hundred acres which had been selected, a lofty plateau, a glorious, inspiring prospect, unexcelled in outlook short of the Blue Ridge. But soon another obstacle arose. Martindale who owned land adjoining was unwilling to sell the quantity required except for a larger sum than the Government was willing to pay. At this critical point Controller Carmichael again called at the Williams home and found the old man in bed. Carmichael explained the case.

"Mr. Carmichael, why not condemn the land?" said the sick man.

"We dare not, Professor, the jury would size our pile."

"Well, Mr. Carmichael, what do you propose to do?"

"Why, Professor, we want you to go out and see Mr. Martindale. You are the only man who can handle him."

"Do you think so, Mr. Carmichael?"

"We know it, Professor."

Almost before the words were out of Billy Carmichael's mouth Old Horace was up, out of bed, and putting on his shoes. In a few days the grand scheme was put through, and Chapel Hill had secured the requisite quantity of land for an airport. In an incredibly short time the "Horace Williams Airport" became an actuality, the pride of the State, one of the most extensive university ports in all the land. The United States had put hundreds of thousands of dollars into the project.*

* Thousands of fine young pre-flight cadets are now at Chapel Hill, in training to defend their country.

Nearly every Sunday afternoon Old Horace would walk around the neighborhood and call on old friends, the Coateses, Cobbs, Kennettes, Umsteads, Bradshaws, and also on later ones, the Kenfields, Stuhlmans, Millers, and others. On these visits he would be as saucy as in days of old. As he was passing the home of Mrs. Miller she called him in to see the new wallpaper on her sun parlor.

"Don't you think it is pretty, Professor?" she queried.

"Nor," he grunted.

"Why, Professor!"

"It's too loud."

"But, Professor, it matches up, it brings the trees and the flowers right in the house."

"No. Tear it off and leave the bare walls."

One day, while Billy Carmichael was calling, Old Horace tackled him.

"Mr. Carmichael," he drawled, "I see you are going to make a speech."

"Yes, Professor. Down on Roanoke Island."

"What's your subject, Mr. Carmichael?"

"The Lost Colony, Professor."

"What's the good of that?"

"Why, Professor, they were the very first white people to land in America."

"Yes, Mr. Carmichael, but they failed. Speak on a success not a failure."

"Why, Professor, didn't Jesus fail and win too?"

"Mr. Carmichael, you talk like a Baptist preacher!"

Habits of promptness and punctuality still dominated. One afternoon the old gentleman invited the Coateses and Mrs. Hall, mother of Mrs. Coates, to tea, fixing the hour at five o'clock. The guests did not arrive until fifteen minutes after five. "Come in," the host politely greeted them at the door, conducting them into the dining room. "You are late so I've had my tea."

It pleased the old philosopher to drop by and have a

chat with Mary Manning and talk of old days in Chapel Hill. Or to cross the street and sit with Mrs. Roberson, relict of the good old village doctor, long gone to his reward.

In his eighty-second year he had a most agreeable surprise. One May day, Julien Wood and wife, none other than the adorable Mary Anderson, the Highland Mary of his young days, called. This man and this woman, finest expression of North Carolina culture, had been drawn to each other and in old age had carried out Horace Williams' prophecy of fifty years earlier. They had married, and were living in historic Edenton. A sight of Julien Wood, his old college mate, and Mary Anderson, the aspiration of his college days, warmed the cockles of the Old Man's heart. Memories of the visit lingered and in a few days he wrote,

CHAPEL HILL
May 18, 39

Dear Mrs. Julien Wood,

You gave me a delightful surprise. I was in college with Jule Wood. I remember the night when he came to Chapel Hill. Don Gillam and I welcomed him. There was no finer boy in my day. Unfortunately I have seen nothing of him since leaving college. I have thought of him and wished our paths might cross. He was always a gentleman. Please tell him for me that the same adjectives apply to Mary Anderson. I knew her as a girl. She was always delightful, often brilliant, never commonplace. I am wishing for you both the beautiful things that go with a happy marriage. Tell Jule to let you indulge your aesthetic self. Mrs. Williams was an artist and delightful memories are associated with her artistic joys. I caught some of the glow. My regret is that I did not do more for her artistic soul. Many thanks for the invitation to visit Edenton. It would be delightful to be in your home and see the happiness of two such friends. I have never lost the thrill of seeing Edenton. As a boy I drove through the main street and we came to the view of the bay. My impulse was to pitch my tent there. I had not seen anything so beautiful. Wishing you the joys that go with a happy, beautiful marriage, I am,

Affectionately yours,

Horace Williams

The Old Philosopher's eighty-second, and last, summer was entirely satisfactory. His affairs were settled up. His will had been made and he was ready to "play the angel." In the afternoon he would ride out and see the Horace Williams Airport in the process of construction, with steam shovels and steel plows tearing up the ground where lately sheep and cattle had been grazing. Occasionally he would send letters, written in his own hand, to old students, invariably harking back to earlier days and praising the work of George Washington and the marvellous Convention of 1789.

But it was apparent that the end was approaching. Now and then he would lapse into semi-consciousness. One night, he walked a short way out of doors and on the return dropped senseless on the steps leading from the study to the bedroom. There, on the floor, he lay, fully dressed, until morning, when Celia, the cook, arrived and aided him to bed.

Not alone the physical condition of the patient but also his spiritual condition alarmed his thoughtful nurse. She had never seen him on his knees.

"Mr. Williams," she anxiously inquired, toward the end. "Don't you ever pray?"

"No, Mrs. Vickers, I don't need to pray. My life is a prayer."

A pause ensued. Then the old man added, in the most casual manner, "Mrs. Vickers, I want to ask a favor of you. I want you to go out and see me buried."

"No, no!" sobbed the kind nurse, "I couldn't do that. I couldn't bear to see you put under the ground."

"Mrs. Vickers," rejoined the dying man, "Christians

now-a-days have a wrong idea of death. Dying isn't death, it's life."

Manifestly the old philosopher's thoughts had turned to the time when he had said to his friend Ross that a man's quality is immortal: from the dead grain of wheat there will spring twenty grains, thirty grains, forty grains.

Shortly afterward a period of semi-consciousness again set in. The end had come. The last moment—simple, courageous, individual—was true to the austere life he had led. The watchful nurse, observing no sign of life, approached the couch and whispered, "What is your name?" Far away the voice answered, "Horace Williams."

www.ingramcontent.com/pod-product-compliance
Lightning Source LLC
Chambersburg PA
CBHW032221010526
44113CB00032B/196